THE PRICE OF MISFORTUNE

The Price
of Misfortune

Rights and Wrongs in Indebted America

Daniel Platt

THE UNIVERSITY OF CHICAGO PRESS

CHICAGO AND LONDON

The University of Chicago Press, Chicago 60637
The University of Chicago Press, Ltd., London
© 2023 by The University of Chicago
Published 2023
Printed in the United States of America

32 31 30 29 28 27 26 25 24 23   1 2 3 4 5

ISBN-13: 978-0-226-73398-2 (cloth)
ISBN-13: 978-0-226-73403-3 (e-book)
DOI: https://doi.org/10.7208/chicago/9780226734033.001.0001

Library of Congress Cataloging-in-Publication Data
Names: Platt, Daniel, author.
Title: The price of misfortune : rights and wrongs in indebted
America / Daniel Platt.
Description: Chicago : The University of Chicago Press, 2023. |
Includes bibliographical references and index.
Identifiers: LCCN 2022058884 | ISBN 9780226733982 (cloth) |
ISBN 9780226734033 (ebook)
Subjects: LCSH: Debtor and creditor—United States—History—
19th century. | Debtor and creditor—United States—History—
20th century. | Debt—Moral and ethical aspects—United States. |
Consumers—Civil rights—United States—History—19th century. |
Consumers—Civil rights—United States—History—19th century. |
Finance, Personal—Social aspects—United States.
Classification: LCC HG3756.U6 P538 2023 | DDC 332.7/50973—dc23/
eng/20230103
LC record available at https://lccn.loc.gov/2022058884

♾ This paper meets the requirements of ANSI/NISO Z39.48-1992
(Permanence of Paper).

Contents

INTRODUCTION

What does it mean for a person to owe? Newspapers, novels, and films are replete with tales of the drama and pain that often surrounds the obligation to repay. A 2021 editorial in the *New York Times* describes the $54,000 that the author, Lori Teresa Yearwood, owed after being homeless for two years. Hospital expenses, tax penalties, and misdemeanor fines were the inevitable consequences of Yearwood's poverty and a burden against which she fought as she worked to return to the "world of the housed." Sixty-year-old Jack Connolly, a high school English teacher profiled in *Slate* in 2020, narrates the decision to move in with his son and the challenge of dating and making friends while still carrying $200,000 in student loans. "It's not exactly where I thought I would be," he laments. In the 2018 thriller *Widows*, four women turn to theft to pay off their husbands' debts—owed to a local crime boss who threatens them with violence—while the protagonist of Catherine Lacey's 2017 novel *The Answers* is driven by medical bills and mountainous credit card balances to take work in an experimental form of emotional prostitution. In these tales and others, those who owe are forced to work in ways they would rather not. They struggle to build and maintain intimate relationships and to make ordinary moral decisions. Altogether, they appear to lose command over their life trajectories and their selves. To dwell on their deprivations is to ask: Is the debtor a self-possessing individual? Is the debtor truly and wholly free?[1]

These questions have been heard time and again in the United States in the twenty-first century. They have been inspired by crises fast and slow. The subprime lending bubble that burst in 2008 saw four million houses pushed through foreclosure—taken back by the banks when their owners could not pay—and more than twelve million borrowers burdened by underwater mortgages (in which the loan is worth more than the home). Personal and household finances—particularly for Black and Hispanic families—took years to fully recover from the resulting Great Recession, and at lower income levels are still impacted. On the ledger of gradual crises, there is the staggering burden of medical debt. Nearly a third of adult Americans carry some kind of health-related balance, while one-fifth of Americans regularly struggle to pay off healthcare bills and one million medical debtors file for bankruptcy each year. Education debt is similarly characterized by dismal constancy and, worse, steady increase, jumping from $480 billion nationally in 2006 to $1.7 trillion in 2020. These borrowers cannot escape their debt through bankruptcy and, if their obligation endures long enough, can see their Social Security pension garnished by their creditors. Wage stagnation and ascendant income inequality nourish quieter financial hardships as well, such as rising credit card balances and a growing reliance on payday lending. State and local governments increasingly turn criminal justice debts—fines, fees, and court costs—into pretexts for harassment and abuse. In Florida, felons who have served their prison sentence but who have not paid back their monetary debts to the state are denied the right to vote. Most elsewhere, these open balances are reported to credit bureaus and can provide a legal basis for discrimination in housing and employment.[2]

In this context, new movements for financial reform have launched and radical voices have grown in influence. Activist groups now press for the formation of debtors' unions and the organization of repayment strikes. Their claim is that debt is an illicit form of constraint—a check on the borrower's freedom and capacity to flourish. Their demands for massive debt forgiveness, and the building of a less debt-dependent economy, are issued in the language of emancipation and jubilee. These calls are not new to the United States. Indeed, they have a long and tangled history. Between the Civil War and the Great Depression, concerns for debtors' freedom possessed a kind of moral urgency that presaged the activism of today. In that era—the Age of Capital—a range of political actors, including feminists, agrarians, civil rights advocates, and urban progressives, drew profound analogies between slavery and imprisonment for debt (both recently abolished) and the more ordinary experiences of owing, such as violence, intimidation, and dispossession. Those actors tried to protect borrowers from the unfreedom of debt using the tools of law, securing against creditors and the volatile market the debtor's person, labor, and experience of dignified homelife. Their efforts constituted a distinguished expression of liberalism and were seen as consonant with "the progressive spirit of the age." Yet tensions arose across this era as reformers encountered debts that were rooted in other, sturdier, and more naturalized inequalities, such as the hierarchy of marriage, the oppression of Jim Crow, and the dependency of the wage. If securing the debtor's freedom meant challenging these social systems, would the law embark on a program of radical and ambitious change? Or would it tolerate financial coercion in order to preserve an unequal social order? These are the questions that animate this book—a critical history of debtors and their rights at the dawn of modern America.[3]

In 1882, a Nebraska farmer bemoaned his condition to a relative in the East. "I would like to be with you on a visit," the westward settler wrote, "but our debts must be paid, and of course while they remain unsettled, my time is not my own." The concerns that came together in the farmer's lament—the sense that debt impinged on family relationships, forced one to work when one wished to retire, restricted movement, and robbed one of the ownership of one's time—would not have been unfamiliar to Americans of earlier eras. As an agricultural nation, in which expenses were constant yet payment for the harvest came once a year, credit was an integral part of economic life for many, from the small farmers of the North and West to the large planters of the South. Merchants and artisans relied on debt to sustain themselves and turn the wheels of commerce as well, while the urban poor became experts in how to pawn their few possessions and stretch their credit accounts with grocers, retailers, and landlords. These experiences of indebtedness gnawed on their own, but the ideology of republicanism—with its suspicions of distant power and aristocratic rentiers—enriched them, inspiring a popular debtors' politics as early as the Founding era. Shays' Rebellion, an uprising of poor debtors in western Massachusetts in 1786 and 1787, found its moral legitimacy in the claim that in a democratic nation, finance should serve productive industry rather than master it. State efforts during the early nineteenth century to enact stay laws—statutes that suspend foreclosure proceedings during moments of economic depression—continued this tradition and gave it legislative form. Andrew Jackson's battle against the national bank in the 1830s carried the project into the antebellum period and joined the ethic of small finance to the era's other democratic aim, the movement for universal suffrage for white men. Yet while the Nebraska farmer of the 1880s could have no doubt found a sympathetic peer in Shays' New England or Jackson's Upper South, the meaning of the debtor's plight in the late nineteenth and early twentieth centuries was fundamentally different, owing both to new material qualities of the debt relation and to new social contexts in which the problem of debt was read.[4]

In part, the change was that the debt that bound the Nebraska settler was simply different from the obligations faced by borrowers in earlier eras. The introduction of a national currency and a national banking system during the Civil War inaugurated a period of decline for small financial institutions, particularly those on the rural periphery. Unable to meet new minimum capital requirements or to pay new taxes on note issuing, such institutions went out of business in droves. When they did, national banks stepped in to satisfy the demand that the older establishments had serviced. These new banks were impersonal lenders, often based in or associated with firms in New York. They had few social connections to their borrowers and less at stake in the long-term health of the local community. Mortgage debts and seasonal notes thus became colder, more legalistic obligations— experienced not as investments in a person, town, or region but as contracts that had to be met, lest one face serious consequences. The emergence of secondary mortgage markets compounded this transformation, as lenders increasingly sold their financial assets to speculators, tethering the borrower to a stranger whose interest in the debt was purely economic. What this meant to many debtors—especially small farmers in the South and West—was that there were fewer social resources to draw upon for softening the edges of their obligation. In the event of a poor harvest, a personal tragedy, falling commodity prices, or a mass financial panic—all developments that beset American borrowers during the late nineteenth and early twentieth centuries—it was harder to secure a special dispensation to relax the terms of the loan. The problems that faced the large debtor (the planter or the merchant) were often shared and passed down to the small debtor (the worker who took a cash advance or the tenant who owed back rent). This meant that all who borrowed increasingly found themselves entangled in firmer and less forgiving bonds. When John F. Armstrong, a cotton farmer from Georgia, was returned to his state by the sheriff after fleeing a debt in 1892 and being sued by his lender, he described the modern mortgage system as a form of unfree labor: "I worked and toiled from year to year and all the fruits of my labor went to the man who never struck a lick."[5]

For legal and economic reasons, personal debt thus felt different than it had in earlier eras. Armstrong was resolute in declaring it a species of "slavery." Yet debt also acquired new public meanings in this period that were shaped by several overlapping social contexts, in which the stakes of financial loss were raised. The farm-mortgage crisis that developed in the West following the Civil War, for example, threatened not only the mass of independent farmers but also the vast social project of continental expansion and settlement. Between 1840 and 1890, hundreds of thousands of migrant families poured from the East into the Great Plains and onward toward the

Pacific. Some were drawn by the promise of fast wealth through gold mining or land speculation, but most sought a basic agricultural competency consisting of "freehold ownership, command over household labor, and control over the resources of the farm." Free-soil ideology celebrated this movement as a measure of national strength and a source of civic renewal. Western settlement nurtured republican virtues, forestalled industrial class divisions, and enacted racial privilege and domestic hierarchy. The state was committed to aiding this project, both through the acquisition of western territory and the distribution of those spoils in measures like the Homestead Act. Yet while the successful settler vindicated these profound political and symbolic investments, the indebted farmer squandered them. In his loss of landed independence and liberal self-possession—with an emphasis on the gendered pronoun, which is consciously used throughout this study to reflect the maleness of the idealized victim of debtors' rights discourse—he endangered the vaunted inequalities of home, nation, and empire. The dominance of white settlers over the Indigenous West was thrown into question, as was the order of the republican household, as children lost their birthright in the land and wives were denied the fabled virtues of the private sphere. The continental expansion that Walt Whitman had celebrated as an "empire grander than any before" risked devolving into a vast landscape of impoverished tenants and broken homes. In this setting, personal debt and the threat of dispossession carried a new significance for the individual, the family, and the nation at large.[6]

This meaning was informed by developments in the East—for what continental expansion was expressly intended to avert was the precarity, landlessness, and wage dependency that increasingly characterized laboring life in the industrial city. There, the small shop had given way to the factory, and the factory was giving rise to a new terrain of urban poverty. The poor were crammed into "wretched tenements [like] smoked herrings in a grocer's box," and husbands worked twelve-hour days while their wives took in laundry to make ends meet. Before the Civil War, one could imagine, as Abraham Lincoln had, that the "prudent, penniless beginner" who "labors for wages awhile" would eventually "save a surplus with which to buy tools or land . . . and then labor on his [own] account." By the late nineteenth century, however, observers of the urban condition discerned the clear emergence of a permanent hireling class. Reformers and charity workers investigated whether the resources of philanthropy—or, perhaps, the state—could improve the lives of common laborers. Working people gathered into unions and battled for raises in wages and control over the shop floor. These were conflicts first and foremost about the emergent industrial order; within them, debt was often used to describe and appreciate the permanency of class division and the paucity of the wage. "How much money had you left?" asked one member of the Senate Committee on the Relations between Labor and Capital of a precarious wage earner in 1883:

A. Sixty dollars in debt.
Q. How did you do that?—A. I don't know, sir.
Q. Can you not think of something more you have wasted?—
    A. No, sir.
Q. Have you been as careful as you could?—A. Yes, sir.
Q. And you have come out at the end of the year $60 in debt?—
    A. Yes, sir.

Here, debt measured the essential inadequacy of the wage—its inability to sustain the worker as an individual and a head of household. One could not save one's way to independence on the wage alone; one could not even necessarily survive. A host of anxieties converged on the figure of the hireling in the wake of the Civil War: that of a person who lacked autonomy; who could not participate freely and wisely in politics; who could not support a family in dignity; and whose poverty made him vulnerable to radicalism and crime. Debt both signified the worker's unsettled status and materially amplified it, by adding another expense he could not afford. Protecting the wage earner from debt and insolvency was thus interpreted as a necessity if reformers were to resolve the profound contradictions of the dawning industrial age.[7]

Finally, and perhaps most important, there was the experience of national slave emancipation and the questions it raised about the meaning of freedom and the persistence of racial hierarchy and control. Between 1862 and 1865, four million Black men, women, and children passed from bondage to freedom—legally, through such devices as the Emancipation Proclamation and the Thirteenth Amendment, and practically, through resistance and flight during the Civil War. Slave emancipation ended the profound moral contradiction of holding people as property in a free and modern nation. It ennobled a public philosophy of liberal self-possession, premised on the individual's fundamental right to labor freely, to form a family, and to make contracts. In this worldview, however, debt stood as a troubling bond: a voluntary pact that often eroded these signal expressions of autonomy. Before emancipation, African American newspapers had carried tales of freedpeople who had fallen into debt and were thrust back into bondage. On the plantation, insolvency had routinely been linked to some of slavery's worst abuses, as the master's unpaid debts inspired the sale of human chattel and the separation of enslaved families. In the wake of the Civil War, prescriptive texts like Clinton Bowen Fisk's *Plain Counsels for Freedmen* (1866) warned the formerly enslaved against contracting for debt. Credit, Fisk explained, was unlike contracts for wages or marriage, which honored labor and romantic partnering and defined the content of freedom in the wake of emancipation. Debt, on the other hand, was something darker. It offered opportunity and convenience, but also compulsion and submission. Interest could eat into wages, making the purchase of land unlikely. The workday could grow long as the borrower sought higher pay through greater toil. Tools and domestic goods might need to be sold to meet demands, jeopardizing self-employment and the integrity of the home. Independence could quickly be replaced by a servitude to the lender, "and let me assure you," Fisk warned, "a creditor is a very hard master." To protect the debtor in this freighted moment thus meant more than giving expression to familiar republican critiques of monied interests and the virtue of landed labor. It also served to bolster and secure the "new birth of freedom" realized through the Civil War.[8]

Americans of the late nineteenth and early twentieth century who bemoaned the debtor's condition participated in a tradition of economic moralism that traced back as far as the classical era. Aristotle considered credit at interest to be a crime against nature, since it bred wealth out of barren coin. The Old Testament instructed merchants to lend money only "unto the stranger," in order to prevent greed and duplicity from poisoning community affairs. Religious authorities in the medieval and early modern periods repeated these claims, and they were echoed in the eighteenth and nineteenth centuries as well, with debt often likened to other sinful markets, such as the leasing of church pews and the selling of dead bodies for medical research. Yet modern critiques of finance took shape across these centuries as well. They described indebtedness as a form of dependency, a check on reason and virtue, and an obstacle to mobility and choice. "What can be added to the happiness of a man who is in health [and] out of debt?" asked the liberal political economist Adam Smith. What more could be taken from the hopeless insolvent, who could not work and could not provide for a family? Was he even a "free agent," asked a New York judge in 1847, or rather a tethered subject, "the slave of the lender"?[9]

The new political economy of the postbellum United States rendered the debt at the center of this discourse colder and more impersonal, and a changing social context invested the debtor—whether a homesteader, a precarious wage earner, or a freedperson—with heightened meaning. Cultural currents mattered as well, for if it was true that the borrower was in any way "the slave of the lender," then how could a country that had abolished slavery leave the debt relation untouched? A vision and a politics of debtors' rights thus developed in this period that looked not backward, toward a vanished moral past, but ahead, toward a moral goal that the nation had not yet achieved. In keeping with "the liberal thought of the day," a range of men and women called for substantial legal guards to be raised around the debtor, insulating that vulnerable figure from risk, dependency, and loss. "Freedom of the person" meant little if the twists of fortune could grant the lender access to that "sphere of activity the individual creates for himself, and with which his existence is inseparably blended." An essential task in the Age of Capital was thus to build a wall around this sphere, marking out the line "beyond which no creditor shall invade."[10]

This book explores the cause of debtors' rights in the late nineteenth and early twentieth centuries. It argues that debt—often discussed in relation to Populism, rarely plumbed much further—was central to the era's debates about what freedom meant and who was meant to enjoy it. The narrative opens at the dawn of the postbellum era. It follows the analogy commonly drawn between slavery, imprisonment for debt, and more ordinary financial pressures and penalties, and it traces how the conviction that debt endangered free labor and domestic integrity inspired important protections for the vulnerable borrower. Yet while all debts might constrain, the law divided on whether all people were entitled to live free of constraint. This tension is explored in greater detail in the book's three interior chapters, which span the 1870s to the 1920s and deal with the problem of extending financial rights to wives, African Americans, and industrial wage earners. Each of these groups saw their freedom diminished by creditors. For each, though, the captivity of debt was but one expression of a larger and sturdier inequality: the hierarchy of marriage; the architecture of white supremacy; and the poverty of the industrial wage. Poised between the modern commitment to debtors' rights and these steadfast social structures, how would the law proceed? Across these distinctive histories, two patterns emerge: the granting of some genuine rights and protections to these imperiled groups, but also, and more so, the emergence of new cultural scripts for defining their financial experiences as acceptable to, if not emblematic of, the modern liberal age. The book's final chapter describes the close of this era and the dawn of a new one, as the market crash of 1929 and the onset of the Great Depression returned the debtor to the main stage of social thought. Calls to surround the borrower in protective law were once again heard, but national policymakers, instead of heeding them, embraced a different moral narrative: the notion that it was not vulnerable people who needed to be guarded from the high-risk market but rather the vulnerable market that needed to be guarded from high-risk people. The guiding light of the law (and the liberalism) to emerge from this moment—most clearly in the National Housing Act of 1934—was the belief that in matters of borrowing and lending, it was not more protection but "more discrimination" that was necessary.[11]

The pages that follow thus consider the rights of the debtor across several decades and social contexts. They examine many types of debtors and many expressions of legal power: state legislation, municipal reform, judicial interpretation, and administrative policy. Two important limits should be noted. First, this book is concerned only with personal debts, primarily those incurred by poor and working people. These included cash loans issued by professional lenders; wage advances issued by employers; book credits furnished by retailers; and use expenses that became debts when they went unpaid, such as back rent owed to landlords. These were obligations that touched the borrowing person and implicated his or her property—easily, if the debt was secured by a mortgage, or with greater difficulty, if the debt was unsecured and required a court judgment to resolve. What is not included here are discussions of corporate debts or public debts, though they inspired moral and political debate in this era as well, regarding the size of government, the power of big business, and the ability of collective entities to make promises that obligated their members. These were significant issues, but ones that were experienced separately from the debts at the center of this study, which bore on the meaning of freedom for the individual.[12]

Additionally, this book addresses the problem of debt only in the United States. Americans did often look to foreign experiences—real or imagined—to measure their advance from more exploitative financial regimes. In India, "if a person owes, and cannot pay, he is compelled to resign his wife to his creditor as security," the *National Citizen* reported in 1881. Slavery for debt in Africa and Latin America, and the financial dimensions of tenancy in Ireland and serfdom in Russia, were invoked by debt reformers as well. These allusions propelled domestic legal changes *and* could be used to assure Americans that the dispossessions caused by debt in the United States were less extreme than those encountered elsewhere. Further, Americans also appropriated technologies of financial reform that had first been refined in other countries. They drew inspiration from English bankruptcy law, for example, and from the credit cooperatives of Germany, Italy, and Canada. How the tensions that Americans detected in debt were felt in other countries, however, lies beyond this book's focus. This is not because those tensions were exceptionally American. In England, the notion that modernity demanded freedom for the debtor was realized in metropolitan measures like the Debtors Act of 1869 and in colonial debates about bonded

labor. In France, liberal jurists of the nineteenth century considered it a tru-
ism that "the more civilized the society, the more it relied on the debtor's
property, rather than his body, as collateral"—a conviction that energized
the elusive distinction between persons and things. Yet in all instances, the
problems of debt, even in their broadest constructions, keyed into distinctive national histories, including forms of government, legal family distinctions, social movement activity, and the experiences of slavery and empire.
This book limits itself to those of the United States.[13]

The forces that have driven a renewed politics of financial activism in the
twenty-first century have also inspired an outpouring of scholarship attending to the nation's financial history. This literature has explored the
controversial lives of major financial instruments, from the life insurance
contract to the municipal bond to the credit score, and the financial context
of watershed events, from the panics that inspired the Populist revolt to the
fiscal crises that inaugurated the neoliberal era.[14] This book joins this compelling body of work and aims to enrich it in three ways. First, it narrates a
financial history from the bottom up, examining not elite money managers
but working people who participated in finance in direct and modest ways:
by putting their sewing machine in pawn, by requesting advances on their
wages, by mortgaging their land, furniture, or tools, or by falling behind on
bills and owing money to grocers, doctors, and landlords. These exchanges
were an essential part of economic survival for ordinary people in the late
nineteenth and early twentieth centuries. One cannot account for the profound transformations that characterized working life on the western farm,
on the post-emancipation plantation, or in the industrial city in this era
without attending to the everyday economies of borrowing and lending.
Further, to train on these small and deeply personal transactions is to see
the close connection between finance, personhood, and labor. This book
does not portray a speculative marketplace unmoored from the quotidian
struggles of the sharecropper, the farmwife, the department store clerk, or
the railway brakeman. Instead, it demonstrates that financial relationships
often reduced to starkly material questions of work: Who would toil for
whom, at what times, and on what terms?[15]

    Second, this book shows that when Americans endeavored to answer
these questions, they did so by using the power of law. Borrowers and lenders of this era were not adrift in the market. When they joined in a transaction, the modern ideal of free contract—in which two autonomous actors
bind themselves according to their will—did not prevail. Instead, personal
debt was an intensely legalistic entanglement. Reformers worked to ensure

that it was governed by restrictions on allowable interest rates; prohibitions on loans that compelled personal service; exemptions on the creditor's seizure of land, home goods, and tools; protections for the debtor's income; limits on what kinds of debts could implicate a farmer's crops and whether such debts could apply to subsequent harvests as well; statutes and common-law traditions that dictated how the husband's debts affected the wife and how the wife's debts affected the husband; and provisions that allowed insolvent individuals to escape their debt through bankruptcy. This book documents this legalism and argues that it constituted an important effort to wall off the market—full of risk, avarice, desperation, and dispossession—from the liberal (and liberated) person, with the power to control his labor, maintain a home, and make independent moral choices. The emergence of the rights-bearing debtor in this period was an expression of what Karl Polanyi has narrated as the modern struggle to defend the social world against untrammeled capitalism. Determining what one could pledge and what one could lose in debt—what price one might pay for misfortune—was an attempt to constrain the power of the market. It was also an exercise in defining the content of freedom.[16]

Yet debtors' rights advanced only so far. For the most privileged subjects, the struggle to protect the debtor as a laborer, a patriarch, and a moral agent encountered resistance that was both political (from organized creditors) and ideological (in the ethic of promise keeping). For those people whose financial vulnerability was part of a deeper social vulnerability—the dependency of marriage, the oppression of Jim Crow, or the poverty of the industrial wage—the law was even more reluctant to act. Coercions remained in the lived experience of debt that the law would not or could not take away. We can "limit the extent of a creditor's claim on the debtor's person," one turn-of-the-century economist explained, but "we cannot make it zero." Thus did there emerge an important cultural task adjacent to the project of legal reform: that of justifying the limits of reform and explaining why the coercions that persisted in debt *did not* offend the conscience or deny to debtors—especially the most disfavored ones—the experience of freedom. This book's third contribution, then, is to argue for the importance of ways of seeing and unseeing that concealed or effaced debt as a relation of power. An economy of borrowing and lending could not be accepted in an emancipated nation so long as debt was regarded as a breed of dependency and the debtor as a figure whose liberty was impaired. Resolving this tension, through law as well as culture, was a central preoccupation in the United States in the years between the Civil War and the Great Depression. It bore not only on the institutions of credit but also on the status of women,

African Americans, and wage earners, whose indebtedness provided a testing ground for determining the freedoms to which they were entitled. Finance was central to the social politics of the period, and social politics, in turn, were central to the financial economy that took shape in the Age of Capital—one that, in important ways, endures to the present day.[17]

1

JUBILEE

On October 30, 1871, Judge George G. Barnard, justice of the New York Supreme Court, ordered an investigation of the conditions at the Ludlow Street Jail in Manhattan's Lower East Side. At least thirty-seven men were there imprisoned—some for days, others for months—for failing to pay their debts. One had neglected to pay alimony. Another had defaulted on a court judgment. The rest had been interned because of the failure to pay back ordinary cash loans taken to fund business risks or to meet the expenses of living. "Technically, these [men] are within the grasp of the law," the *New York Times* reported. Their lenders had sworn to a magistrate that they were planning to flee the city, empowering officials to issue a warrant for their arrest. Yet "according to the spirit of our code they are . . . illegally restrained of their liberty." Their true fault lay in having suffered the twofold misfortune of failing in the market and owing money to parties eager to punish them to the fullest extent of the law. Judge Barnard's interest in the issue stemmed from the reputed state of the jail, where many inmates were said to endure "filthy quarters, bad food, harsh treatment, and close restraint." For the *Times*, however, the injustice was the practice of imprisonment for debt itself. Inmates interviewed by the newspaper attested to their misery. They explained that their failings owed to bad luck and not to reckless borrowing or want of industry. Misfortune joined to legal restraint now resulted in the twin tragedies of being unable to work and unable to provide for their families. "But for the malice of enemies who put me here . . . I could and would have been doing well now," one assured. Another maintained that when his credit had been good, he had been capable of earning thousands of dollars each year. For a third, the loss had been felt most at home. His wife had been forced to pawn everything, "even the family Bible, and had it not been for the kind offices of the City Mission she and the little ones would have starved."[1]

Readers of the *Times* might have been surprised to learn that the debtors' prison still existed in their city. They may have recalled the campaigns to shutter the institution in the 1830s and 1840s—efforts that had likened civil incarceration to slavery and had contributed to its prohibition in New York in all instances other than those involving fraud or attempted flight, of which the Ludlow inmates were accused. Upon discovering that delinquent debtors could still be thrown into the prison's hold and locked away, many no doubt wished for its final demise. Critics had long insisted that imprisonment for debt was a vestige of barbarism. It conjured images of medieval dungeons, feudal justice, and even the savagery of the slave plantation. It was "wrong in principle" and harkened "the ignorance and tyranny of the darker ages." "The power of a creditor to imprison his debtor, is the only case in the United States, where, among free men, one citizen has legal authority to deprive his co-equal fellow citizen . . . of the right of personal liberty," the prison's antebellum opponents had insisted. "For the mean and contemptible sum of one hundred dollars, a single exasperated creditor may treat his debtor worse than a criminal." He may confine him to "a filthy cell behind ponderous doors—grated windows—massy [*sic*] locks—and damp walls, [and] thus actually [purchase] . . . the positive but useless slavery of a free citizen." Even as the practice of arrest and imprisonment had faded as a common financial remedy, reformers had cast its formal excision from the law as a necessary measure of the nation's moral progress. The federal government had banned the practice (for interstate debts that fell under federal jurisdiction) in 1833. Many states had abolished it before the Civil War, while others announced the closure of their debt prisons soon after. Its gradual eradication was heralded by Americans across the political spectrum as a decisive step in the "struggle for human liberty." It was a triumphant star in the constellation that stretched from "the Declaration of Independence and its successful assertion [to] the emancipation of 4,000,000 slaves."[2]

Even as the debtors' prison was shuttered during the mid- and late nineteenth century, however, there were those who questioned whether its closure meant that the debtor's body had truly been freed. It was a fact that the debtor could, in most instances, no longer be seized and caged; the lender could not summon the sheriff or bailiff to lock the debtor away, isolating him from family and friends. Surely, however, freedom required more than the possession of one's body. Most agreed that it also included the rights to own and control one's labor, to form and maintain a family, and to make independent moral choices. These liberties the creditor could still take away—formally, using writs, attachments, and foreclosure proceedings, and informally, by harassing the borrower, impugning his reputation, or threatening him with violence. In the late eighteenth century, William Blackstone, the English jurist, had described the debtor's condition as falling somewhere between that of the free citizen and that of the criminal. Theophilus Parsons, in his *Law of Contracts* (1853), counted the insolvent among those persons whose legal agency was "disabled in whole or in part," along with children, married women, soldiers, and slaves. "At one point the debtor might be sold into slavery," a Wisconsin editorialist mused in 1848. Eventually he was freed from the threat of bondage, but "the fangs of the law fastened upon his corpse and forbade its burial until his relations or friends had paid his debts." Later, the corpse was freed, but the living debtor "might be buried in jail during his life." In the modern era, imprisonment was increasingly abolished, yet the borrower's hands remained "effectually bound" so long as his wages could be garnished, his "bed, pillow, and blankets seized," and "his wife and children made into houseless, homeless beggars." Narratives that suggested lingering traces of incarceration in the seizure of property, the pressure to make payments, the impoverishment of the family, and the ruining of one's name highlighted a moral goal that the nation had yet to achieve. The debtor should have the right to exit financial relationships when they became burdensome and oppressive, and he should be able to protect from seizure those possessions deemed essential to the experience of freedom.[3]

The era's discourse of finance did not universally frame debt as an illicit constraint. Liberal evangelists celebrated credit and promise keeping as signal expressions of self-possession. Yet profound anxieties, also rooted in liberal thought, stalked the personal loan as well, likening indebtedness to imprisonment and bondage. These concerns acquired particular urgency in the wake of the Civil War: as westward settlement cast the debtor as a homesteader and entwined his freedom with the project of national expansion; as industrialization refracted the debt question through anxieties about the dissolution of craftwork, the decline of the family, and the dependency of the wage; and, most important, as slave emancipation—and resistance to that achievement by southern elites—inspired debates about what freedom for African Americans would entail. Several legislative initiatives of the postbellum moment gave legal form to these concerns and sought to shield the debtor from power and dispossession. The Peonage Act of 1867, passed under the auspices of the Thirteenth Amendment, prohibited financial contracts that compelled the specific performance of labor. It announced that debt could not command work and bind the borrower to toil for a private master. The Bankruptcy Act of 1867 created a federal legal process for discharging debts that had not been repaid. It announced that no promise could obligate the borrower forever against his will. The act also nationalized a raft of state-level property exemption laws that shielded the debtor's land, home, and tools from seizure by creditors. Collectively, these measures girded the debtor in law. They set out to secure his power to labor freely, to form and maintain a family, and to make independent moral choices. While the postbellum period has often been characterized as witnessing the unleashing of the capitalist economy, as national policies and a new free-market creed fueled industrial development, the saga of debtors' rights suggests an important countermovement: a commitment to placing limits on the market by protecting people, property, and family life from the threat of financial dispossession. At the dawn of the Age of Capital, a range of reformers converged on the figure of the debtor. They declared it an urgent matter to invest that person with rights and to guard him with the law, "like a sea-wall uplifted against the tide."[4]

The Civil War inaugurated the end of slavery in the United States. With the Emancipation Proclamation of 1863 and the Thirteenth Amendment of 1865, human beings could no longer be held as property. Labor could not be commanded by a master, and families could not be divided and separated by sale. African Americans celebrated emancipation in the language of the Old Testament. Sang one Black preacher in Boston, "Sound the loud timbrel o'er Egypt's dark sea, Jehovah hath triumphed, his people are free." Yet in the wake of abolition, as antislavery forces considered their victory and as revanchist whites resisted its reach, important questions emerged about the legal boundaries of freedom and the abuses and inequalities that might remain in African American life. Many dilemmas centered on self-government. Did emancipation entail a moral right to vote and hold office? Or was political participation a privilege that southern whites could reserve for themselves? Civil rights were similarly contested, as African Americans and abolitionists asked whether discrimination in public spaces was a vestige of slavery or a separate indignity, untouched by emancipatory law. Violence—and the right to be protected from it—was significant as well, as subordinations that could not be impressed by the state were imposed extralegally by terror groups like the Ku Klux Klan. Many of these postemancipatory questions reflected longstanding tensions within law and liberal thought concerning the rights of the individual and the powers of the local and federal state. They were amplified in the postbellum moment by social struggle, as African Americans sought their own experience of freedom, as white allies sought to aid (and discipline) their efforts, and as many in the South sought to "contest," by whatever means, "the Emancipation of the Negroes." In the Fourteenth and Fifteenth Amendments, as well as the Civil Rights and Enforcement Acts, Black freedom was formally substantiated to include the rights of citizenship and universal male suffrage. The Radical Republicans who enacted such measures sought to ensure that at the level of the law, the end of slavery would mean more to African Americans than "the bare privilege of not being chained."[5]

Articulating the difference between slavery and freedom was no less fraught in the domain of work. Certain badges of forced labor were clear. The Thirteenth Amendment surely prohibited one's being born into a status relationship in which one was bound to toil for no reward. But what was that system's opposite? What did it mean to labor freely? Did it mean that one owned land and tools and answered only to oneself? Or could a person be free and yet serve another, toiling in someone else's factory or on someone else's farm in exchange for a wage? If such labor was acceptable, then what rights would the worker need to ensure that service did not devolve into servitude? These questions surfaced throughout the nineteenth century, as new ideals of freedom confronted a new industrial order. In popular and moral culture, they inspired meditations on the virtues of landedness and the sanctity of contract. In law, arcane debates about workplace accidents, the employer's right to discipline, and the employee's right to organize bore responsibility for explaining how the sale of labor was different from the sale of self. Even in the North, where wage labor most closely approached its formal liberal ideal, many observers struggled to see the conditions of workers—poor, desperate, and embattled—as wholly free. In the postbellum South, the defects of the wage system were compounded by the planter class's commitment to purging it of any residual freedoms it might confer. The Black Codes, which limited Black mobility in order to prevent African Americans from choosing new employers and driving up their wage, were one expression of this goal. Planters also introduced compulsion into the labor contract directly, by providing workers with wage advances that required them to work for the planter until the debt was paid. As African Americans reported these arrangements to officials with the US Army and the Freedmen's Bureau, and as those reports made their way to the abolitionist press and Radical Republicans in Congress, a question took shape on which many of the moral achievements of the Civil War appeared to rest: Was labor still free when it was coerced by the obligation to repay?[6]

It was a question that had been considered earlier, in the antebellum era, when state courts in the North were asked to release indentured servants from contracts that they no longer wished to fulfill. If the servant had received travel expenses from a lender in return for a term of labor, would the law compel the servant to pay the debt through the specific performance promised? Or did the enforcement of such contracts create a condition of servitude, illegal in those states that had abolished slavery? At issue in these cases was a tension in modern contract law—indeed, in liberalism itself—between the right of entrance and the right of exit: whether freedom was defined by the power to commit oneself to whatever one wanted, or whether it required the ability to escape a commitment when it no longer accorded with one's will. Facing this question in 1843, the Illinois Supreme Court privileged the right of entrance, ruling that the enforcement of an indenture agreement "simply holds parties, who being free to contract, had voluntarily done so, to a specific performance of their contract." Absent "fraud, misrepresentation, or coercion," a debt that compelled a person to serve was fully enforceable, and doing so did no injury to the indebted individual or the principle of free labor. In Massachusetts in 1856, however, the Supreme Judicial Court found that such a "sale of service" was wholly "inconsistent with the first and fundamental article of our Declaration of Rights, which, *propio vigore*, not only abolished every vestige of slavery existing then in the Commonwealth, but rendered every form of it thereafter legally impossible." Once the debtor was "willing to serve no longer," any policy that compelled the specific performance of labor created a condition of bondage. Across the mid-nineteenth century, other state courts took up the issue and divided, as Illinois and Massachusetts did, with partisans on either side of the issue claiming the mantle of modern moral progress. In the postbellum South, it was far from clear whether wage advances would be contracted freely and whether the debt would be calculated fairly and faithfully. Yet even if it were, a genuine question remained as to whether such pacts honored the debtor's freedom or violated it.[7]

In the wake of emancipation, tales of coerced labor near and far suggested the need to settle the paradox decisively. In 1865, an American diplomat in Mexico reported the passage of a new law, "drawn up solely . . . with the view of inducing our southern planters to emigrate," that promised to reinstall involuntary servitude through personal indebtedness. Slavery had been abolished in Mexico in 1829, and the conservative architects of the new policy assured that abolition would remain the law of the land. All "men of color" would continue to be "free by the simple fact of treading the Mexican soil." Yet if any laborer in Mexico became indebted to his employer in any way—through a cash loan or through the provision of food, shelter, clothing, or transportation expenses—then he would be obligated "to remain with the master" until the debt was paid. The servant would work for "very small wages," inadequate to the task of retiring the loan, under a system that claimed to respect the worker's freedom but effectively indentured him. It was "an extraordinary thing, and almost incomprehensible," the diplomat wrote, "that when slavery . . . received a death-blow" in one country, an "attempt to reestablish that odious system" might emerge in a neighboring nation through the institution of debt. Similar narratives emerged from within the United States, in accounts of Indigenous peonage in the Southwest, indentured Chinese labor in California, and the practice of wage advances and merchandise credits to Black farmworkers in the South. "We suppose it is natural," one antislavery activist wrote of such reports, that a person "who has been accustomed to steal the whole labor of his slave, should continue to steal a part of it when the whole is no longer at his mercy." Holding the worker in a state of indebted coercion might even be more appealing to the erstwhile master, for financial servitude urged no reciprocal obligation. Should the laborer "get disabled, become permanently an invalid, or grow old and useless upon our hands," one editorialist ventriloquized for the planter, "then we can show our generosity by remitting the balance of the debt and turning him loose again."[8]

It was as the master class—at home and abroad—appeared to mock the antislavery faith in contract as an embodiment of freedom that Republicans in Congress acted to codify the right of exit in federal law. In 1865, Senator Charles Sumner of Massachusetts had championed the ratification of the Thirteenth Amendment, which declared that "neither slavery nor involuntary servitude, except as punishment for a crime . . . shall exist in the United States." In 1866, he brought to his colleagues a letter from N. H. Davis, assistant inspector general of the US Army, explaining that the military was powerless to eradicate Indigenous peonage in the Southwest because indebted labor was considered by his office to be a form of "voluntary and not involuntary servitude." Sumner disagreed with the inspector general's interpretation, but he acknowledged the need for Congress to clarify what was contained within the category of slavery and what was prohibited by the Thirteenth Amendment. Accordingly, in January 1867, he introduced a bill "to abolish and forever prohibit the System of Peonage in the Territory of New Mexico and other Parts of the United States" under the authority of new constitutional law. The measure defined peonage as "the voluntary or involuntary service or labor of any person . . . in liquidation of any debt." It declared that any contract or law that gave rise to such an arrangement was null and void. Any person who held another in a condition of peonage could be fined up to $5,000 or imprisoned for as many as five years, and any member of the military or civil service who obstructed the enforcement of the act would be subject to court-martial and discharge. The Peonage Act meant to empower state officials to extinguish debt bondage from the nation's imperial periphery and to prevent its emergence in the postbellum South. Moreover, it would settle a longstanding ambiguity in the American law of labor and contract, by declaring that freedom did not include the power to mortgage one's laboring self.[9]

Congressional debate on the proposal was brief. The loudest voices were those that supported the bill. Senators Henry Lane of Indiana and Henry Wilson of Massachusetts—whose respective state courts had long vindicated the indentured servant's right of exit—affirmed that labor obligated by debt was just as objectionable as labor expropriated under slavery. Both systems offended the individual's rights and the nation's republican principles and should be prohibited "where[ever] the power of this Government can extend." Most of the Republicans in the Senate and the House of Representatives agreed, and no Democrat spoke for or against the measure. One novel perspective was issued during debate, however. It was sounded by Senator Garrett Davis of Kentucky, a former Whig, future Democrat, and present member of the short-lived Unionist Party. Davis announced that he had spent most of his life in debt. He had owed money to bankers and shopkeepers, and there had been times when the service on his loans had consumed "all of the proceeds of my labor." He had not pledged himself to the lender formally, like the peon, and his exertions had not been commanded by a master. Yet he had nevertheless been bound by contracts that required him to toil and saw most of his earnings given over to someone else. "A man's *working* to pay the debts that he owes" was in fact how most obligations were retired, Davis explained, and it was thus ordinary, rather than exceptional, for debt to challenge the free-labor ideal. Davis did not argue that all debt was equivalent to peonage or that coerced labor should not be prohibited by Congress. But he did suggest that there were deeper tensions within the ideology of free labor and contract that Sumner's bill did not address. Much as moral critics had asked whether abolishing the debtors' prison meant that the debtor's body was truly free, Davis intimated that one could banish peonage and yet still find people worked and ruled by debt.[10]

His was a small protest, and it did little to slow the passage of the bill. The measure was approved by both bodies of Congress in the spring of 1867 and was signed into law soon after. Its most direct impact was in the Southwest, where the territorial government promptly declared all persons "held to service or labor by any statute or custom heretofore in force" to be free. Emancipation was not immediate, but over the next year, more than three hundred prosecutions were undertaken against individuals who retained debt peons, and by end of the 1870s the practice had been largely suppressed. In the South, the more significant policy was the placement of the former Confederacy under military control, commencing with the passage of the first Reconstruction Act in March of 1867 and continuing as late as 1878. African Americans, with their ability to vote and hold office protected by the federal government, were able to repeal the Black Codes and pass debtor protection laws, which limited the duration of secured loans, exempted from seizure and forced sale certain kinds of property, and allowed for the kind of physical mobility that was needed to contract on fairer terms. Indeed, it was in this period that the debtors' prison in the South was fully abolished (having previously been shuttered only for whites). The problem of African American debt would not go away—its trajectory into the twentieth century is considered in the third chapter of this book—but its most coercive form was temporarily forestalled by the federal prohibition against peonage and by Black political work during Reconstruction. Yet Davis's comments on the Peonage Act as it was debated in Congress highlighted a contradiction in more ordinary experiences of indebtedness that called for further reform. Even if debt did not compel the borrower to serve the lender, as a slave or a peon to a master, it nevertheless required the borrower to work if he wanted the obligation retired. The farmer, merchant, or craftsman who toiled under a loan was not formally bound, but neither did he experience his laboring condition as self-possessed and free. The right of exit enshrined by Sumner's law was limited to contracts that explicitly mortgaged labor. Even then, it left the debt intact and barred only the specific performance of work. For borrowers coerced in less direct ways, a different approach would be needed. Freedom for debtors would require the power to exit the contract entirely when it could no longer be justly repaid.[11]

The Peonage Act was the first piece of legislation passed by Congress that drew on the authority of the Thirteenth Amendment. It prohibited loans that mortgaged the labor of the debtor and made it the property of the lender. In early 1867, as the measure made its journey from bill to law, it was trailed by parallel piece of legislation, shepherded by Representative Thomas A. Jenckes of Rhode Island, that would extend the right of exit beyond debts that obligated the debtor to serve. Article I of the US Constitution authorized Congress to enact "uniform Laws on the subject of Bankruptcies throughout the United States." At the time of the constitutional framing, those words had referred to a specific and controversial process in English law whereby a group of creditors could petition a court to discover all a debtor's assets, liquidate them, and divide the proceeds among the creditors. Bankruptcy was a process that happened *to* the borrower, rather than a process that he initiated. It offered lenders the opportunity to terminate a stagnant financial relationship and recover what they could of the debtor's remaining funds. For the debtor, bankruptcy was a fraught ordeal in which the achievement of financial release was offset by the procedure's involuntary nature, as well as the loss of one's valued possessions. It was "the Hell of the English," in one scholar's estimation. In the United States, these demerits had long discouraged the passage of statutes that followed the English example. There were also concerns that a federal bankruptcy law would weaken the power of the states to govern insolvency locally, and that the availability of the bankruptcy process would encourage speculation by lessening the hazards of borrowing and lending. For these reasons, Congress had failed to embrace its constitutional authority on the bankruptcy question for much of the nation's history, outside of four years (1800–1802 and 1841–1843) in which temporary bankruptcy laws had been established following financial panics.[12]

Yet Jenckes believed that the Civil War had changed these political and philosophical dynamics. In part, he recognized that the conflict had inspired new and urgent needs for financial relief throughout the nation. Secession had severed the commercial relationships that stretched from North to South. Yankee businesses that relied on southern agriculture were instantly imperiled, as were firms that prospered on furnishing the plantation economy. Military mobilization upset the availability of ordinary business resources, from raw materials and rail transportation to money and laboring men. "Melancholy derangements and upheavals" in economic life were natural to war, one New England newspaper reported, and commercial failure was sure to follow in its wake. The refusal of southern planters to honor the debts owed to northern shippers, factors, insurers, and salesmen compounded the situation. It meant that many northern businesses faced not only an inhospitable market but also an unexpected evaporation of the funds they had loaned to the South. Additionally, all these developments took place amid the ongoing recovery from the Panic of 1857, a reversal triggered by the collapse of the Ohio Life Insurance and Trust Company that had reverberated throughout the nation, particularly in the mercantile North and the agricultural West. In this context, the scope of financial failure in the United States was catastrophic, with a basis in developments—panic, secession, and war—that lay far beyond the individual's control. "I am one of the victims who lost my property in the South," one debtor wrote to Abraham Lincoln in 1863. "Mine is not an *isolated case* but one among thousands," another insolvent explained. "I am living on the hope that Congress will break our chains and restore us to the activities and ambitions of life," a New York debtor affirmed, while others pled for an opportunity "to be of use to themselves, their families and society." In a moment of unprecedented failure, the nation's commercial men begged to be released from their obligations and allowed to begin their financial lives anew.[13]

Jenckes's bill proposed to meet this demand by allowing the federal district courts to hear petitions of insolvency and to grant debtors a full financial discharge. Such petitions had to concern debts that exceeded $300. They were primarily to be initiated by debtors themselves—a form of *voluntary* bankruptcy that had been unknown at the time of the constitutional framing. Involuntary proceedings could be commenced as well, but only when the debtor was believed to be transferring property to someone else or leaving his state of residence "with intent to defraud his creditors." In all instances in which failure was confronted honestly, the choice to enter bankruptcy would remain vested with the debtor. If he chose to seek liquidation and discharge, he would file a petition with the judge declaring his inability to pay and his willingness to "surrender all his estate and effects for the benefits of his creditors." He would present evidence of all outstanding obligations and a full inventory of his property. If his creditors demanded it, he would have to submit to a public examination, in which an officer of the court would search out undisclosed possessions. Bankruptcy would not be a quick process. Indeed, Jenckes imagined it would take several months to complete, stipulating in the bill that perishable property—which would lose its value if it spoiled—should be sold at the earliest possible moment, even before an inventory of the rest of the estate had been completed. During the pendency of the proceedings, the debtor could not be arrested or imprisoned for debt if he lived a jurisdiction where such actions were still legal. Once the court had knowledge of all the insolvent's assets and all the people with a right to them, a distribution schedule would be produced and the property would be disbursed. At that point, the creditors' claims would dissolve and the debtor would walk away free.[14]

The bill was a response to the financial distress engendered by the war. Congressional action was needed to restore the nation's economy and revive the circulation of credit. Yet the moment also supplied important ideological reasons for reform as well. These stemmed from the achievement of slave emancipation and the larger historical arc that it was believed to form. Several analogies connected these themes to the bankruptcy bill, proposed not as a temporary measure, like the earlier bankruptcy acts, but as a permanent addition to American law. They appeared at different points in congressional debate. First, there was the free-labor notion that all who worked were entitled to a just and fair reward—that "every man—so far as . . . he can accomplish it—should be allowed to have the fruits, and all the fruits of his own labor." This was an axiom of liberal political philosophy and of American antislavery discourse, which defined the sin of slavery as the expropriation of labor without wages or consent. In the bankruptcy debate, the debtor was cast as being similarly denied the due profits of his industry. While the debtor wore "no visible chains," an editorialist with *Hunt's Merchants' Magazine* declared, his labor was effectively owned by his creditors, who could readily use writs and attachments to "sweep off [his] earnings" whenever they so desired. The fruits of daily exertion did not make their way to the debtor's account, as they were meant to in liberal and republican theory, but instead were diverted to the lender until the debt was paid. Jenckes acknowledged that this did not constitute a formal condition of servitude, but he did believe that it amounted to a kind of "pecuniary bondage"—one that trespassed against the principles of free labor and possessive individualism. Bankruptcy legislation would emancipate the debtor and permit him to again engage in "a career of industry and enterprise, *with its reward.*" It would allow him to draw a line beyond which his misfortunes could not travel and where the fruits of his industry would be his. "As this is a year of jubilee for those literally enslaved," the abolitionist congressman and bankruptcy advocate Owen Lovejoy declared, "so let it be signalized by the disenthrallment of those who are entangled by pecuniary obligations," by the passage of the bankruptcy bill.[15]

A second defense of the bankruptcy law placed it in the mainstream of the age through a novel synthesis of free-labor ideology and free-contract beliefs. The claim was not that the debtor was forced to work for the benefit of others, but rather that he could not work *at all*. In particular, entrepreneurial labor became impossible for the insolvent debtor because, as an insolvent, he was unable to secure new lines of credit with which to fund his risks. He had no property left to mortgage and no reputation on which to trade, and any capital he did acquire could be seized by prior creditors. The debtor was thus consigned to languish in commercial purgatory, standing idle as profitable opportunities came and went. In Lovejoy's estimation, there was "a vast amount of business talent, enterprise, and commercial integrity throughout the country that may be said, in sort, to be imprisoned." It was tragic and immoral, Jenckes agreed, that "the energies of the unfortunate debtor are lost to his family and his country" under a legal system that provided no path for the release of insolvent individuals from their prior obligations. "Although the actual imprisonment of the [debtor] has been abolished . . . in most of the States," the congressman explained, "there still exists that life-long incarceration, more terrible to the honest and sensitive mind than the other, in the chain network of insoluble debt." The insolvent debtor thus joined the prisoner and the enslaved person as an individual who had been made ineligible for normal commerce. All three stood outside free society; all three required positive acts of law to participate fully in the "life and prosperity" of the nation. Like the abolition of the debtors' prison and the eradication of slavery, bankruptcy expressed the individual's moral right to enter and exit the market at will.[16]

These analogies emphasized the debtor's relationship with work. They described bankruptcy as a tool for restoring the labor and entrepreneurial power taken from the borrower by insolvency. They envisioned a different type of debtor than the opponents of peonage—one entrepreneurial and middle class rather than poor and waged—yet they shared a common language of moral progress rooted in the ownership of one's laboring self. A third line of reasoning defined the unfreedom of insolvency as a trespass against the debtor's right to form and maintain a family. At the center of this complaint was the belief that free society both required and promoted a balance between the public realm of commerce and the private realm of the home. The former was a world of contract, peopled by formal legal equals, whereas the latter was a world of affectionate dependency, arranged hierarchically from men to women to children. Domestic inequality did not offend the ethic of liberal self-possession but instead expressed it for its ideal male subject. Just as a man was entitled to sell his labor freely in the market, so was he entitled to the refuge of the home, with the gendered subordination of woman and children signaling domestic integrity. This vision gained clarity in the antebellum period through comparison with the sexual disorder of the slave plantation, as abolitionists summoned child separation, rape, adultery, and incest to index the moral distance between North and South. Bondage cultured depravity, they argued, while freedom assured the triumph of the well-ordered home. This claim helped mobilize support for the antislsavery crusade, but it also presented an opportunity for moral critics to advocate for reforms that would protect the family from the market wherever it was found to struggle.[17]

Insolvency was readily incorporated into these narratives. In popular and prescriptive literature, debt had long been pictured as a threat to the sanctity of the home. Men who were saddled with debts were said to be unfit for marriage until their loans were paid, and those debtors who were married were depicted as witnessing their relationship strain and break under the weight of financial misfortune. Fathers might be forced to leave their families as they hid from creditors or sought a fresh start in another state, and children might be sent to live with more prosperous relatives until the hard times had passed. Most common were stories of wives sent to work outside the home, in mills and factories or as domestic servants or prostitutes. Advocates of bankruptcy law seized on such tales. "Can anyone imagine a slavery more absolute and more heart-rending," asked Senator Reverdy Johnson of Maryland, than that of the insolvent man who "sees in his own household . . . the utter hopelessness with which his wife and children from day to day live?" What meant freedom for the patriarch who could not prevent his commercial failures from invading the private home? What, indeed, meant patriarchy? As Jenckes reported to his congressional colleagues, the debtor who desired to return to business but could not contract on his own account would hide "behind all sorts of subterfuge." He might advertise himself "as agent for his father, son, or, in some States, even his wife." This was a narrative not only of the loss of autonomy in the market—the ability to work, trade, and take on risks—but also of its effect on the home, as insolvency imperiled the right of the grown son to escape the empire of the father; the right of the husband to rule and provide for the wife; and the right of the father to govern the child. Financial abjection turned on its head the hierarchy of the family, which to many was the quintessential expression of high liberalism. By allowing the insolvent patriarch to dissolve his obligations, bankruptcy would offer him an opportunity to reclaim his familiar and natural powers. "All the law proposes," Senator Johnson declared, is "that he who is in that condition of human thralldom shall be permitted to escape from it and be again a man."[18]

The advocates of bankruptcy legislation thus aligned their cause with the emancipatory spirit of the age. By providing the debtor with a release from existing obligations, they would restore to him the rights of free labor, entrepreneurship, and family maintenance that were taken by insolvency. Slavery offered a rhetorical foil for the liberated borrower in its dependency, licentiousness, and pain. Yet the victim of unfreedom pictured in the bankruptcy debate was a decidedly more privileged subject than the chattel bondsman or the debt peon. He was a head of household accustomed to earning a living through business rather than toil. He was also, in the imagination of bankruptcy advocates, explicitly white. It was not only the case that bankruptcy legislation would be of the greatest benefit to white men—those craftsmen, farmers, and merchants possessed of the standing to become substantially indebted before and during the war. It was also that their suffering was signified in bankruptcy discourse through their alienation from the supposed birthright of whiteness. For some, the law was said to demonstrate that freedom would be allocated evenly in the postbellum United States. "I ask the gentleman from Pennsylvania," Jenckes put to the abolitionist Thaddeus Stevens, "whether after so many years during which he has been known as the champion of the black man, he will now in his old age vote [against the bankruptcy bill and thus] for the enslavement, the continued enslavement, of the white man." Outside Congress, the language of racial resentment cut more sharply, as newspaper editorialists questioned whether the federal government would extend "to more than 100,000 *white men*" the liberty that it was "*apparently* so anxious to grant to the colored race." The captivity of indebtedness was even said by some bankruptcy advocates to represent a greater moral offense than plantation bondage because of the capacities of the people it affected. Insolvency was "far more galling [to the white man] than slavery to the colored man," this argument went, because the former constrained those who were "high minded, honest, [and] ambitious," whereas the latter bridled only those "uneducated or refined." Reported one probankruptcy memorial, "The poor African, without the knowledge of his wants, devoid of the intellectual torments which are produced by dependence and subjection . . . stands on ground far more enviable than that maintained by the insolvent debtor . . . who has known better days." This was not a separate claim from narratives that described insolvency as an infringement on individual rights and liberties. Instead, race was woven into the liberal discourse of debt, serving to define the essential rights of freedom through the familiar privileges of whiteness.[19]

Indebtedness had long been analogized to the captivity of bondage. The debtor was not, in most instances, the servant of the lender, but neither did he enjoy the rights of contract, property, free labor, and mobility experienced by his solvent peers. Legal theorists often likened the insolvent's condition to the disabilities of the child, the wife, the soldier, and the slave. Bankruptcy advocates embraced this language to argue for a federal law that would allow debt contracts that no longer accorded with the borrower's will to be dissolved. They suggested, in terms both highly liberal and profoundly conservative, that to pass through this age of emancipation without creating a formal right of financial exit would be a betrayal of the era's principles and a concession to dominance and power. Jenckes's bill had a longer legislative history than Sumner's Peonage Act. The proposal was put forth and defeated in 1864 and 1866, but it finally passed in 1867—in the same session of Congress in which the Peonage Act was passed and, in the first Reconstruction Act, the Radical Republicans asserted their control over the postwar South. The law's effects were both broad and ironic. In its first year of existence, more than seven thousand insolvents had their debts discharged by the federal courts; by 1870, the number had swelled to nearly forty-three thousand. Among those who received the privilege of financial release were northern merchants, western farmers, and white southern planters—a class of debtors excluded from bankruptcy in the bill's earliest drafts but eventually embraced in an attempt to salve sectional tension and restore commercial union. Indeed, the promotion of trade and the cultivation of business, even to the point of aiding former Confederates, was a central object of the act. Bankruptcy was of a piece with other Republican initiatives that sought to foster industrial development and promote financial markets, through taxes, land grants, and currency legislation. Yet bankruptcy's approach was unique: it encouraged business and enterprise by limiting each, investing the individual with the right to exit oppressive entanglements and walk away from pacts that he no longer wished to keep. Risks could be taken because their consequences were defined. Promises could be made because they could more easily be broken.[20]

The Bankruptcy Act enshrined a right of exit in federal financial law. It assured that no promise—and no misfortune—would bind the debtor forever. Once a loan became too burdensome to repay, the borrower could petition a court to have the obligation satisfied as best as possible and then be declared discharged. Yet as the act was debated in 1864, 1866, and 1867, an important question emerged: Should there be limits on what could be taken from the debtor to settle the account? That is, did bankruptcy fulfill its moral vision if, in liberating the debtor, it dispossessed him of all his belongings? For many lawmakers, a freedom that was earned by draining the insolvent of the materials of labor and the comforts of homelife was unworthy of the name. Thus, they included in the Bankruptcy Act a section stipulating that the debtor who petitioned for release would not be deprived of all his possessions. Instead, he would be permitted to keep "necessary household and kitchen furniture," basic clothing, and any items that were "exempted from levy and sale upon execution . . . by the laws of the State in which the bankrupt has his domicile." Bankruptcy was a federal legal experience. It was authorized by the Constitution, legislated by Congress, and administered by the federal courts. Yet it would also be shaped by the local law of property exemption, with the debtor secure in those belongings that state legislatures had deemed inaccessible to creditors. In part, exemption law was incorporated into the act as a political concession. It was meant to appeal to those congressmen who cherished the local property exemptions as embodiments of community values and who feared that bankruptcy without exemption would lead to the transfer of land from small settlers to large financial concerns. Yet exemption's inclusion in the federal law also represented a positive moral endorsement of the exemption principle itself. If bankruptcy was to deliver true and meaningful freedom to the debtor, then it could not allow him exit the obligation with nothing, granting him only the autonomy of the beggar. Instead, it would need to preserve his ownership of land, tools, and the familiar comforts of home and therein allow him to earn a living again and thrive.[21]

Property exemption law was a creation of the mid-nineteenth century. It emerged as one of the ways that states could provide relief and protection to debtors without running afoul of the Contract Clause of the Constitution, which reserved the right to alter or dissolve existing debts exclusively to Congress. What was left to the states was the power to set the terms of enforceable contracts—an authority exercised in usury laws, for example—and the power to govern the remedies that were available to creditors if the debtor defaulted. The abolition of the debtors' prison was one expression of this prerogative, as states removed a remedy that creditors had previously employed to motivate the debtor—or his family and friends—into finding the means of repayment. The passage of stay laws, which temporarily suspended foreclosures and forced sales of property during periods of panic or depression, was another. Yet the most popular regulation of the remedy was for state legislatures to declare certain kinds of property to be permanently—in all economic moments—exempt from execution.[22] If a debtor defaulted on a loan and the creditor petitioned a court to seize and sell the debtor's assets, the bailiff would leave untouched those items that were shielded by statute. If the exemption was ignored or misinterpreted and a piece of protected property was taken, the debtor could file a lawsuit—sometimes against the creditor and sometimes against the offending state official—to have the property returned. And in many states, if the debtor attempted to borrow money on the security of protected property and did not take the required steps to waive the exemption, then the discerning lender would deny the loan, as the mortgage was in fact an empty pledge. Property exemptions were not absolute. They did not protect items that had been purchased with borrowed funds, and they could be defeated by debts owed to the state (for taxes) and debts owed to hired workers (for wages). Yet for the ordinary loan that the craftsman or the farmer undertook to have cash until a sale or harvest, the exemption was an effective device. It drew a bright legal line around cherished pieces of property that the market could not imperil and the creditor could not seize.[23]

Geographically, state exemption laws first appeared in the South and West and gradually made their way to the Great Lakes region and the Northeast. Chronologically, they were enacted and enhanced in two waves. During the first, in the 1840s and 1850s, jurists and lawmakers prioritized the protection of the debtor's homestead. Their model was a measure passed by the short-lived Republic of Texas in 1839, which declared up to fifty acres of family-occupied property to be ineligible for levy and forced sale. The exemption would last for the lifetime of the debtor and of his dependents, so long as they continued to live on the property. States that followed Texas shielded not only the home itself and the land on which it rested but also those items deeply associated with family life, including decorative objects, heirlooms, books, musical instruments, and other possessions that aided in the raising of children. Reformers who championed these laws celebrated the home as a space of tranquil refuge and virtuous repose, where men were entitled to enjoy the "feelings of security and pride" and where women should be able to add "comforts to conveniences" without fearing that it all could be swept away. Judges in the newly annexed state of Texas expanded the exemption law in 1857, widening its protections to land not currently used or occupied by the family but that the family owned and envisioned developing into a home in the future. In Kansas, at the constitutional convention of 1859, an argument took shape over whether there should be any limits on the size and value of the exempted homestead. Against the charge that many debtors were wealthier than their creditors and that an unlimited exemption would perpetuate its own form of injustice, a contingent of conventioneers asserted that "a home is a home—good or bad—valuable or valueless. Even if the value of a man's home stands up to five hundred thousand dollars, let him have and enjoy [it] and the society of his friends." For many reformers, it was better that the family be protected even to the point of injuring the honest lender than that some homes be unguarded and left subject to the whims of economic life.[24]

A second way of regulation arrived in the 1860s and early 1870s, with exemptions expanded—by both statutory amendment and judicial interpretation—to include protections for property that bore on the debtor's status as a laborer: specifically, as a farmer, mechanic, artisan, or professional. The thread of moral reasoning behind these provisions often began with the illicitness of imprisonment for debt, in which the borrower's laboring capacity was controlled by the creditor, and moved on to the need for protections for the material of work itself. Just as it was wrong for the lender to own "the future labor of a man," one reformer explained, so was it unjust "that you should take from him all means of [laboring] in the future." On this basis, the exemption for family land—itself a productive resource as well as a site of domestic maintenance—was enhanced in the years surrounding the Civil War to include protections for those items that "enable a person to carry on the business in which he is principally engaged" and to secure "the means of making a living." Included in this category were the medical instruments of a doctor or dentist; the horse, harness, and plow of a farmer; the lumber, hammer, and shingles of a carpenter; the safe, cabinet, and drafting table of a surveyor; the ink and press of a printer; and the bucket and lantern of a miner. The goal of these protections was to secure to the working person "a competence when he has once obtained it [and] to make him what God designed he should be, a free man."[25] The law was likewise committed to shielding the rewards of labor, exempting the wages of service against garnishment by creditors. In some states the exemption was fixed by cash value—with the creditor permitted to claim monthly earnings above, for example, $25—whereas in others the protection covered the wages in whole. In the North and West, the exemption was generally limited to "persons who have to provide for the entire support of a family," whereas in the South it tended to be available to all "journeymen, mechanics, and laborers." The premise of the law in both instances was that no man (and especially no householder) should "make merchandise of his wage-earning power," just as he "may not sell himself into slavery."[26]

Exemption law had much in common with the federal bankruptcy and antipeonage laws. All three aspired to protect the debtor against coercion and dispossession. Each was narrated and naturalized through the language of bondage and freedom. Bankruptcy and exemption law were positively conjoined in the Bankruptcy Act of 1867, with the state laws acquiring federal significance and helping to legitimize the more controversial bankruptcy process in the eyes of suspicious legislators. In the South, both would be used by indebted planters seeking to maintain their social power. Important differences separated property exemption from its national counterparts, however, for while the right of exit could be distributed to debtors with relative uniformity, the exemption laws protected property that had particular meaning to the insolvent borrower. Enforcement thus required knowledge of who the debtor was and what identities and relationships the vulnerable property supported. Land became a homestead, for example, only when it was settled and occupied by a family. There was thus space for the creditor to challenge the debtor's claim to household headship—to say that he had no family and that the land was hence unprotected—and a competing need for the insolvent borrower to defend his householder status. Exemptions for the materials of productive work could be similarly contested. As a Minnesota judge observed, "The tools and instruments of a dentist, surgeon, or watch-maker, could [do little to] relieve the distress, or add to the comfort, of an insolvent farmer." Courts and creditors routinely investigated cases of deliberate fraud, in which the delinquent debtor falsely claimed a trade so as to shield more valuable belongings. Yet even in the absence of outright deception professional identification presented challenges, as the event of financial default inherently meant that the borrower was not earning a living in the way he was accustomed. What domestic furnishings were appropriate to a bankrupt's social station? Asked one creditor's attorney in an Illinois lawsuit in 1873, what tools were "'suited to the condition or occupation in life' of an insolvent debtor"?[27]

Such dilemmas flooded the courts in the 1860s and 1870s. They arose both when exemptions were used in federal bankruptcy proceedings and when they were used in state courts, to shield property from the ordinary process of levy and sale. To determine where in economic life the debtor fit and which items were required to keep him there, judges often considered the person's work history, skill, and future prospects. In *Harris v. Haynes* (1874), for example, an insolvent hardware dealer in Michigan sought to have his tinning tools returned to him after they had been seized by the county sheriff. While he had never been gainfully employed as a tinner, he had been learning the trade for several years and had agreed to manufacture some tinware for a client in the future. The sheriff and the creditor insisted that the debtor was "not so engaged" in the occupation as to render "said tools and machines exempt from sale," but the court found that his knowledge and intent in the trade was sufficient to protect the items. "It is not presumed [by his present unemployment] that he means to become an idler," the judge concluded. In other cases—concerning debtors transitioning between occupations, debtors claiming multiple occupations at once, and debtors making novel claims on personal possessions as the tools of their trade (for example, a gold watch as being essential to running a business in an era "when everything moves on scheduled time")—the courts similarly tended to favor the most generous exemptions the insolvent could reasonably defend without doing gross injustice to the lender.[28]

Questions of identity were no less challenging when the role in question was family head—a designation that granted debtors access to the most expansive safeguards for land and domestic belongings. The law's ideal in this regard was a man who led a household comprising a wife and children. Debtors who approached the courts in this condition were easily recognized as deserving and entitled subjects. Yet what of the man whose wife had died and whose children had been hers from another marriage? What of the husband who had abandoned his family, or the wife he had abandoned? Did either of them have a claim to the status of head of home and thus to the law's most robust protections? Adoption, composite households, estrangement, and separation all tested the legal definition of the familial in different ways. Two cases from 1870s demonstrated the complexities of family identification, as well as the profound conservatism that often guided the law. The first concerned an immigrant widow, Louisa Oldridge, who became indebted to her landlord after failing to pay rent for several months on a large apartment in Chicago. The second dealt with a Black woman, Lettie Marshall, who lived and worked on the land owned by her former master, B. G. Marshall, who had died indebted to several men in Fort Bend County, Texas. In the first case, Oldridge's landlord had secured a creditor's warrant from a local justice of the peace and had seized the widow's household furniture with the intention to sell it. In the second, Marshall's former master had bequeathed to her a portion of his estate, but the land had entered probate and was claimed and divided by the testator's creditors, leaving nothing for his heir. Both women were dispossessed of property, and each sought relief in the exemption statutes of their state. Yet neither was the debtor whose freedom was most legible to the law—a laboring man whose earnings supported his dependents. Each thus embarked on a novel legal performance in order to make their suffering meaningful to the court.[29]

Oldridge challenged her landlord's levy in the Circuit Court of Cook County and, on appeal, the Supreme Court of Illinois. In both venues, she told a tale of mastery lost. First, she explained that at the time of the levy, she had been subletting several rooms in her apartment to tenants. This made her the matron of a boardinghouse—a gainful occupation—and entitled her to shield up to $100 of business property from creditors, which she sought to apply to the domestic furniture taken by her landlord. Second, she contended that at the time of the levy she had been acting as the head of a family. She was thus entitled, by Illinois law, to protect an additional $300 worth of property that was familiar to home. Oldridge did not have any children, and her husband had been dead for several years. Her claim for family headship did not rest on any connections made by blood, sex, or marriage. Instead, she offered her relationships with three individuals who lived with her: two waged servants and one female friend who neither paid rent nor was in her employ. She urged the court to recognize these relationships as familial by using the classical definition of the family as all the persons who "live in one home and under the authority of another." The family, in this reading, was a unit defined by proximity and power rather than by affection or kinship. It did not require marriage or consanguity, and it often encompassed such connections only because they overlapped with the essential characteristics of the family: order and mastery. Indeed, the word *family* derived from the Latin *familia*, Oldridge reminded the court, which meant "the whole of the slaves of the household." Because Oldridge's friend and servants depended on her for support and responded to her commands, they constituted the membership of her household. Her headship thus made her eligible for the most generous entitlements afforded by the law.[30]

Lettie Marshall's lawsuit—heard by the Fort Bend County Court and, on appeal, the Supreme Court of Texas—relied on a parallel narrative of dominance and submission. Marshall's former owner had bequeathed to her a portion of his estate, but he had died indebted to several local creditors. His property had entered probate, and in the order of distribution, the creditors would receive their shares before Marshall, who would ultimately be left with nothing. Marshall challenged her place in this sequence by arguing that she had been the lone, constitutive member of her former owner's family. As such, the estate was required to be treated as a homestead and, under Texas law, should pass directly to her, sustaining her until her death and only at that point becoming available to the creditors. Her challenge was not based on any claims of romantic intimacy with her former owner or any evidence of common descent. Instead, she argued that, "for thirty years, bond and free," she had tended to her owner in the manner of a family dependent. He had been "a cripple, and [had lived] the last years of his life [as] a helpless invalid," unable to care for himself. Marshall had risen to the task, serving as his "housekeeper, nurse, and general domestic manager." The relations that began in slavery had continued after emancipation, with Marshall pressing beyond the contractual obligations of a waged employee and fulfilling "all of the duties . . . of mother, sister, and daughter." Such labor "supplie[d] the place of inheritable blood" in constructing a family unit that the law was bound to respect. It invested both the debtor and his dependent with rights that could not be violated by creditors or the law. Even—if not especially—in death, the debtor was entitled to protect his family from destitution. Marshall thus deserved to receive that protection in the form of land that would provide for her in her old age.[31]

Property-exemption law aimed to shield the debtor from the ravages of creditors and the vagaries of the market. Advocates analogized the exemption's protections to the shuttering of the debtors' prison and, in some contexts, the abolition of slavery. Yet property became meaningful under exemption law only through its personal significance to individuals—as a means of supporting free labor or as the material for a dignified and orderly home. As in the case of bankruptcy law—with its implied connections to domestic hierarchy and race privilege—exemption law often warred against the dependency of indebtedness in order to preserve more familiar expressions of power and subordination. Oldridge and Marshall thus sought to make themselves legible to the legal order by performing those unequal relations. They were not anonymous persons besieged by creditors. Instead, the former was a household authority, upon whom others relied for direction and care, and the latter was a household dependent, deserving of continued support from her deceased provider. Rather than understanding the cases as questions of aid for two single women—one Black, one white—the legal narrative framed the cases as aiding a deceased master and affirming the principle of (male) family headship as a form of domination, respectively. Both women prevailed at the level of the local court. The Cook County judiciary awarded Oldridge her property, and the Fort Bend County judge recognized Marshall's life title to her former owner's homestead. In each instance, the creditor appealed. The Supreme Court of Illinois reheard the case and vindicated the lower court's judgment, holding that "the friend of the appellee and her two female servants were each a part of the family," rendering Oldridge a qualifying head. Marshall was not as fortunate. The Supreme Court of Texas heard her tale and accepted that her relationship with her former owner had exceeded the bounds of conventional employment. It deferred, however, to the claims of the lender: that in freedom, Marshall was "not in the power" of her former owner. "He had no authority over [her, and she] had no claim for support upon him." Their arrangement thus fell short of the familial, leaving her to collect her bequest after the estate had been liquidated by the creditors.[32]

The outcomes in the Oldridge and Marshall cases were no doubt shaped by race and region. If Black men and women like Marshall could be legally recognized as members of their former owners' families—as slavery's apologists had long insisted they were—then property across the South might pass to African Americans as the last generation of slaveholders died out. This would be a reversal in the social order more unsettling to most judges and lawmakers than the passage of planter estates to creditors, and so the definitions of the family that could be accepted in Illinois proved untenable in Texas.[33] Yet the fact that Marshall's case found success at first, and that both Oldridge and Marshall based their pleas for relief on the language of mastery and servitude, highlighted an important element of the exemption principle and, indeed, the cause of debtors' rights more generally. Exemption law, like the Bankruptcy Act, promised to protect the debtor's freedom. While bankruptcy provided an actual release from the debt—an emancipation or jubilee—exemption law divided the debtor's possessions in two and shielded those that supported the debtor in productive labor and domestic dignity. In this way it would ensure that he would always be "what God designed he should be, a free man." This vision was at once liberal and universalistic but also deeply conservative, for the freedom that debt most readily drained (and thus that the law most eagerly sought to protect) was that which was enjoyed by the nation's most privileged subjects: white, propertied men. Exemption law promised the greatest benefits to those who had the most to lose. Oldridge's and Marshall's novel legal performances underscored this point, as a white widow and a formerly enslaved Black woman framed their claims around the rights of husbands, fathers, and masters. To rule for them individually was also to rule for the hierarchies of race, class, and gender that elsewhere left them vulnerable and marginalized. Oldridge and Marshall sought freedom from debt not in defiance of an unequal social order but, ironically, in its defense.

In 1872, the year after the revelations of imprisonment for debt at the Ludlow Street Jail in New York—a saga that ended with a judicial order discharging the debtors then imprisoned—Mark Twain and Charles Dudley Warren published *The Gilded Age: A Tale of Today*. The novel depicted a nation freshly removed from slave emancipation in which most every-thing was for sale, from land, labor, and consumer goods to political influ-ence, reputation, and even human bodies. Many of these transactions took place through the medium of credit, with objects of perceived value being pledged to lenders in exchange for present funds. No character embraced the promise and peril of finance as fully as Laura Hawkins. Hawkins hailed from a midwestern farming family that was perched between wealth and in-digence. Her father had gone deeply into debt to buy an unproductive tract of land, and the family waited to see if the property would acquire value be-fore the mortgage swallowed them whole. In the novel's opening chapters, Laura set off for the nation's capital with a plan to have the estate purchased by the federal government as a site for the education of freedpeople. Indebt-edness inspired her journey and enabled her rise as she climbed through Washington society by coining the appearance of status into social and po-litical currency, trading on the promise of approaching wealth rather than the wealth itself. Yet in the market, all were vulnerable to chance, and in the novel's concluding chapters, misfortune mounted for the overly leveraged protagonist. First, a lover's quarrel ended with Laura slaying her companion and facing trial. Then, her chief political patron was caught in a corrup-tion scandal that sapped his influence and scuttled the land purchase that would have enriched the Hawkins family. Finally, with obligations to repay, Laura was forced to seek an income on the lecture circuit. Upon learning that her first address would be given to an empty auditorium—the public uninterested in the recollections of yesterday's belle—Laura spontaneously expired, enacting her belief that in the gamble she had undertaken, "if I lose, I lose everything—even myself."[34]

The existential threat of debt—its power to crush the individual—was a common theme of late-nineteenth-century literature. Novels and serials dwelled on the unfortunate borrower who was driven to crime, alcohol, forced labor, or suicide after his financial failure. These were not only the concerns of popular fiction, however. They preoccupied the law as well. While important cultural currents in the postbellum period ennobled free contract and speculation—the right of the individual to embrace an uncer-tain fate—freedom was also defined by the debtor's ability to exit oppres-sive financial relationships and to do so with his property and personhood intact. In the wake of the Civil War, several legislative initiatives gave in-stitutional expression to this faith. The Peonage Act forbade contracts that mortgaged the labor of the borrower. The Bankruptcy Act permitted the debtor to petition a federal court to have his current obligations discharged. State-level property exemption laws, which were nationalized under the Bankruptcy Act, shielded the debtor's homestead, tools, clothing, and domestic adornments from levy and forced sale. These concentric rings of protection for the debtor rested on the view that the abolition of imprisonment for debt—a cause adjacent to the abolition of slavery—was incomplete without safeguards for the most cherished experiences of freedom: the ability to own and sell one's labor, to form and maintain a family, and to make independent moral choices. Some physical and figurative possessions could be pledged for debt and lost, but others should never be taken away. Against tales of past and distant lands where, "it is said, the creditor may not only reduce the debtor himself to slavery, but . . . may even violate the chastity of the wife," these reforms told an important moral tale. They taught that debt in the United States had been made modern. By extension, the United States was thus modern as well.[35]

In the decades ahead, this commitment to the debtor's freedom would be tested in two ways. At the center, a history unfolded that pitted debt reformers against one another, against creditors and their political allies, and against the belief—also rooted in liberalism—that people should be free to bargain for what they wished and live with the consequences of their choices. In the face of these interlocking challenges, some of the institutional architecture of debtors' rights would fall. The Bankruptcy Act, for example, was rescinded in 1878. Many Americans would increasingly look to private devices for hedging against risk and forestalling the possibility of loss, like the life insurance contract and the mutual aid society. Yet so too would they continue to press for legal protections, yoking the moral precepts of debtors' rights to campaigns to revive the escape of bankruptcy (enshrined in the Bankruptcy Act of 1898); to govern the national currency so as to do justice to debtors in a deflationary era (an effort that animated the Populist challenge of the 1890s and the creation of the Federal Reserve in 1913); and to preserve and expand the property exemptions. Indeed, state-building progressives of the early twentieth century would draw on the tradition of the exemptions for a kind of historical legitimacy, as evidence of a longstanding American belief that "property rights yield to human rights when the home, the family, and the minimum of subsistence are at stake." That commerce in a moral nation required limits on what fortune could take and what the debtor could lose—that it was "in harmony with the liberal thought of the day" for society to draw a line "beyond which no creditor shall invade"—thus endured as a compelling faith and influenced the law at its normative center.[36]

Yet debtors' rights also had a history at the margins, in cases like Oldridge's and Marshall's, where freedom for the debtor did not align with accustomed hierarchies but challenged them. The male homesteader lost some of his familiar power when debt impinged on his ability to support his family. What, however, did debt do to his wife, when she was forced to work to service the mortgage or when the home that she had tended was taken away by the bank? Could she be protected from her husband's debts without upsetting the inequalities of marriage? Or did including her in the project of financial reform require a reckoning with the gender of American freedom? In the South, debt was gradually transformed—as the abolitionists had cannily predicted—into an instrument for tethering freedpeople to the land and compelling their labor for little reward. It did so, however, as the nation sought to transcend the hostilities of Reconstruction and leave sectional conflicts to the past. How, then, would national legal institutions respond when they were forced to confront the unfreedom of the Black debtor at the turn of the twentieth century? Would they push against Jim Crow and reassert the debtor's rights across the color line? Or would they accept that white capital had successfully subverted the achievements of the war and that in many corners of the South, "the spirit of the Thirteenth Amendment [was] sadly broken"? In the industrial North, the issue was the dependency of the wage earner and his reliance on pawnshops, installment houses, and exploitative loan sharks to pay rent, weather unemployment, and meet unanticipated expenses. Did the sharks indicate the fundamental inadequacy of the wage? Could the worker be freed from high-interest finance without securing a fairer income? Or would reformers need to choose between labor rights and debtors' rights in the industrial city? In many ways, these uncertainties reiterated the social questions of the day. They were not debates about debt alone but about the boundaries of belonging and citizenship in the modern United States. Yet debt provided a legally important way of engaging with those dilemmas—of measuring the coercions that women, freedpeople, and wage earners experienced and of imagining the freedoms that they might be owed.[37]

2

THE DEBTOR'S WIFE

Ella Gertrude Thomas was born to an affluent Georgia family in 1834. She married her husband, Jefferson, in 1852, and the two drew on her fortune to establish themselves as planters. They purchased land, built a home, had children, and owned slaves. The onset of the war unsettled their position, and the peace initiated their decline. The Thomases lost the money they had invested in Confederate bonds and the wealth they had stored in human chattel. Jefferson borrowed from relatives and mortgaged their estate in order to rebuild the plantation on a free-labor basis, but crop yields were low and repayment deadlines were missed. Slowly the household's debts amassed, and lawsuits were filed that resulted in the seizure and forced sale of the property. At one point, before Jefferson's creditors had started taking him to court, Thomas's mother wrote to her daughter to warn her of Jefferson's mounting difficulties. She assumed that the wife did not know the extent of her husband's entanglements. "Not know it?" Thomas journaled incredulously in her diary. "Heavenly Father! Thou knowest, and thou alone, how much I have known it—how the knowledge of it has deepened the lines upon my face—furrowed my brow & aged my heart."[1]

Thomas was not cloistered in the home. She was not shielded from her husband's public failings by the sanctity of the domestic sphere. Instead, she was witness to and participant in the financial misfortune, and her diary narrated her family's descent into insolvency and her interpretation of the events. She reflected on the origins of their decline in the Civil War and emancipation. "If one word of mine would restore the institution, I would not utter it," she insisted. "Better to have debt to encounter than slavery." She also recorded her discomfort with her husband owing a great deal of money to her cousins, fearing that it strained the bonds of family and might precipitate the cousins' insolvency as well. She wrote of her sadness over losing familiar property and the embarrassment of being seen in town after parts of their estate had been advertised in the foreclosure column of the newspaper. Above all, she meditated on the ambiguity of her role as the wife of an insolvent debtor. Jefferson's obligations were not hers. She had not contracted them, and, legally, they saddled her with no formal liabilities. Yet it was with those debts that her fate was entwined. They threatened the property she had brought to the marriage and all that she had acquired therein. They shaped her standing in society and her access to a lifestyle to which she had grown accustomed. In ways formal and indirect, they made claims on the labor she had invested in maintaining the home and nurturing the family. There was an emotional component as well. "I have read a great deal of woman's endurance under pecuniary trials," she wrote, "a great deal . . . about cheering a desponding husband [and] soothing his dejection." She wondered "if it ever occurred to anyone to realize or imagine how a proud woman feels under such circumstances[.] A woman who is identified so completely with the interest of her husband that his success or failure is hers."[2]

Thomas desired recognition. She wished for her contributions to be seen, foremost by her husband, who she believed took no note of her efforts to save money through sacrifice and thrift. She also prayed for separation—not for an end to her marriage but to the circumstances that tethered her financial life to her husband's. Men hated to acknowledge that their wives had independent personalities, she believed. When they discussed their land and their business, it was "all the masculine 'my' and 'my own' which they use." Yet the wife was ever present in such affairs, and Thomas saw an injustice in her future being held captive to the financial choices made by someone else. "I heard one of the farm hands illustrate the idea forcibly a few days since," Thomas wrote. "She (Mollie) wished her account separate from her husband's so she would know how she stood. 'What's mine is mine,' she said 'and what's tother folks is tother folks.'" Like Mollie, Thomas wished for a line to be drawn that would distinguish what was Jefferson's from what was hers. She wanted that line to partition not only their labor and property but also the debts that might lay a claim to both. Thomas sought to author her own financial fate and receive acknowledgment—from her husband and the culture in which they both lived—that she was an independent economic person with "an individuality of my own."[3]

Thomas's journal illuminated a dilemma of women's rights and debtors' rights in the United States in the Age of Capital. Men who borrowed money and could not repay it lost their claim on a liberal bounty entwined with their status as men. When their earnings were seized, their home invaded, and their ability to make independent choices compromised, it offended their rights as self-possessing persons and as male heads of household. Was there a slavery more heartrending and absolute, one bankruptcy advocate had asked in 1867, than that of the insolvent husband and father who saw in his own home "the utter hopelessness with which his wife and children from day to day live?" Women like Thomas might have answered that their experience was the worse, for they suffered the same indignities as their spouses—the alienation from labor and the assault upon the home—plus the added unfreedom of having had no formal say in assuming the debt and few options for building an economic life outside their husband's horizons. The backdrop of the wife's condition was the common law of coverture, under which marriage dispossessed her of her right to contract and her ability to control and acquire property. Where coverture prevailed, the husband's success or failure was truly the wife's as well. The dominant culture of marriage, work, and business also shaped her experience, closing off opportunities for an independent competency and leaving women like Thomas effectively bound by their husbands' fates even as the stricture of the common law relaxed. Those who found the situation offensive could call for women to be protected from debts in ways that paralleled the rights more readily granted to men. Yet the problem of the debtor's wife was more complex, because her vulnerability to dispossession stemmed not from the chaotic market or the grasping creditor directly but from those forces as they were channeled through the medium of her spouse. How could the married woman be shielded from the injuries of debt without shielding her from the husband himself? What would drawing a legal line between husband and wife in such a way mean for the institution of marriage? If the law was forced to choose between debtors' rights for the wife and the familiar domestic hierarchy, how would it proceed?[4]

These questions were not wholly contained to the late nineteenth century. They were part of a perennial conversation, dating to the antebellum period and earlier, about the subordination of women in a free and modern nation. They took on heightened significance, though, in the decades following the Civil War: as impersonal debts and economic volatility thrust more indebted households into default; as slave emancipation ennobled both the family and free contract in liberal thought; as westward settlement invested the solvency of the homestead with imperial meaning; and as the rights of the debtor in general became a signal measure of the nation's moral progress. In this context, lawmakers and courts struggled to determine how and whether to bring the promise of debtors' rights to wives. They often did so quietly, in legislation that received little attention and in rulings that were rarely reported far beyond the legal press. This was not, in the main, a history of organizing and popular protest. Feminists of the era were more focused on suffrage, and then on temperance, than on the plight of women like Thomas. Yet it was in debt law and debt litigation that the moral (and legal) boundaries between men, women, and the market were redrawn for the modern age. That process began with the work that the debtor's wife was regularly compelled to perform—the labor of solvency undertaken by elite women such as Thomas as well as ordinary farmwives, wage-earning women, and Black women of the South. It continued into legislation that was passed to improve the wife's condition—laws that promised a measure of financial separation between husband and wife but which were often sapped of their strength by judges and subsequent legislatures, who were reluctant to substantially challenge the family, the home, or the husband. The yield of this conservatism was not only the continued financial sub-ordination of the wife—the stubborn endurance of "the masculine 'my'" in matters of borrowing and lending. It was also, across these years, the emergence of new ways of seeing and unseeing the debtor's wife that summoned her sentimental traits to imagine indebtedness as feminine and fa-milial. Protection from debt—for the wife as well as the husband—might be unneeded. Debt itself could be domesticated.[5]

"From the grain that feeds the horse to the butter that spreads the bread, I pay for everything. I often think that I am the heart, I feed the arteries, I fill the veins, [and] if I stop pulsating it is death, for debt is death." Thus did Harriet Bailey Blaine of New England describe to a relative the financial responsibilities she assumed in widowhood in 1879. Death of a husband was one path that led women to enter the credit economy in the nineteenth cen-tury. Letters and diary entries like Blaine's abound, documenting the ways that women took control of financial lives left intestate by a spouse's aban-donment or passing. Yet widowhood was not the only point of entry into the market for married women of the era. Wives with living husbands often assumed a range of roles related to the management of debt as well. Under the law of coverture, married women were denied the power to forge finan-cial contracts. Those who traded on credit accounts with merchants did so as proxies for their husbands, who were obliged to retire any debts incurred by their wives. Technically, even the husband's liabilities did not attach to the wife where coverture prevailed, for she was without legal personality and thus could not be bound or sued. Within this framework of supposed exclusion, however, many women performed important duties in the cir-culation of credit and capital. They kept account books, interfaced with creditors, serviced their husband's debts with their earnings, and provided their husbands with valued financial counsel. In these ways, they became involved in the masculine sphere of market life, laboring to sustain financial relationships that implicated the home at the behest of husbands, creditors, and a larger culture of marital duty. That their consent had not been needed to tether their fate to the lender did not diminish their burden.[6]

Many married women were charged with keeping records of household incomes, outflows, and debits. The daybook of Sarah Browne, a merchant's wife in Salem, Massachusetts, maintained from the antebellum period until after the Civil War, for example, captured a complex ecology of simple transactions joined by open credit accounts with the family's grocer and doctor. These obligations were not interest bearing or secured—meaning that their threat to the home was less direct than a mortgage—but they were nevertheless significant. If left unpaid, they could result in higher food and medical prices, the denial of credit in the future, and exposure to legal proceedings. At stake in retiring them regularly was the solvency of the household and the cherished impression, real or imagined, that the home was sufficiently insulated from the market. Browne took seriously the task of managing these entanglements. She assiduously documented amounts owed, and to whom, and made sure that the family income was not stretched so thin as to be unable to cover them when payment was due. Other wives undertook similar labors. They wrote of their dedication to recording household transactions "regularly & correctly" in their "beloved expense book." Some enrolled in bookkeeping courses, so as to better chronicle the complicated features of credit in a maturing economy. Others refined their own accounting techniques. "These all belong to different objects," one woman wrote of a collection of purses which each held funds committed to certain expenses. "When my money comes in, I apportion it according to its amount [and] I never borrow from one to use for another, for fear that I might sometimes be tempted to be unjust." Those of the middle and professional classes typically embraced more formal bookkeeping, while for those of the urban working class, accounting could consist of knowing which "pawnbroker was likely to give the most on account for clothing" and "how long a bill . . . could be stretched before the credit was exhausted." For families of all stations, these efforts helped keep the home free from financial troubles that owed to profligacy or neglect. They also served to maintain the circulation of household capital, to the advantage of borrowers and lenders.[7]

Wives also interfaced directly with household creditors, mediating financial relationships in which they might have no formal role. Luna Kellie, a Nebraska settler, recalled a visit she once was paid by "Mr. Linnegar of the firm Linnegar and Metcalf, a big machinery company," who had come to see her husband "about the payment on the binder." Her husband was

FIGURE 2.1. *Household Accounts*, from Emma Churchman Hewitt, *Queen of Home* (Philadelphia, 1889), 36.

away, and Kellie and the creditor "sat there and talked quite pleasantly so I felt quite at home with him. [I] told him just how we were fixed, how much wheat [we had] to thresh, how we had to fix some kind of house, and how afraid I was of sod houses. How [my husband] had worried about the debt he owed them and expected to pay it soon as we could thresh and haul off the wheat." The conversation left an impression on Linnegar, in Kellie's telling, and he volunteered to change the terms of the obligation. "He could see we would not have much to fix a house let alone get through the winter, but I guess he felt we were honest for as he rose to go he said, 'Tell Mr. Kellie not to worry about the note to us. I will mark it extended for another year and tell him I want him go ahead and fix up a better place for you and the baby before it gets cold.'" Kellie's experience was echoed in the private writings of many women who found themselves at home when lenders came to call. Some wives reached out to creditors directly, when their social standing provided a more meaningful point of contact than their partner's. Others drew on gossip and other forms of semiprivate knowledge to discern which debts were urgent and which could likely be extended or delayed. Like the work of bookkeeping, these communicative labors helped keep household finances in balance and prevented them from getting out of control. They also, as in Kellie's case, personalized and even sentimentalized the debt contract, softening the edges of bonds that otherwise might be enforced with black-letter severity.[8]

Household solvency could not always be assured by careful bookkeeping and personal appeals. Large disruptions to the regular rhythms of economic life, such as panics or droughts, frequently forced the borrower into a bind that could not be accounted away. At such a point, the wife often resorted to the tenets of domestic economy. "How often I heard [my mother] tell of the straits in which she found herself during those cruel times," one memoirist recalled, "how the clothes were turned, and twisted, and made over many times, because new ones were not to be thought of." Other labors of conservation—from mending old linens to stretching the grocery budget—took on new meaning within the context of the husband's indebtedness. Many wives also pursued remunerative work, either to pay down debts directly or to maintain a familiar standard of living while their husband's income was diverted elsewhere. Many wrote of planting gardens, taking in laundry, and marketing handcrafts in order to earn extra money and keep the family's lenders at bay. "I sold turkeys last fall and got $25 for them, all told," one woman reported to her relatives in the East. "I have not the figures in poultry but for the year before I sold 344 pounds of dressed chickens at 5 and 6 cents a pound," another recounted. In charity surveys of women in the industrial city, it was not uncommon to encounter wives earning a wage to help service a debt owed for medical or housing expenses. In private writings, such as letters and diary entries, women tended to omit whether they had been asked to perform such tasks by their spouses. They may have taken the initiative themselves or may have wanted to guard their husbands' reputations as diligent providers. In such narratives, the choice to engage in compensated labor was often urged by female friends and tended to lead wives to markets populated primarily by female consumers. Yet while gendered networks provided a point of economic entry for the wives of struggling debtors, they did not lay a claim to the remuneration those efforts yielded, all of which was generally asked to moderate the experience of the husband's indebtedness and to facilitate the family's return to economic solvency.[9]

Married women also assumed a final role in the labor of household solvency: that of domestic financial adviser. In many families, it frequently fell to women to help determine whether money could be responsibly borrowed for land, tools, or improvements to the home. John Ise, in *Sod and Stubble* (1936), a narrative of the author's childhood in rural Kansas in the 1870s, recalled his mother's efforts to steer the household between prudent debts and incautious ones. When Ise's father wanted to borrow money to finish construction on their farmhouse, it was his wife, Rosie, who assured that they could "get along without plastering the upstairs for a while" if it meant staying out of debt. "If we get a few bad years," she explained, "we will be glad we are not tied with a mortgage anyhow." When they considered borrowing money to purchase a windmill, she "made some rough calculations" and determined that the obligation "would at least be no extravagance." Nevertheless, the risk left her unsettled. "Interest is a terrible thing," she reminded her spouse, "the way it eats and eats, due twice as often as it ought to be, and always at the hardest time." In many households, such discussions were ordinary events. It was considered an unexceptional matter of weekly routine to conference on "those little domestic arrangements on which so much of the future was to depend." Yet the woman's role in these conversations was to perform the labor of counsel and persuasion rather than to grant her formal consent. When wives advised and husbands ignored—or when the husband did not even solicit advice and undertook a large financial transaction on his own—the customary fact of patriarchy was reiterated. Married women's counsel was welcomed, and sometimes even demanded; but rarely was it required to authorize or sufficient to reject a prospective contract for debt.[10]

Ella Gertrude Thomas's diary chronicled her embrace of these familiar forms of financial labor throughout the 1870s and 1880s. Her husband's early indebtedness had relied on her presence twofold, in that it was her cousins from whom he had borrowed and her inherited land on which he had secured the loans. To his wife, Jefferson Thomas thus owed his connection to capital and the property that made him an acceptable risk. As his business stagnated and the loans became more onerous, Ella Thomas guided her husband through his financial choices. She sometimes wished she was "not burdened with my husband's confidence in money matters . . . but then I console myself with the idea that I am what every woman should be—his friend and counsellor." Thomas kept track of household expenses and indicated to her husband which comforts they could go without. When her cousins became impatient and threatened litigation, she persuaded them to grant her husband more time and to delay filing suit for as long as they could. Twice she gave her husband permission to sell property that had been bequeathed to the family specifically for her support and that of her children. She also eventually took on schoolteaching—a labor she detested—in order to "pay the drygoods bill of the family" while her husband's earnings were diverted to lenders. In 1880, she drew on her social standing to help her husband secure a new line of credit with which to forestall further dispossessions and operate the plantation for another season. "For several months Mr. Thomas has made effort after effort with the various city merchants to advance money or supplies but in vain." He even appealed to his mother-in-law for support, "but she did not wish to run any risk." Eventually, Ella Thomas called on an old friend and "told him how much I wished to make an arrangement to supply us this year." The friend asked Thomas to instruct her husband to reach out—without any mention of the advance work his wife had done—and an arrangement was effected. "He charged us eight per cent," Thomas reported, "and I am *truly grateful*."[11]

Thomas's labors were uniquely well documented in her diary, and as the matriarch of a planting family, her connections to debt were more complex than for those who had no land to mortgage or wages to pay. Yet the work of accounting, earning, advising, and saving was performed by married women of a wide range of social and economic stations across the late nineteenth century (and, of course, earlier). In middle-class households, a special emphasis was placed on the management of credit with doctors and grocers. It sometimes included the management of family bank accounts, particularly in the larger cities of the North. For the wives of industrial wage earners, the labor of solvency often entailed taking in boarders, earning a supplementary income, and, especially, circulating domestic goods in and out of pawn. For some, the pawnshop was a space where women initiated transactions—putting in "the family's Sunday best on Monday morning in order to cover the week's food and rent." For others, it was an institution to which they were practically bound against their will. In the mid-1870s, a fisherman in May Port, Florida, wrote to his family about a man in town who, each week, pawned his violin in order to pay his debts at the saloon, only to have his wife, each week, take "the money she earns Washing" and hand it over to the broker to redeem the instrument. For Black women in the rural South, family solvency amounted to a different kind of challenge, as debts were often manipulated by white lenders to obligate African Americans indefinitely. No amount of prudence or economy could ensure that the loans were retired. Yet if anything, the context of white supremacy placed more weight on women's financial labors, as every dollar not borrowed and every cent repaid made the Black household that much less vulnerable to violence, theft, and fear. "To keep down debts in the ensuing winter, Mother cooked and washed and Father felled trees in the icy 'brakes' to make rail and boards," the novelist William Pickens recalled of his parents' shared labor during his youth. William Holtzclaw, the Mississippi educator, described a time when white creditors invaded his childhood home, determined to seize all the family's corn, and his mother insisted they leave some for the household's sustenance. "She said that was the law," Holtzclaw observed, and "the white man who was getting the corn respected her knowledge . . . and left there the amount of corn that she demanded."[12]

When Ella Thomas's mother wrote to her to warn her of Jefferson's declining position, she keyed into the belief that wives knew little about the financial entanglements of their husbands. Theirs was the realm of the home, and they had no need or reason to follow the public affairs of their spouse. Said Senator Eugene Hale of Maine, during an 1890 debate on a bill instructing the US Census Office to survey the amount of household indebtedness held in the country, not more than "one woman in a hundred" would be able to report how much of their family's property was mortgaged and what proportion of it was "free from debt." To ask the wife about her husband's obligations was to burden her "with questions which cannot in the nature of things be answered." Such assertions reflected not the truth of women's experiences, however, but the world as a range of political and moral traditions wished it to be. In practice, women at all levels of society were implicated in their husband's finances. The debts might lay a claim to the property a woman had brought to marriage. They would often compel her to additional labor, as she turned to bookkeeping, domestic economy, and even wage work to keep the lenders at bay. The embarrassment, anxiety, and hopelessness that bankruptcy advocates interpreted as an injury to the husband—his loss of domestic peace and successful household headship—was in the first instance an injury to the wife, whose legal existence and economic horizons were largely determined by her spouse. Ella Thomas may have desired the ignorance that her mother had presumed—not as an expression of gendered confinement but as a privilege of independence. In January 1870, amid a period of dramatic financial decline, the debtor's wife began a journal entry midsentence, asking "if we will ever live to know this feeling of freedom." Who was the "we" to which she referred? It might have stood for one of several collectives: planters, southerners, or the embattled Thomas family. Yet it also may have called to the mass of married women who were bound by law and custom to debts they did not contract and fortunes they could not control.[13]

The married woman's labor of solvency was not confined to the late nineteenth century. In earlier periods as well, she tended the account book, counseled her indebted husband, and cycled household items in and out of pawn. Yet her labors became uniquely problematic in the Age of Capital for several reasons and from several perspectives. In the most conservative framing, the republican patriarch was responsible for providing for his dependents. The wife's labor of solvency measured his inability to fulfill his duties and thus his alienation from the status of patriarch. Her struggles indexed his; her dispossession took from him as well. Hamlin Garland's short story "A Good Fellow's Wife" (1891) gave expression to some of these fears. Garland's fictional husband becomes insolvent and the wife, by dint of economy, enterprise, and ingenuity, manages to service the debt on her own. "Let's begin again, as equal partners," she proposes to her spouse after the debt is repaid, holding "out her hand, as one man to another," in a gesture depicting the evacuation of hierarchy from marriage that was possible when debts touched the wife. From a liberal and feminist perspective, the debtor's wife troubled because she was burdened by obligations she had had no formal role in creating. It was a hallmark of the modern creed—ennobled in the context of slave emancipation—that no man should be placed in debt "against his will." Yet for the wife, this was the normal state of affairs, with loans and mortgages implicating her person, her labor, and her property at all times, with or without her consent. Thus did women's movement leaders and their allies call for the wife to be freed "from liability of any debts, except those contracted by herself or for which she [had] voluntarily made herself responsible." Between these positions—that the indebted wife represented an injury to patriarchy and that she represented an injury to the woman as a liberal subject—were interpretations that worried in a more general way about the health of the family unit. They imagined that a wife with some financial rights might ballast the speculative adventures of the husband. She might not need or deserve financial autonomy, but she, her husband, and their children might benefit if she had a store of wealth or a source of income that her spouse's creditors could not touch.[14]

These ideas shaped a variety of debt reforms in the mid- and late nineteenth century. The pitiable wife was marshaled in discussions of usury, bankruptcy, and exemption laws as well as debates about farm policy and the currency standard. To protect the husband from insolvency was, by extension, to protect the wife, many debt reformers insisted. Yet the primary vehicle for addressing the debtor's wife specifically was the Married Women's Property Acts, a genre of state legislation that was passed in several waves between the 1840s and the 1880s. These laws sought to relax the strictures of coverture and grant the wife some amount of financial independence. Indeed, the acts all had "for their object the accomplishment of the same general purpose," one jurist wrote in 1887. Their goal was the "protection of the married woman . . . from the control of an improvident, unfortunate, or profligate husband, and his creditors." This they sought to achieve in three ways. First, the laws permitted the wife to hold real property—land—that was separate from the husband's holdings and could not be used to satisfy his debts. Lawmakers often imagined that women would receive this property from their fathers, who would hope to provide their daughters with a fund for family maintenance that the husband could not traffic away. Second, the laws permitted the wife to use her separate property for ordinary commercial transactions. She could not only hold property but could "bargain, sell, convey, and contract" with her estate "as fully as the husband can as to his." Third, in the earning laws—an addition to the property laws enacted in most states after the Civil War—the wife was granted the right to contract for wages. This reform did not give wives the right to enter a labor market that they previously had been barred from. Many working-class women already toiled in homes, mills, and factories. Rather, the earnings laws announced that those wages—and whatever was bought with them—belonged solely to the wife and could not seized or garnished by "the rich, shoddy creditors of the husband."[15]

These reforms all promised to set the husband and the wife apart in matters of household finance. They were often enacted in lockstep with prohibitions on imprisonment for debt and the state-level property exemption laws, which set limits on what creditors could mortgage, seize, and sell. In the debates that surrounded the various married women's property legislation, partisans readily drew on the image of the poor debtor's wife to articulate the injustice that the new laws would prevent. Yet a diversity of social visions in fact converged at marital law reform—from the conservative to the feminist and the liberal—and there was little agreement on how emancipated the wife was intended to be (and for what purpose). The economic volatility of the 1870s and 1880s—an era in which legalistic debt contracts tethered borrowers to impersonal lenders in a chaotic environment—precipitated financial failure on a massive scale. This, in turn, flooded the courts with insolvency conflicts, many of which implicated the debtor's wife and her newfound financial rights. In determining who would prevail in litigation pitting the creditor against the husband or the creditor against the wife, the woman question and the debt question joined as one, and the scope of the wife's freedom—financial and otherwise—was set in law. Two questions proved particularly vexing in this period. First, did the wife have the right to forge her own relationships with creditors? Could she take on debt herself, thus making herself vulnerable to dispossession but also accessing a financial path separate from her husband's? And second, was she truly permitted to be untouched by her husband's debts? Or was financial separation too great a challenge to the familiar structure of marriage?

Promissory capacity—the wife's right to take on debt herself—was perhaps the more divisive of the two concerns. In the state of New York, the question was decided in favor of the greatest financial independence possible. In 1873 and 1878, the New York Court of Appeals heard two cases concerning the married woman's right to voluntarily assume financial obligations. In the first, a creditor sought judgment against a woman who had signed a promissory note to borrow money with which to purchase a small business. The woman defaulted on the note, but she argued before the court that she could not be held liable because the state legislature had not explicitly granted wives the right to take on debt. Similarly, in the second case, a banker sought to foreclose on a separate estate that had been mortgaged by a wife, who claimed that the mortgage was void because no statute explicitly endowed her with the right to mortgage. Where the statutory text ended, these women insisted, the common law of coverture prevailed. Yet in both contests, the court sided with the creditor—which, ironically, meant siding with the more expansive rights of wives. Under New York's Married Women's Property Acts of 1848, 1849, 1860, and 1862, the wife had received the right to perform labor or services "on her sole and separate account." For the court, this implied a right to enter into all contracts made in the ordinary pursuit of business, including those for debt. "The new legislation assumes that [the wife] is capable of managing her own interests," it announced in the 1873 ruling. She was "no longer regarded as [being] under the tutelage of the court." Indeed, if she wanted, she could "incur the most dangerous, and even ruinous, liabilities . . . and they will be enforced against her to the same extent as if she was unmarried." In the clearest terms, the Court of Appeals affirmed that the wife was now a financially autonomous subject. The right to be untouched by the husband's financial fortunes carried with it the right to assume her own risks and bear her own responsibilities.[16]

Yet New York's position was an exception to the general rule of the age, with most states interpreting the wife's financial freedom as narrowly instrumental rather than broad and absolute. In 1871, Judge Thomas Cooley of the Michigan Supreme Court was asked to evaluate whether a married woman had the right to endorse a promissory note originally contracted by someone else (in this case, her husband). Cooley acknowledged that his court had constructed the relevant statute generously in the past, sustaining some contracts that "might not come strictly within the terms" of the state's legislation. Yet for three reasons he believed that the wife's endorsement stood outside the legal and moral bounds. First, the wife in question possessed no separate estate. She was not attempting to charge a piece of property but rather was binding her person directly. It was unclear if she technically had the right to do so, based on the doctrine of charging. Also unclear were the consequences for marriage, in theory and in practice, if a wife could implicate her person the same as a man. Could her personal services become the property of the creditor? If imprisonment for debt were reestablished, could the wife be placed in prison? Second, the wife in question had not received anything in exchange for her endorsement. Endorsers in general were not required to profit from their promise—amid the rise of the will theory of contract—but the court worried that to permit married women to bind themselves thus would be to give them license to gift their wealth away. This offended the legal conscience for a third reason: Cooley understood the purpose of Michigan's married woman's property law not as emancipating the wife fully but as relaxing her confinement partially "for the benefit of herself and her family." Her disabilities had been "removed only so far as they operated unjustly and oppressively; beyond that they are suffered to remain." The wife, in other words, was not meant to be free enough to fail. She was not to be the sovereign of her economic destiny. She was rather to be shielded from her husband's failings, instrumentally, for the good of the family and home.[17]

Many other state courts followed the Michigan example. Unless the wife's promissory rights were named explicitly by statute, judges preferred to recognize them only to the extent that they appeared consonant with the health of the family. Indeed, even when legislation did name the right to take on debt, courts might defer to the purpose for which the wife's specific separate estate had been created, reasoning that because a mortgaged piece of property had been given "to provide and to secure a home . . . not for the wife only, but for the children," the mortgage was unenforceable.

Legislatures embraced this vision by making the wife's promissory capacity contingent on the consent of the husband. In Massachusetts, the husband had to write a letter giving the wife permission to borrow and file that document with the local court. In other jurisdictions, such as California, the wife was required to receive a special dispensation from a judge or magistrate, based on a demonstration that "the husband's income is not sufficient for support of the family." Only then would she be empowered to enter the market as a fully capable individual—when it was evidenced that she did so not to pursue wealth for its own sake or to chart a path out of the home but instead to draw the domestic unit closer together and nourish it with her industry and enterprise. Even when these legal obstacles were surmounted, the tangle of rules that could potentially invalidate the wife's promises made her an unappealing risk to lenders, who feared that the courts would not help them collect. "Who wants to transact business with a person thus law-crippled?" asked one reformer in 1876. Who would trust that the married woman's promise would not be later voided by a solicitous and conservative court? "It proves to be no mere parlor pleasantry, no false rumor, but very truth that many of the wealthiest corporations issue orders to every office and every agent in their employ under no circumstances to loan money to a woman," the Indiana suffragette May Wright Sewall observed in 1884. With only a tenuous grasp on promissory capacity, it remained safest for lenders to continue regarding the wife as ineligible to borrow, as she long had been under common law.[18]

The wife's separation was thus not so great as to allow her to freely take on debts herself. She could not absent herself from her husband's fortune to the point of creating her own. Yet the law also proved reluctant to effectuate the more limited goal of insulating the married woman from her spouse's creditors—of preventing her from being bound by debts "in contracting which she had no part nor lot." In some scenarios, her right to independence was incontrovertible. A wife who had inherited a piece of land from her father could likely keep it safe from the husband's debts. A married woman who had been abandoned by her husband and "lived alone, subsisting by, for example, making suspender straps or doing housework for another man," had a strong claim to protecting her daily wages. Beyond such simple cases, however, lay ambiguity. The specter of fraud loomed large in insolvency contests, with the married woman's claim to independent ownership often impeached by the suggestion that her spouse had manipulated feminist law reform to keep wealth from honest lenders. Gifts passing from husband to wife had to be commensurate with the husband's financial condition, and wives eager to shield their holdings were encouraged to publicize their separate estate. The tenor of the day's decisions, one jurist observed in 1878, "is that the wife should take some steps to protect herself, and that she has no rights against her husband's creditors after she has been a passive or willing instrument in his hands to deceive them." Even when deliberate fraud was not suspected, the commingling of the wife's property with the husband's had the effect of rendering it vulnerable to lenders. "We readily admit [that] so long as the wife holds the property in her hands, just as she received it, it cannot be taken for the husband's debts," one feminist explained in 1880, "but the moment she permits her husband to convert the property into another shape, it becomes his, and MAY be taken for his debts." A jurist, writing in 1884, echoed the point: "Though a married woman's separate estate is no longer liable for the debts of her husband, yet where husband and wife live together, the presumption of law is that the personal property on the premises belongs to the husband. Should the household goods actually be the property of the wife, she must be prepared to rebut the presumption against her by showing [her title] clearly . . . else they may be swept away from her by her husband's creditors."[19]

Where there was doubt or confusion as to ownership, the old rules of coverture thus generally adhered. However, even clarity of will and ownership was not in all instances sufficient. In 1880, Mary J. Follet, a furniture dealer in Chicago, sold several pieces of furniture to Elijah Dicks on credit. Dicks's wife, Ruth, refused to sign the promissory note and did not offer any evidence of support for the purchase. Indeed, she explicitly "objected to the purchase of the furniture proposed" and told Follet before the sale that "she was the only one in the family who had any means, and [she] would not be responsible for the price." Nevertheless, when the note went several years unpaid and Follet chose to bring suit, she named not only Elijah but also Ruth, charging the wife's separate estate with nearly $100 in outstanding expenses. During the trial and appeal, no one denied that Ruth had positively forbade the note. There was no accusation of fraud or commingling of wealth. Instead, Follet looked to an 1874 law enacted by the Illinois legislature that held that "the expenses of the family and the education of the children shall be chargeable upon the property of both husband and wife, or of either of them, in favor of creditors therefor, and in addition thereto they may be sued jointly or separately." It was on this authority, of recent vintage, that Follet brought suit against the penniless Elijah Dicks and his more monied wife. The court sided with the creditor, finding that because the furniture had been bought to enhance the home and provide comfort to the family, it could be credited against Ruth's account. How was the furniture's familial status known to the court? It was evidenced by the husband's decision to buy it. "Notwithstanding the numerous statutes in favor of married women, the husband [is] still the head of the household . . .

[and] his judgment could be assumed to be the better as to the expediency or propriety of a purchase for family use, even when . . . his wife was of a contrary opinion." For debts that pertained to family support, the will of the married woman was irrelevant. She could not authorize or inhibit a debt from attaching to her property. In matters of family maintenance—as attested by her spouse—she could "neither assent or dissent as to exonerate her separate estate."[20]

The Illinois case was not unique. Many legislatures enacted similar family-expense laws during the 1870s and 1880s, mostly in the West but also in the Northeast. In some states, such as Connecticut, while both husband and wife were responsible for debts contracted to support the family, it was the husband's property that was to be "first applied to satisfy any such joint liability." In others, such as Missouri, the wife could enjoin the husband from charging her account if she could prove that he was "drunken and worthless." Yet, in most cases, the law simply made husband and wife equally liable, without exception, and left it to the creditor to determine whose estate to pursue. Those who selected the wife's were often successful. In *Marquardt v. Flaugher* (1882), a jeweler was permitted to bind a wife's separate estate to settle the bill for a watch purchased by the husband, defeating the wife's claim that the item had been used only by her and thus was a personal, rather than a familial, expense. In *Watkins v. Mason* (1883), the Supreme Court of Oregon held that a wife was jointly responsible for a grocery debt incurred "for the meat used in the family." In *Frost v. Parker* (1884), the Iowa Supreme Court rejected a wife's novel argument that a piano had not been "purchased by the husband for use in the family, but for the purpose of 'speculation,' that is, for sale at a profit." That it had become family property after the husband failed to find a buyer rendered it sufficiently familial to vindicate the creditor's claim, the court found, permitting the creditor to assess the expense to the married woman's estate. Lenders did not discover boundless rights under such laws. Plows, buggies, and reaping machines—despite being tools that could help the husband support the family—were generally held to stand outside the category of family expense and thus could not be chargeable to the wife. In other instances, though, items that seemed far less related to family maintenance—like an "expensive stick-pin purchased and used by the husband exclusively"—were debited against the married woman, and in one case a wife's property was declared liable for a debt for which the husband had escaped responsibility via bankruptcy.[21]

Advocates for the household-expense laws defended them with various arguments. They marshaled the language of equality, suggesting that in the modern age the husband's customary duty to provide should be distributed evenly to both spouses. They described the injustice that could be done to lenders without such reforms, in which "the vendor may be ignorant of the manner in which the property of the parties is held" and would extend credit to the husband on the assumption that the wealth in the home was his. Primarily, however, lawmakers cast family-expense legislation as a confirmation and continuation of the husband's traditional authority. "Our law is liberal in protecting the rights of the wife in relation to her property," one midwestern jurist explained. "But it has not gone so far as to abolish the headship of family, nor to take from the husband the right to exercise best judgment and discretion in the management of his affairs. [Husband and wife] are alike interested in the education of the children and the support of the family. For the expenses thereof it is both right and proper that the property of each or both should be liable. She, as a rule, *must be governed* by his contracts in relation to these matters." In this reasoning, the wife's advance as a responsible and propertied subject joined with the husband's enduring right of command to naturalize her involuntary indebtedness. Both components of the argument were necessary because family-expense legislation, while in many respects conservative, had effected a radical change. Under the common law, the feme covert had not known formal financial liabilities. Because she had had no legal personhood against which such claims could be made, the burden of domestic provision had pressed solely on the husband. Family-expense law embraced the wife's newfound autonomy as a means to subvert the same. As an independent agent, she could be charged with obligations that had once been reserved for married men. As wife and mother, it was "right and proper" that any household obligations attach to her regardless of her consent.[22]

The Married Women's Property Acts aspired to resolve a moral dilemma. In a turbulent economic environment in which even prudent debts could lead to insolvency, laws granting women a measure of financial self-possession forestalled the tragedy of wives and mothers being beggared by their husbands. Gone would be "the old fossil footprint of Feudalism" that bound married women to their husbands' obligations and made them vulnerable to creditors. A more modern and moral arrangement was promised by reform. Yet two visions of the modern joined in the married woman's property acts only to diverge as the laws were tested and observed. Some reformers and lawmakers believed that woman was entitled to the same autonomy enjoyed by man, the right to be freed "from liability of any debts, except those contracted by herself or for which she [had] voluntarily made herself responsible." Others saw the home and family kept in order through the person of the wife—an internally contradictory ideal that wished for the wife to be absented from her husband's debts only to the point that the family appeared to benefit. Promissory capacity (the right to borrow money on one's own account) lay beyond that point for many lawmakers and jurists. Thus did the wife remain "law-crippled" when dealing with lenders—forced in many states to meet different legal standards in order to realize her promissory capacity and in many instances denied it altogether. Family-expense statutes returned the wife to the responsibility for debts contracted by her spouse, at once embracing her emancipated status and using it to assign her liabilities not formally known to the married woman under the common law. Those who feared the centrifugal forces of reform could take comfort in measures that bound the family together as one and resisted the financial separation of husband and wife. Those who believed it unjust or unnatural for the married woman to be present in the husband's debts and misfortunes found only partial satisfaction, however, as legislation and the courts retreated from the goal of freedom for the debtor's wife.[23]

Married woman's property law purported to separate husband and wife in matters of financial responsibility. This it undertook for several reasons. It endeavored to protect dynastic wealth that was held in the woman's line; to guard the family from the profligate or unfortunate husband; and to recognize the wife as a liberal individual. Yet in few states was the separation of spouses permitted to grow too wide. Wives were generally not recognized as having full promissory capacity. They could not borrow money on their property or their person without the forbearance of the courts, which left them substantively tethered to their husbands' financial fortunes. Nor could they uniformly shield themselves from responsibility and liability for their spouses' debts. The specter of fraud clouded all their claims to independent ownership, and any incidence of commingling returned their property to the husband's keep. Family-expense laws, meanwhile, created new obligations for the married woman, mandating that she "as a rule, must be governed by [the husband's] contracts" when they were intended to provision the home. This was not a common-law burden extended into the modern era but rather an original disability premised on the wife's newfound rights of property and contract. Feminists were not wrong to celebrate the married woman's property reforms of the mid- and late nineteenth century. With good reason did they place them in broader emancipationist narratives that included the expansion of popular democracy, the eradication of the debtors' prison, and the abolition of slavery. Yet women like Ella Gertrude Thomas were all too aware of the limits of such measures. Beyond the fact that the new rights often foundered as soon as the property in question showed the least sign of being the husband's, Thomas believed the legal reforms had been instituted only once many women had had nothing left to lose. It was "like locking the stable door after the Horse has been stolen." In theory and in practice, the married woman's property laws thus effected modest change, leaving many instances in which the wife could still be bound by the debts of others.[24]

Wives such as Thomas did have an additional tool at their disposal, however, for governing their household's entanglements and grounding their financial labor in choice: the state homestead exemption laws passed in the mid- and late nineteenth century. These measures drew a circle around family-occupied property and freed it from the threat of dispossession by creditors. Their purpose was to assure residents that their household was established and their "place in the community [was] fixed." Debt and misfortune could not deprive them of domestic sanctuary or their interests in the state, which by the homestead exemptions were "anchored and strengthened." The laws typically defined the amount of protected property by monetary value but occasionally limited it by acreage, based on the principle that "a home is a home" regardless of its market worth. In many jurisdictions, the homestead became exempted automatically by virtue of family occupancy, while in others, the head of household was required to register the property with local officials. The family estate, once exempted, became unusable as collateral for a loan, either because the law explicitly prohibited mortgaging it or because creditors recognized that the protected home was an empty pledge, as it could not be seized. The exemption thus amounted to both a shield and an encumbrance, preventing the head of household from alienating his property freely. Almost universally, however, an escape provision was written into the law that allowed the homesteader to shed the impairment and reacquire his right of unfettered conveyance. The exemption could be renounced in most jurisdictions on the condition that the wife agree to waive it.[25]

The waiver privilege was extended to wives in thirty-three of the thirty-nine states to enact homestead exemption legislation in the mid- and late nineteenth century. It resembled another gendered entitlement in American law, the dower. This was the wife's right to take possession of one-third of her husband's real property at the time of his passing. It was meant to protect the widow from destitution by mandating a marital bequest and barring the husband from trafficking it away. In order to surrender the dower and permit her spouse to alienate the promised property freely, the wife was required to affix her signature to the deed of transfer. This mirrored the process required by the exemption waiver. Superficially, the two privileges thus had much in common. The waiver even annexed some of the precedents of dower adjudication, including the tradition of the private examination, in which the wife met with a court official apart from her husband to determine whether her signature genuinely embodied her will. Yet as jurists of the age often noted, the two devices diverged at the deeper level of spirit and function, with the exemption waiver standing as the more substantial tool. The dower was an inchoate right. It was realized only once the wife entered widowhood. If her life estate was sold or seized without her permission during her marriage, she was powerless to stop it. Many husbands were thus inclined to ignore the waiver and alienate their property as they so desired, with buyers and lenders trusting that the dower would never activate or that the wife would lack the resources to enforce her right later in life. The exemption waiver, in contrast, recognized the wife's present interest in the homestead. It was an entitlement of "a higher character" and "more in the nature of a vested interest or a title." If it was ignored—if the wife's signature was not secured before mortgaging the land—then the wife could bring suit immediately to interrupt and void the illicit transaction. She was thus granted a discretionary power over her husband's promissory capacity that exceeded what might have been required for family maintenance. Once the home was exempted, it could not be pledged without her permission. Debt could not threaten the home or invade the private sphere unless the wife decided to allow it.[26]

Support for the waiver privilege rested on one of two genres of claims. The first was rooted in a liberal discourse of property and labor rights. It held that the home was a store of the wife's exertions—both as a physical estate and as a site of maternal care—and that the waiver privilege allowed her to determine whether those exertions would be pledged (and potentially lost) in the market for debt. As one lawmaker addressed a fictive husband-critic in 1876, the wife had no doubt "taken care of you and the children beside during all these years [and] you have no right to complain that you cannot dispose of your property as you like without *her* consent." In moral if not legal fact, the argument suggested, the homestead belonged to the wife. It had been made hers through labor—she had earned it, even if she had not purchased it—and she was entitled to control its exposure to chance. This narrative appeared in legislative debates about the waiver and in the columns of the popular press. Yet it was not the primary claim marshaled in the waiver's defense. The second and more telling narrative emphasized caution and sentimental difference. It held that the wife was not possessed of the same sensibilities as her spouse but instead was inclined toward financial conservatism and prudence. She brought these traits to the consideration of debt and, if granted a contracting veto through the law, could militate against the husband's reckless gambles. Whether her distinctiveness owed to natural disposition, maternal sympathies, or her inexperience in trade, the wife was cast as uniquely reluctant to authorize excessive borrowing and thus well equipped to supervise the boundary between home and market. It was to woman's uses, rather than her rights, that this argument looked to advance the waiver privilege in the late nineteenth century, legitimizing the extension of new powers on the basis of familiar inequalities.[27]

Domestic economists had made such claims since the antebellum era. Prescriptive writers like Catharine Beecher and Lydia Maria Child had sought to ennoble woman's domestic confinement by defining household responsibilities broadly and casting them as purposeful and scientific. The home, for them, was a space where women might claim a measure of expert authority on par with male professionalism in public life. At the same time, they often invested the home with explicitly public significance, as a site of republican mothering and virtuous repose, and thereby accorded women a critical role in the fate of the national project. From both vantages, financial supervision was natural and essential, for it was only in solvency that the distinctiveness of the home could be preserved and its moral gifts nurtured and delivered. It therefore became incumbent on women to ensure that family finances were kept in balance. Such duties attached to women because they implicated the home, and to women went the concerns of the private sphere. Holding that space at "the happy medium between prodigality and parsimony" was one of the tasks which lay before the wife, announced one postbellum text, and was "therefore given her to do." It was also a category of duty for which many believed she was temperamentally inclined. Beecher, for example, linked women to finance via their obligations to the home, but she also suggested that wives were likely to excel in financial tasks because they were inherently cautious and "disposed to be systematic" in matters of accounting. Others cast the optimism and acquisitiveness that led some persons to borrow heedlessly as fundamentally male conditions, from which women had fortunately been spared. To encounter a female speculator was "an entire novelty," reported an 1867 volume, and an indication that an "unnatural interest" had been cultivated in the mind of the woman in question. Women could "seldom be induced to take . . . chances," proposed another writer, and were "not half as easily 'gulled' by glittering schemes, as are men." So strong was the association drawn between the sentimental woman and financial prudence that some domestic economists cast the account book—that basic instrument of household financial management—as an explicitly gendered object. It was "all we have left by the fairy godmother," S. D. Power declared in *Anna Maria's Housekeeping Book* (1884). "As we keep its pages well or neglect it, we will feel the tap of her angry wand, or we will find her blessing left beside the hearthstone."[28]

Such language identified the stewardship of household credit with the feminine portfolio of domestic responsibilities. Domestic economists generally accepted the wife's promissory incapacity, seeing such thoroughly public engagements as inappropriate for the governess of the home and corrosive of her native virtue. Yet they also suggested that domestic commitments and maternal feelings uniquely prepared the wife to oversee the contest between home and market occasioned by household debt. The exemption waiver's legislative advocates spoke in a similar key. What mother existed, they asked, who "would not prefer carrying to the silent tomb, the children of her bosom, to seeing them thrown upon the chilling affections of a cold world" in order to service a debt? Was not maternal devotion "more strong, constant, and unconquerable, than paternal affection," thus giving the wife a motive for "prudence and judgment" that exceeded that of the husband? The hazardous investment was often sexualized in homestead-waiver debates as a temptress who would "easily seduce" the ambitious patriarch. It was "deceptive, alluring, [and] destroying." If it lay "in the power of the husband" to cede the home "by lien or mortgage," a Kansas reformer predicted, it would surely be pledged away. Entrust financial probity to the wife, however, and it would be secured as if it were fully inalienable at law. The premise of the waiver, insisted one Wisconsin lawmaker, was that "woman is more capable of managing matters than man, or even the constitution." Supporters conceded that the law injured the homesteader as a husband and property owner, taking from his powers and adding to the wife's. Yet they denied that it significantly altered the domestic hierarchy or impinged on the husband's economic freedom. Not only did the wife's natural affections assure that she would honor her husband regardless of her "supervisory power," but her preference for stability over speculation promised to curb her spouse's adventuring spirit and preserve domestic tranquility. "Women are as clear of being operated upon either for better or worse as men," one lawmaker affirmed. "Yet, sir, I do contend that for true merit the female sex stand much higher than the male. They knew but little of the low, truckling, vacillating demagogism that pervades the male portion of creation, and in that their ignorance is a jewel."[29]

The suggestion was not that the wife deserved a voice in financial decision-making because of any embryonic title to her spouse's property. Instead, it was that her guidance, effectively mandated by law, would moderate the husband's cupidity and protect the armature of the public-private divide. Women like Rosie Ise would not have to rely on moral suasion alone. Their counsel would be legally required. As the exemption waiver was debated in the late nineteenth century, the most compelling objections were often nested within this framework of sexual difference. The concern that Joseph Winans expressed at the California constitutional convention in

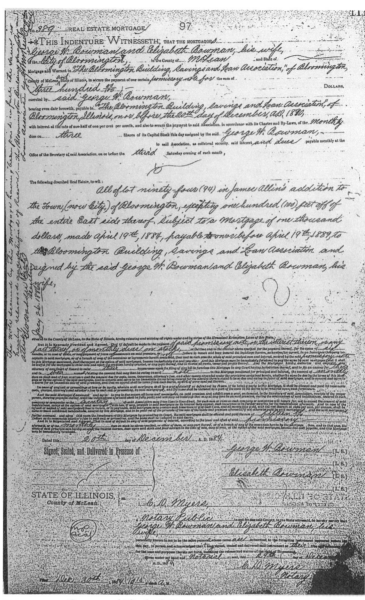

FIGURE 2.2. George and Elizabeth Bowman jointly waive the homestead exemption in 1884 in order to mortgage their lot to the Bloomington Building, Savings and Loan Association for $300. Registry of Deeds, book 97, p. 117, McClean County Recorder, Bloomington, Illinois.

1878 was not that wives would disregard the authority of their husbands
or become mired in speculation themselves. Rather, it was that woman's
commitment to domestic hierarchy would make her reluctant to overrule
her spouse in matters of family business. "When the husband is imperious,
the wife yields to his request," Winans observed, being in most households
"controlled under the oppressive influence of her regard for him." Another
conventioneer submitted that "in nine cases out of ten, if the husband desires to go in debt and encumber the property, he will persuade his wife by
arguments of one sort or another." Such claims challenged the waiver in the
interest of advancing one of two policies: either allowing the homestead
to be thrust into the market without protection or barring it from attachment altogether. Yet they also participated in the gendered narratives on
which the waiver itself rested while doing little to salve the dilemma that
it meant to address. The waiver could be given solely to the husband, who
was liable to mortgage the home for such gambles as "raising money to go
into stocks." It could also be denied to both husband and wife, strengthening the exemption but transgressing more substantially against the rights
of property. Lawmakers here confronted a paradox between the liberal ennobling of trade and the belief that debt imperiled the home and unjustly
bridled the wife. The exemption waiver bridged this contradiction via a vital
compromise. It created a process for alienating the home and stirring the
circulation of finance capital by stamping acquisitive risk-taking with the
imprimatur of moral woman.[30]

Some wives noted the power of the exemption waiver in their private
writings. Ella Thomas, for example, debated with herself whether to allow
her husband to pledge several pieces of property and whether to exempt
another as a recognized homestead. She ultimately decided to cede her
claim to the land not because she thought the debts were prudent, but out
of her sense of duty to her husband's creditors, several of whom were her
cousins. Other wives in different circumstances took the opposing path
and denied their husbands the right to borrow. When such decisions were
tested in court—typically, when the husband had borrowed anyhow and
the creditors then discovered that the wife would not allow them to seize
the homestead—the wife was often vindicated. In 1869, Catherine Ward
brought suit against a mortgage lender who had interrupted the sale of
her husband's property with evidence of an existing lien. The case journeyed through the appellate process and eventually arrived at the Kansas
Supreme Court, which ruled in Ward's favor. "The homestead was not intended for the play and sport of capricious husbands merely," the judgment
announced; instead, it was meant to nurture and sustain the family, whose
interest was safeguarded in the law by the volition of the wife. To circum-

vent her counsel was to raze a bastion of domestic sanctity demanded by
the age. This court could not allow, and so it quashed the lender's claim.
In 1873, Samantha Helm, also of Kansas, prevailed in a similar action against
her husband and his brother. The two had secured her signature on a homestead conveyance, but only by making false promises and threatening her
with violence. Again, the court came to the wife's defense, voiding the conveyance and insisting that the exemption waiver was more than a technical
barrier against alienation, easily hurdled by lies and force. Its purpose was
to involve the wife in financial decision-making and to ballast the force of
improvidence. Even when the homestead had passed through many hands,
the married woman's claim to it endured if she had not properly waived
her rights. In 1879, the Supreme Court of Illinois ruled that a man who had
purchased a tract of land at a foreclosure auction was obliged to allow Sarah
Brooks to continue to use the property as her home, as she had not released
her right of homestead when her husband mortgaged the estate in 1876.[31]

Partisans of the woman question divided on the significance of the exemption waiver. To many social conservatives, the institution transgressed
against the republican family even more stridently than the married woman's property reforms. Not only did it tend to enhance the "individuality"
of the wife at the expense of the husband, but it placed her in a position of
power over him. "Instead of being the head of the family, to provide for
it out of his own property according to his own judgment, and to govern
his family according to the established notions of civilization," a West Virginia judge declared in 1879, the husband was to be "made subject in many
instances to the whims of an inconsiderate wife." The waiver struck such
critics as an affront to traditional gender relations, even if it might shield
the household from dispossession and destitution. For many feminists,
on the other hand, the measure warranted a more muted appraisal. Jane
Slocum, writing in the *Woman's Journal* in 1874, characterized the waiver
as an instrument primarily meant to help the husband evade his creditors
while making more "comfortable and attractive" the wife's "condition of
dependence." To Slocum, the waiver belonged only vaguely to the chronicle
of woman's advancements and certainly achieved none of the radical objectives previsioned by its critics. If the experience of Elizabeth Roach, a
farm wife of the West, was typical, then the ambivalence of observers like
Slocum was well deserved. "No one read the mortgage to me, and no one
explained the nature of the mortgage," she explained to a court in 1877 of
her decision to waive her homestead rights. "I did sign the papers," she
conceded, but thinking they only concerned "some notes my husband was
giving" and not her interest in the family estate. "He told her it was none of
her business," a friend of Roach's reported, and "that the paper offered her

to sign did not amount to a row of pins." Limited literacy, the complexity of finance, and the trust she placed—or was coerced into placing—in her husband neutered the waiver right for Roach and others of similar station. Absent more comprehensive revisions to woman's power in American life, the waiver on its own could not affect dramatic changes to sexual hierarchy or the flow of credit, as Slocum and others anticipated.[32]

There was thus much truth in the claims of the California convention-eers who insisted that the waiver was likely ineffectual. To give the husband "the privilege of reasoning his wife, or teasing his wife, or forcing his wife into signing mortgages for the incumbrance" was, in many instances, to give the family no homestead exemption at all. Indeed, it was perhaps to doom the wife to more coercion and abuse than debt itself would impose. Yet the institution endured, weathering the challenges from those who wished to fully exempt the homestead in California in 1878, Florida in 1885, North Carolina in 1889, New York in 1894, and South Carolina in 1895. In the early twentieth century, states such as Massachusetts even incorporated the waiver principle into wage-assignment laws, with stipulations requiring that loans secured by an assignment of the borrower's wages be, when the borrower was a head of household, "consented to by the wife of the as-signor." Such measures accorded with the interpretation of one editorialist that the purpose of the waiver was to occupy "a middle ground between the entire abolition of the . . . exemption" and its absolute extension, to the point that debt could no longer imperil the home. "It is a pretty solemn piece of business to put a mortgage upon the farm," Senator J. C. Spooner of Wisconsin explained during the census debate of 1890. The wife "knows it," he assured, and she "signs it."[33]

In requiring that gesture, the waiver law did grant women like Ella Ger-trude Thomas a degree of control over their husbands' fortunes and thus, in turn, their own. Yet this was neither its primary goal nor its central function. Instead, the waiver approached two imposing features of modern American life: the home, invested with terrific moral meaning in the context of west-ward settlement, industrialization, and slave emancipation; and the chaotic and impersonal financial market, feared by many as "deceptive, alluring, [and] destroying." The homestead exemption had brought the tension be-tween these worlds under the purview of law. With the waiver, however, it devolved that oversight to the prudent woman, compelling a narrative of feminine sanction to financial risks that threatened the home. Feminists such as Slocum were right to note the social conservatism of the law. On the financial side, however, the work of the measure was more complex. Ex-emption law had envisioned a public and private sphere properly set apart. When coupled with the wife's waiver, however, it acted not to maintain that distance but to collapse it, in a careful, guarded way. The combination functioned to effect a moral process *through* woman—tender, maternal, and prudent—for bringing home and market together.[34]

In an 1887 essay in *Harper's Bazaar* entitled "The Honesty of Women," Thomas Wentworth Higginson, the abolitionist and women's rights advocate, recalled the wish of the white patriarch of *Uncle Tom's Cabin* (1852) that a "new race of black men" be bred to embrace the life of service. Higginson invoked the decades-old tale because he believed there was a "tendency among some of the ardent apostles of progress to assume that such a class of human beings has been found, for commercial and philanthropic purposes, in women." The evidence Higginson cited was not the labor of solvency performed by women on the farm, nor the wife's discretionary power over household borrowing extended by the exemption waiver. Instead, he meditated on women's growing employment in finance, as bookkeepers and cashiers, based on the notion that they were "more honest" in the handling of money than men. At present, Higginson confessed, it was possible that they were, and their advantage might last for years to come. Their instincts were higher and "their temptation less, on the side of perilous indulgence" than speculative men. Yet in all probability, Higginson reasoned, women's financial conservatism owed to their discomfort in trade, their fear of making a mistake, and not to any bequest of nature. The grounding of sexual difference was environment, and home and market, the traditional domains of women and men, cultured divergent sensibilities. The selflessness of woman reflected the influence of her station and not the other way around. It was a mistake, Higginson believed, to suppose that her distinctive traits would long survive in the public realm of men.[35]

"The Honesty of Women" contemplated the subjects of gender and finance. Its moral orientation was toward women's rights on the basis of sameness, and it located its counterpoint in plantation fantasies of mastery and subordination. Higginson's liberalism echoed many architects of postbellum debt reform—those men and women who believed that the wife should be treated as an autonomous agent, free "from liability of any debts, except those contracted by herself." It was a conviction heard in the desires of women like Ella Gertrude Thomas, who wished to be seen as having "an individuality of my own," and those like the farmhand Mollie, who prayed for "her account [to be] separate from her husband's so she would know how she stood." Nature did not destine women for dependence, these voices insisted, and it was wrong for spouses, creditors, and the law to regard them as such. Yet Higginson's target in "The Honesty of Women" was not the conservative strictures of coverture. He did not, like Thomas and Mollie, bridle against codes and conventions that made the wife's financial horizons coextensive with the husband's. Instead, he detected a similar conservatism at work in the push to employ women in finance—to make them present in the business of borrowing and lending on the basis of their inherent difference. Ironically, it was with this cause that a new generation of feminists, sentimentalist in tone, cast their lot. "I am not an advocate of woman's rights in the opprobrious sense of that expression," Mary Lipscomb declared at the Congress of Women in 1893. "I do not care to see—hope never to see—the women of America leave the quiet sanctity of their homes and thrust themselves out into the political world." Yet, Lipscomb suggested, woman's native prudence could be of service in finance—to borrowers, lenders, depositors, and the economy—and her selflessness thus a reason to include her in public life. "I have asked the question many times, 'Does the money that passes through your hands appeal to you as money; do you ever feel that you would like to possess it?'" one champion of the female banker wrote a few years later. The answer given by the growing number of women who worked in finance, facilitating transactions of credit and debt, was reportedly no.[36]

This was an important language of feminist politics at the approach of the twentieth century. It measured woman's advance by her incorporation into the market as a distinctive type of economic actor—one untempted by wealth and intrinsically devoted to service and care. It was a fundamentally different tale than that which prevailed in the decades following the Civil War, when reformers sought to free the wife from debts over which she had no control. While the opening of financial work to women owed something to those earlier struggles—to the ways that reformers had sentimentalized the plight of the debtor's wife rather than upsetting the hierarchy of marriage—it also eclipsed them, offering narratives of progress in which women left the farm or town and found employment and independence in the cosmopolitan city. Increasingly, the idea was seized by bankers as well, in an attempt to portray their businesses as feminine and familial. In this reframing, debt did not dominate the borrower, as it had in the discourse of debtors' rights. The lender's object was not the recovery of his investment at any cost—through repayment ideally but, in its absence, by seizing home goods and garnishing labor. Instead, like the women they increasingly employed, bankers sought to care for the borrower. They were a substitute for the "friend or relative" who in the past had been there to "tide us over our difficulty." Lenders did not need to be walled off from the debtor, because their interest was coextensive with his and his family's. "Sympathy" and "sincerity" characterized their work rather than the cold enforcement of contracts. Their aim was not to make money but rather, like the wife, to serve "one to another, and always above the self."[37]

What did these changes—in a new feminism's relationship to banking and in the creditor's new presentation of his trade—mean to the woman still in the farmhouse or the urban tenement? What did the debts contracted by her husband deliver to her? "It may be summed up in two words," said a woman interviewed by the Department of Agriculture in 1915: "drudgery and economy." These were the themes that defined her life in debt, pursuing her "from the time she signs her name to the mortgage . . . until that other time when, weary and worn, she gives up the unequal struggle and is laid to rest." Many wives continued to handle the ledger, to trim expenses, and to take up helpmeet work to cover the bills into the twentieth century. "I managed thus to pay $200 on the mortgage every year," said one woman of her crocheting, "but the strain was too great, and overwork ruined my health." Perhaps the powers the wife acquired in the preceding decades made the debt feel more freely contracted. Perhaps, as the culture of coupling changed, she felt that the family's fortunes reflected her will as much as her mate's. Yet there was also reason to see her tethered as before by the home and the husband's debts. The two in concert narrowed the wife's horizons and "[robbed] the farm woman of much." It was a dilemma that took shape at the intersection of debtors' rights and the hierarchy of marriage and would pass through the age unresolved.[38]

3

ACCOUNTING FOR FREEDOM

Ned Cobb was born in eastern Alabama in 1885 to formerly enslaved parents. His earliest memories of work were of being hired out by his father to a series of local landowners in payment for various debts. At first he labored for a man who had sold his father a cow. The next season, he and the cow were sent to another man, who had furnished the family with tools and seed. In 1906, at the age of twenty-one, Cobb started working as a sharecropper on his own, but "sorry land [and] scarce fertilizer" left him with little cotton to sell at harvest and a large bill that the landowner carried over to the next year. In 1907, he moved to a richer patch of land and "worked it all in cotton," with a little corn for his sustenance. "Well, I made six pretty good bales . . . out there for Mr. Curtis and myself [but] when I got done gatherin, wound up, by havin to buy a little stuff from Mr. Curtis, [that] it took all them six bales of cotton to pay [the debts.]" Cobb was discouraged. "In the place of prosperin I was on a standstill." His wife, Hannah, "was dissatisfied at it, too," reminding her husband that despite all their labor, "we weren't accumulatin nothin." Over the next several years, the two moved from one Alabama farm to another. Sometimes their old debts trailed them. Occasionally new creditors elected to pay off their outstanding loans. At one point, Cobb was raising a good crop in a strong market for cotton. But a boll weevil infestation destroyed his plantings, leaving him further behind. In another instance, he had paid off his note with his primary creditor and determined to "sign no other," but the lender "run to every guano dealer [in the area] and told em not to let me have no guano," a necessary fertilizer. "He said, 'I aint goin to let you have no guano less'n you sign that note.'" Cobb resisted the coercion for a while, but eventually was forced to borrow from the same creditor again. "You want some cash above your debts," he explained later in life, outlining his impressions of credit and work. "If you don't get it, you lost, because you gave that man your labor and you can't get it back."[1]

Cobb's experience was a common one in the turn-of-the-century South. When W. E. B. Du Bois toured Dougherty County, Georgia, after moving to the region in 1898, he found a place where the richness of the soil belied the poverty of the people. "[A] pall of debt hangs over the beautiful land," he observed. "The merchants are in debt to the wholesalers, the planters are in debt to the merchants, the tenants owe the planters, and the laborers bow and bend beneath the burden of it all." Small farmers in the region relied on credit to buy seed, purchase tools, and maintain themselves until the harvest brought cash. They borrowed primarily from furnishing merchants and larger landowners, on whose property they might rent space or labor for shares. Yet the prices of crops were volatile and trended sharply downward in the decades following the Civil War. Even when market prices were high, a crop was always vulnerable to natural hazards like drought and disease. While the risks that growers faced were abundant, the money that they needed was scarce, with isolated farmers relying on just a handful of local lenders who charged "not less than 25 percent yearly" for credit and often far more. Behind these extortionary demands lay not only the usual dynamics of power and desperation, but also a complex of laws and informal legal practices that left the borrower with little choice as to who to borrow from and at what price once he or she had gone into debt. Property was poorly shielded from seizure and forced sale. If the lender chose to take it, the debtor would be ruined. In some states, failure to repay constituted not simply insolvency but a criminal act of fraud, on the premise that the borrower had intended to default on the debt all along. Working hand in hand with sheriffs, judges, and jailers, the lender in these situations could have the felonious borrower incarcerated and then made to work on the lender's farm, transforming an ordinary cash loan into a positive obligation to serve. Even apart from these more egregious coercions, debt in the rural South invited harassment, intimidation, and abuse. As Cobb described it, indebtedness diminished one's free choice, invaded the home, and forced one to toil with little to no reward.[2]

These indignities pressed on all poor farmers in the region to varying degrees. In 1893, George K. Holmes, chief statistician of the US Census Office, reported that credit in the South tended to beggar Black and white alike, with "the merchants, who advance plantation supplies, [replacing] the former masters and [making] peons of them [and] of their former slaves." In 1905, the journalist Herbert Ward insisted that rural indebtedness was "neither a race nor a negro problem any more than astigmatism is." In the cash-poor agricultural South, such claims were in many respects accurate. Yet it was also the case that Black southerners had fewer rights of mobility, lower rates of literacy, and less access to legitimate legal protection when creditors manipulated their accounts or threatened them with extralegal violence. Plainly, observed the novelist George Washington Cable, the system of extortionary crop liens was "unknown in our free land except in States where the tenant class is mostly Negroes." The unique historical context of Black indebtedness also raised a set of pressing moral questions. "Why should he strive," Du Bois asked of the Black tenant farmer, when every year found his earnings taken away by the lender? Was this the freedom fought for in the Civil War? Had the promise of emancipation truly been realized for men and women who labored without pay, whose homes were routinely invaded, and who could only leave one employer if another volunteered to pay off their debt? And how could a nation that permitted these practices regard itself as one that had abolished human bondage and authored a "new birth of freedom"? The matter of southern Black farmers' indebtedness bore on the meaning of freedom itself and the moral legacy of the Civil War. Was it the case, asked Du Bois, that in remote corners of the regions, where "the telegraph and the newspaper [end], the spirit of the Thirteenth Amendment [was] sadly broken"?[3]

Unlike the saga of the debtor's wife, which dated to the antebllum period and earlier, the problem of African American debt was of more recent origin. "Colored people never had no debt to pay in slavery times," one freedwoman declared. Yet a similar dynamic prevailed, as the law was pitched between the ideal of delivering freedom to debtors and its investment in a system of inequality from which the experience of unfree debt was inseparable. Here, the law in question was constitutional, as African Americans came to challenge the criminalization of default as a violation of the Thirteenth Amendment. The inequality was that of the legal and economic system of white supremacy and the national culture of reconciliation, in which peace between North and South was premised on the former Confederacy's relative autonomy to govern its social affairs. How would African Americans make their pleas for freedom from financial coercion heard? How would national legal institutions respond? And what would it mean to address the plight of Black debtors as so many other mechanisms of postemancipatory exploitation—such as violence, disenfranchisement, and segregation—surrounded them? Financial law was a primary front in the struggle for Black freedom after the Civil War. Even amid the fall of Reconstruction and the rise of Jim Crow, as African Americans were closed out of representative government, Black leaders struggled for debtors' rights in novel ways, turning to thrift, theft, and flight to achieve some measure of independence from the landowner and the furnishing merchant. Yet law remained relevant to Black debtors, even at the nadir of American race relations, and in *Bailey v. Alabama* (1911), the Supreme Court would rule on the debtor's most basic financial right, the freedom from financial servitude. As in the experience of the debtor's wife, the end results of these efforts were ambivalent. Some protections were extended to the Black debtor, yet many inequalities would endure.[4]

For Du Bois, indebtedness was the original condition of Black Americans as they took their first steps in freedom. Emancipation had liberated them from slavery, but they had exited bondage with no savings, land, or tools, and had been ushered into lives as free laborers in which credit was required. Some had settled into relations of tenancy, renting land from large planters—often their former masters—and owning the value of what they grew. Others engaged in sharecropping, wherein they paid no rent but owned only a share of the harvest, paid to them essentially as a wage. On both paths finance was essential, for any small farmer needed to purchase tools, fertilizer, and seed and to provide for family sustenance until the harvest could be sold. While "the carelessness of the nation in letting the slave start with nothing" may have destined freedpeople to dependence on lenders, the experience of debt was strongly shaped by local law and thus closely tied to Black political power. Under the aegis of Radical Reconstruction, Black lawmakers served in state constitutional conventions—convened by each of the formerly rebellious states as a condition of readmission to the union—and state legislatures. Eighteen African Americans claimed high executive office, including the governorship of Louisiana and the lieutenant governorship of Louisiana, Mississippi, and South Carolina; sixteen served in the US Congress. Black political might was never fully proportional to the size of the Black population, but African Americans in the South were important members of the Republican coalition and worked in that capacity to pilot the rise of more progressive local governance. Many Black lawmakers sought funding to expand public education and to construct other institutions of social welfare, such as hospitals and clinics. They raised taxes on large planters and floated bond issues to finance highway and railroad construction, hoping to free the region from "the plantation's dominance" and furnish "abundant employment opportunities for black and white alike." They also sought to protect the rights of debtors, ensuring that even in a credit-reliant economy, those who borrowed would be secure in their labor, property, and personhood.[5]

It was during Reconstruction, for example, that the campaign to abolish imprisonment for debt in the South caught up with the earlier reforms in the North, with civil incarceration prohibited in all cases other than those involving fraud or suspected flight. Republican lawmakers, Black and white, effected this change through ordinary legislation and in the constitutional conventions of the late 1860s. Like northern reformers, they drew an analogy between the institution of the debtors' prison and the bond of chattel slavery. Just as we "have said there shall be no involuntary servitude," B. F. Whittemore of South Carolina explained, so have we "abolished the barbarous law of imprisonment for debt" and announced "that the poor debtor should have the free use of his limbs to support his family, and that he should not be shut up in a dungeon." From there, many lawmakers reasoned toward protections for the insolvent debtor's property. "By the old common law, it used to be a crime for a man to owe a debt, [but] all that has passed away," C. P. Leslie, also of South Carolina, insisted. "Now, we propose to create a homestead law . . . to shelter our people from the storm, the rain and the misfortunes of the world." Most southern states had enacted homestead exemptions before the Civil War, but they had tended to privilege large estates and in some instances had explicitly reserved their protections to whites. The Reconstruction governments reprised the exemption principle in the new constitutions and made it applicable to all borrowers, regardless of race. They also tailored the laws to shield the typical possessions of landless freedpeople, such as tools, clothing, livestock, and furniture, and, in Georgia, for example, stipulated that owning land was *not* a precondition for enjoying such personal property protections (as courts occasionally held). In Texas, a Black legislator drafted a measure "exempting from forced sale 200 bushels of corn and 500 pounds of bacon per each and every family"—notionally ensuring that the farmer's power to sustain himself and his household could not be pledged and lost in the market. By setting the cash value for small property exemptions low and clarifying that they could be defeated by debts owed to hired laborers, lawmakers also sought to prevent such measures from being used by large planters to the disadvantage of African Americans.[6]

The appeal of these protections was threefold. First, they were understood as securing to freedpeople—indeed, to all people, "white or colored, it made no difference"—the right to own their labor. Limits on seizure and forced sale meant the protection of a space where work could earn a full and fair reward. Commenting on the Louisiana homestead exemption, which he had helped author and pass, Black lawmaker J. Henri Burch suggested that working power and the tools and rewards of work were one and the same. The new law prevented the creditor "from taking any labor [or] any of [the laborer's] implements—that is, his horse, his wagon, his stock, his wife's furniture, and such as that." Emancipation had announced that the formerly enslaved now had the full title to their toil, and debtor protection buttressed that achievement by assuring that their property in labor would not be taken away. Indeed, the second major appeal of debtor's rights in the South was their contribution to freedpeople's post-emancipation advance, establishing a rung below which they could not fall as they ascended the economic ladder. "I want to see the colored men of this State, and of all the States, whenever they acquire property . . . I want them to keep it," a delegate at the South Carolina convention declared in 1868. "It is one of the reasons I am pressing for this exemption." Finally, debtors' rights were effective politically, firming up the critical alliance between Blacks and poorer whites. As Republicans struggled to maintain their control of state governments against the Democratic resurgence, debtor relief was often seized as a class-based mobilizing issue. Alonzo J. Ransier, running for the lieutenant governorship of South Carolina in 1870, campaigned on Republicans' passage of the homestead exemption, which had freed yeoman farmers as well as the freedpeople from the fear of "being driven out of doors" by avaricious creditors. "Colored men and legislation by colored men" had raised the barrier between the market and private life that found favor throughout the state. Ransier—who would win the contest—emphasized that protection from risk and the security of the home were entwined with the political power of African Americans.[7]

Yet in the late 1870s, Democrats, promising to redeem the white South from the indignity of Reconstruction, began to close those "colored men" out of representative government. Amid the withdrawal of federal troops and the waning of northern interest in southern affairs, white revanchists employed organized violence, formal barriers to voting, and electoral fraud to limit Black participation in government. The Thirteenth, Fourteenth, and Fifteenth Amendments might "stand forever," one spokesman of the countermovement declared, "but we intend . . . to make them dead letters on the statute-book."[8] As Black representation in politics diminished and as the Redeemers' legislative powers grew, the trajectory of debtors' rights reversed course, to the advantage of creditors. Not all debtor protections came under attack. The exemption for land itself, popular with poor whites and large planters alike, often remained in place, recast by the Redeemers as a device for maintaining racial order and guarding "inviolate our social system." On the other hand, the protections for smaller possessions, such as tools, clothing, and furniture, were in many states narrowed or rescinded. "Yes, sir; the Democrats repealed that as soon as they got in," Burch reported on the fate of the Louisiana exemption law that he had helped pass. "The consequence is that there is nothing safe for the laborer now, if [the creditor] chooses to move upon him and take away his goods and implements of agriculture." Du Bois, touring the region at the turn of the century, observed the absence of the small exemption law's enforcement even in the states where such protections technically endured. "I have seen a black farmer fall in debt to a white storekeeper, and that storekeeper go to his farm and strip it of every single marketable article—mules, ploughs, stored crops, tools . . . all in the face of the law of homestead exemptions." This was the very plunder that the original architects of exemption law had sought to prevent—a slavery in which the debtor's hands were "effectually bound" because the creditor could seize his "daily wages" as well as his "bed, pillow, and blanket." In the aftermath of Reconstruction, white revanchists sought not to prevent this suffering but to permit it, repealing protective financial law and leaving Black borrowers to be "preyed upon by these swindlers and rascals."[9]

The retreat of protective debtors' rights was paced by the introduction of new powers for creditors who secured their loans using crop liens. Crops were the primary collateral required by lenders in the South when extending credit to farmers—always when dealing with landless tenants, but often when dealing with landed borrowers as well, as the harvest could be more readily converted into cash for the lender than the land on which it had been grown. The lien gave the lender a right to claim a portion of the farmer's crop if the debt was not retired, in ways similar to an assignment of wages. Credit in the postbellum South was typically provided by furnishing merchants or large landowners, and the early struggles over lien law represented a clash between rival classes of capitalists, for the power to control and profit from agricultural labor in the region rested on determining whose lien claim on the crops was stronger—the landowner's or the merchant's. Later struggles centered on the debtor's rights within the lien, and as Black political strength diminished, so too did the poor farmer's safeguards under the law. There had long been a limit on rolling one season's crop lien over to the next year, for example. This was intended to prevent any one debt from becoming a perpetual bond. In many southern states, however, that protection was rescinded by legislation and court rulings in the 1880s, allowing one misfortune to jeopardize the farmer's harvest indefinitely and to effectively require him to continue contracting with the same lender year after year. Also weakened were limits on the kinds of debts that could implicate the crops—a change that provided more opportunities for creditors to seize the debtor's primary source of income—along with laws that had prevented the lien from extending to other pieces of property, such as tools and household goods, if the harvest was insufficient. The result of these repeals, in the context of declining crop prices, was an indebtedness from which there was often no escape and a labor for which there was little to no reward. It was the lien farmer's belief that "he is always only twelve months away from freedom," one agricultural journal observed; rarely did reality bear this out.[10]

In the 1890s, state lawmakers pressed further in advantaging the creditor, enacting legislation that transformed debt into a positive claim on the debtor's service. Creditors would not only enjoy greater access to the borrower's crops, property, and earnings but would also be able to command the debtor's labor directly. One instrument for effecting this change was the surety laws. These statutes made court-issued fines and fees salable to third parties, who acted as the criminal debtor's surety and could demand repayment for their generosity in labor. What this meant was that if a worker absconded from an employer, the sheriff could arrest the worker on a charge of vagrancy, levy a fine, and then sell the debt back to the original employer, who could command the worker's labor until the debt was repaid. Employers could even market the service they acquired, with "a man who had a debt against a Negro [selling] the claim to [another] farmer who wants more labour," the minister Charles Otken noted in 1894. A second device for weaponizing debt was the false-pretense law. This measure classified the failure to repay wage advances as a criminal action of fraud that could be punished by fines, imprisonment, or hard labor. The sharecropper who had an outstanding debt with a landowner thus could not exit the working relationship without committing a criminal offense. As a sequence grounded in criminal rather than civil law, prosecution under this measure did not violate state constitutional prohibitions against imprisonment for debt. Nor, its proponents believed, did it transgress against the Thirteenth Amendment, which allowed for involuntary servitude when it was imposed "as a punishment for a crime." False-pretense legislation carefully nested the labor it intended to coerce within the legitimizing architecture of due process and the law of fraud. As its supporters calmly assured, all the law proposed was to protect the humble farmer, himself "one of the laboring classes," from "irresponsible helpers" who would "start a crop, get into debt, and then leave the indulgent employer helpless and ruined."[11]

Debtors' rights emerged as a primary front in the struggle to define Black freedom after the abolition of slavery. African Americans understood the law of debt as deeply related to their prospects for economic mobility and as a means of consolidating the gains of emancipation. The rise of Black political power during Reconstruction was coextensive with the rise of debtors' rights in the states of the former Confederacy. White conservatives, in turn, placed the dismantling of those rights at the top of their agenda for the redemption of the region. Indeed, in the wake of Reconstruction, laws rescinding debtor protections and advancing creditor power were enacted in the South before the laws that segregated public facilities, disenfranchised African Americans, and prohibited miscegenation. The debts these codes enhanced did not solely imperil Black workers. White tenant farmers were similarly impoverished by the revisions to lien law, and white immigrants from southern and eastern Europe were similarly ensnared by false-pretense laws, which bound them to work off their travel fees in extractive industry and railway construction. It was also the case that the financial coercions endured by African Americans often exceeded that which the legislatures permitted. No statute gave Cobb's erstwhile creditor the right to force him to borrow again, and no law permitted landowners and merchants to calculate debts unfairly—to lie about what had been paid and what was still owed—or to threaten the borrower with violence. Law and the plight of the Black debtor were thus imperfectly aligned. Yet it had been legal power that African Americans used to shield themselves from the strength of the lender, and it was in the gradual loss of that power that the lenders' command over Black labor steadily grew. "Here and there a man has raised his head above these murky waters," Du Bois wrote of the South at the turn of the twentieth century as the last lights of Reconstruction died out. Most Black workers he observed, however, were "slow, dull, and discouraged." They were tired of tilling the land, reaping the crop, and "fighting a hard battle with debt."[12]

The path of legal change in the postbellum South invested one annual moment with profound significance. This was settlement time, also known as "countin' day," or simply the "reckoning." It was the point just after the harvest when the landowner or furnishing merchant tallied up the workers' expenses and balanced them against their crop's value, determining whether the worker would finish the year with some earnings or, more likely, end up owing more than when they began. Settlement told workers whether they were any closer to buying land, or at the least whether they could pay off the debt incurred to finance the planting in the first place. It was also understood as a reading of the progress that African Americans had made since emancipation—a measure of freedom or, more often, of enduring dependency. "The second year the whole family plunged into work, and made a bigger and better crop," the Black novelist William Pickens recalled of his youth. Yet "at reckoning time history repeated itself [and] there was still enough debt to continue slavery." Another observer explained, "After they have made four or five bags of cotton, and so much corn . . . their landlord or employer [performs] the measuring and weighing of the crop, and the handling and calculating of the orders." Often, they made it out "so that they not only have nothing, but are in debt, with a mortgage on them, as one

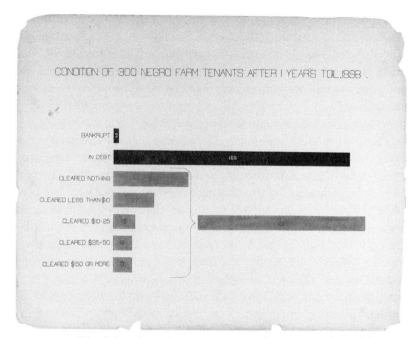

FIGURE 3.1. "Condition of 300 Negro Farm Tenants after 1 Years Toil, 1898," from *W. E. B. Du Bois's Data Portraits: The Color Line at the Turn of the Twentieth Century,* ed. Whitney Battle-Baptiste and Britt Rusert (New York: Princeton Architectural Press, 2018), 122.

might say, for the future." The settlement did not always yield such dispiriting results. "We worked on shares [and] got half . . . and in the fall we paid our debts," one Arkansas man recalled. "Sometimes we had as much as $150 in the clear." Others were able to escape the tension of the settlement altogether. "When my first husband died he did not owe fifteen cents," another woman reported. "He just would not go in debt to nobody." Yet for most Black workers in the postbellum South, the reckoning was a freighted moment in which their captivity to the creditor was extended for another year. As a familiar folk song explained, "You may work around the house / Till the big settling time / It makes no difference / You are coming out behind."[13]

With few legal protections to shield their property and labor, African Americans refined a variety of informal tactics to achieve some measure of freedom in debt. Some took to marketing their harvest in secret, hoping to sell it and keep the earnings for themselves without the creditor claiming them as his own. "So skillfully and so closely has [the merchant] drawn the bonds of the law about the tenant, that the black man has often simply to choose between pauperism and crime," Du Bois observed. Thus when the crop was growing, "the merchant watches it like a hawk," for there was truth in the recurrent tales "of cotton picked at night [and] mules disappearing" as Black farmers tried to make a profit out of sight. Others pursued the mastery of calculation, imagining that if they better understood their contracts, and if their expenses were recorded more faithfully, they might find that they were not as far behind as the lender inevitably claimed. Those who could read and write, for example, often volunteered their services to friends and relatives. "A man that didn't know how to count would always lose," one farmworker reported. Literate and numerate African Americans thus would "check [the] merchants' calculations" on behalf of others and "keep them from taking all our labor away from us." Mary Matthews, who worked with her husband on a farm in North Carolina, acquired an account book and asked her employer to mark their expenses there as well as in his own ledger, so she could keep the debts honest and her family's spending disciplined. "He cussed at me," Matthews recalled, and, as her husband added, "said nobody should keep no damn books on his place, and if we didn't like it, Goddamn it, get out!" Even had Matthews's request been honored, her records most likely would not have carried much weight in the event of a formal legal dispute. As Pickens recounted, when judges were presented with conflicting accounts of an individual's debt, they almost always sided with the lender: "It was understood that the Negro was unreliable, and the courts must help the poor planters." Nevertheless, the reaction elicited by Matthews's request indicated that the creditor's power was not absolute. The account book was a site of struggle, and many African Americans sought to use it in their defense.[14]

Part of the account book's significance may have rested on Matthews's proposed justification for its use—as an instrument of self-discipline and thrift. For many African Americans, credit had initially been experienced as a measure of freedom. It allowed them to purchase goods they desired, provide for their families on their own accounts rather than the masters', and make investments in seed and tools that might yield a sturdier independence in time. There was a dignity in being treated like a responsible person and in being trusted by white lenders as legal equals in the market. "Anything you wanted, you could get if you were a good hand," one laborer said of his first visit to the country store after emancipation. "If you didn't make no money, that's all right; they would advance you more." Another recalled, "In our anxiety to be free, we would gladly mortgage our time to anyone who become our security." Yet a ministry of domestic economy militated in the other direction, teaching that the path of true freedom ran not through credit but through financial restraint. The early exhortations of the Freedman's Savings Bank implored African Americans to save rather than borrow and therein "Be Your Own Master." Toward the turn of the century, this thinking continued in initiatives like the Black Belt Improvement Society, which counseled tenant farmers to labor hard and practice frugality. "It took me fifteen years" to buy property and become independent, one Black farmer recalled, "and during that time I had to undergo all sorts of hardships." Getting out of debt meant "get[ting] up before day and stay[ing] up late at night." It meant missing church to avoid being seen in tattered clothes and denying one's family the comforts they desired. "I feel a little above owing a man now," said one cropper who had worked himself from insolvency to independence. "I was in debt thirty years; now I do not owe any man."[15]

These efforts could be appreciated in a conservative register. They could place the responsibility for preserving freedom squarely on the formerly enslaved, effacing the retreat of Reconstruction and the harassment of revanchist whites. Certainly if the individualization of economic fate inspired African Americans to work longer and harder, drawing more profit from the soil than they otherwise would, it had the support of landowners and merchants. Yet in a political and social economy in which indebtedness was a primary means of maintaining white power, thrift could take on a more ambitious and radical cast. Lenders did not simply permit indebtedness, but compelled it. One farmworker who was supposedly plotting to move to another town was threatened and beaten by a landowner before being made to "go to his store and get a month's supply of groceries" on credit. When another tried to pay back his debt to a merchant, "[the creditor] did not want to take the money . . . [saying] he did not care whether his good customers paid him or not, just so they kept on paying." Ned Cobb was denied the ability to purchase fertilizer with cash in order to coerce him into contracting again with the lender, thus returning him to the type of debt he had labored to escape. In these instances, the ability to avoid credit signified not only a triumph over the desirous self—as in the classical discourse of prudent economy—but also a triumph over a social order that aspired to compel toil through debt. The more that someone like Mary Matthews could challenge the fiction that her family's poverty was rooted in its ungoverned wants, the more that creditors would betray their inability to survive in the market economy without recourse to deception and abuse.[16]

These were gradual forms of resistance. They tested the architecture of indebted labor slowly. Even at their most successful, they brought such achievements as solvency and landedness only after many hard years; often, they delivered neither. A more immediate option—albeit one that entailed greater risk—was the decision to escape the debt altogether. Few Black borrowers owed enough, or had requisite access to counsel and fair courts, to petition for the release of bankruptcy. In any case, it was not clear what formal discharge would mean in an economy in which borrowing again, under the same unequal conditions, was inevitable. Instead, some Black debtors turned to the discharge of flight. Black mobility was precisely what vagrancy laws, false-pretense laws, and other pretextual instruments sought to curb, but many found ways to depart from farm, town, or region and leave their coercive debts behind. Sometimes exodus was collective. In the late 1870s, as many as forty thousand African Americans decamped the South for Oklahoma, Colorado, and Kansas. They were inspired by the exhortations of race leaders like Benjamin Singleton and Henry Adams, who promised a greater, more substantive freedom in the West. Yet they were also driven away by political violence, mounting daily abuse, and a political economy that trapped many African Americans in perpetual debt. "I left the South because I could not make a living," one Mississippi migrant explained to a Senate Committee on the removal in 1880. "If I got half a barrel of meat and some flour, [the furnishing merchant] would take all my cotton for it and still leave me in debt." They "worked year in and year out," a Kansas resident said of his community's new arrivals, "and, notwithstanding they raised good crops, they were at the end of the year in debt." Smaller migrations at the beginning and end of the 1890s spoke to the enduring appeal of challenging debt through relocation to states where credit was not so entwined with mastery.[17]

Flight also happened at the individual and household level. Pickens's childhood memories from the 1880s and 1890s orbited his family's experiences of debt and desertion. When he was born, his parents were living in South Carolina, entangled in a relationship in which "my father worked and another man reckoned." As Pickens recounted, "It always took the whole of what was earned to pay for the scant 'rations' that were advanced to the family, and at settlement time there would be a margin of debt to keep the family perennially bound to a virtual owner." At one point, a hotel operator in town offered to pay down Pickens's father's debt "if Father would be his man of all work and Mother [would be] his cook." The family accepted the exchange and relocated to the city, but the pay at the hotel was low, and the elder Perkins, in search of the kind of income that might one day fund the purchase of land, migrated the family further west, to Arkansas, "where the soil was fertile and wages high." The move was possible, Pickens recalled, "only by allowing some Western farmer to pay the fares of the family through his agent, and by signing a contract to work on that farmer's land until the debt was paid according to that farmer's reckoning." Thus were they again bound to a white landowner, finishing year after year "deeper in debt than on the day of our arrival." For the adults in the family, indebtedness kept them laboring without reward. For Pickens himself, it meant delays in his education, as the children were made to work until the debt was paid. Ultimately, "there was but one recourse—the way of escape," as the family fled the farm and continued to move west, always seeking land or at least a loan on more honest terms.[18]

There were also opportunities, even amid their political exclusion, for African Americans to make novel appeals to the law. The reforms of the Redeemer governments denied poor borrowers the protections of most property exemptions. Local courts could not be trusted to adjudicate debt contests fairly. At a higher level, however, the state constitutional prohibitions against involuntary servitude and imprisonment for debt were sometimes respected, and the writ of habeas corpus could be used to resist the criminalization of default. In *Ex parte Riley* (1891), an Alabama case, an agricultural worker who had been bound to his employer by a wage advance was freed by the state supreme court, which held that abandonment of the advance constituted "mere breach of contract" and not a criminal action. In *State v. Leak* (1902), in South Carolina, a bond of indentured service was invalidated as a transgression against the abolition of slavery. In the same state, in 1907, one "H" successfully contested a misdemeanor conviction for having accepted a cash advance and failing to perform "the reasonable service required of him." In North Carolina's *State v. Williams* (1909), a debtor was likewise emancipated by his state's high court on the grounds that a statute denying "any tenant or cropper" the right to abandon a debt secured by service "without good cause and before paying for such advances" constituted an illegal form of imprisonment. The language of protest in these challenges often hewed to the keywords of classical liberalism. "The patrimony of the poor man lies in the strength and dexterity of his own hands," a 1907 writ of habeas corpus for the brothers Enoch and Elijah Drayton quoted of Adam Smith. Any institution that "hinders him from employing this strength and dexterity in what manner he thinks proper . . . is a plain violation of his most sacred property." As plaintiffs, affiants, appellants, and witnesses, African Americans brought this precept into confrontation with the legal architecture of white supremacy.[19]

Black debtors also attempted to summon the power of the federal state, conveying their allegations of debt peonage in the South to the US Department of Justice (created after the Civil War principally for the purpose of enforcing the Reconstruction Amendments). Some complaints traveled to federal officials by mail, like the letter Andrew Salter of Alabama sent to the US district attorney in Mobile in 1911, reporting on the criminal sentence he had received for defaulting on an alleged debt owed to the county court. Another plea journeyed to Washington addressed to "The United

States Departmental Bureau of Justice and Labor." Often, such accounts were routed through complex networks of family and friends. One woman, whose letter to a federal judge was forwarded to the US attorney general in 1912, described being "told by some good white men to appeal to you for aid in regard to my husband," held in a condition of peonage on a plantation in rural Arkansas. Others sent similar pleas on behalf of wives, siblings, parents, and children, while D. P. Johnson's tale of indebtedness was mailed by B. F. Scott, a white veterinary surgeon Johnson met while working on a farm in Troy, Alabama. Federal officials were also sought out in person. "We are almost daily called upon by negroes in a state of abject fear," informed one official in Georgia. When Lettie James was twice forced by local law enforcement to remain on the cotton farm of her employer, she reached out to the district attorney in Mobile and submitted not only an affidavit detailing the abuse but also a letter sent to her by the employer, in which he made clear that James and her sons "owe me, and I will make you pay it, [and] if I can't the sheriff can." Like those African Americans who filed writs in the state courts, James performed a range of legal labors to resist the pretextual coercions of debt. In contacting federal officials, preserving evidence, and providing testimony, she and other Black debtors nourished a federal legal presence in the South and claimed a form of aspirational citizenship in the early years of Jim Crow.[20]

What power did the federal government have to answer these calls? On what legal authority could it involve itself in the small sums owed by wage workers and sharecroppers, the falsifications of the merchant's account book, and the revisions to exemption and lien law? The ordinary mechanics of contract enforcement and debt collection fell under the purview of state legislatures. Even a Congress that wished to amend the lien law or restore the older exemptions lacked a path toward meaningful reform. The informal nature of many financial coercions also stymied officials. How was federal law enforcement supposed to police the deliberate misrecording of debts, the bad weights and measures used at settlement time, and the illicit pressure that lenders placed on fertilizer suppliers? Two authorities that did exist for the Department of Justice and the federal courts was the Peonage Act of 1867 and the Thirteenth Amendment. These were not tools that could readily target the coercions to which Ned Cobb or the Pickens family were subject. The expropriation of just earnings through a fallacious reckoning was offensive to the free labor ideal but not generally considered to be a form of involuntary servitude. Yet when private contracting merged with public power to force borrowers to work off their debt under the threat of prosecution and imprisonment, the constitutional prohibition on forced labor was potentially involved. Involuntary work was precisely what many observers believed false-pretense laws accomplished, by criminalizing fraud and defining the act of abandoning a service contract as prima facie evidence of duplicitous intent. The courts would have to rule on the technical question of whether such laws sufficiently disguised their command of the insolvent debtor's labor. But major political and moral issues also loomed, as the application of the Thirteenth Amendment to the plight of indebted labor appeared to force a confrontation: between the law's commitment to the debtor's freedom and the nation's political commitment to sectional reconciliation and white supremacy.

The debt that would force that confrontation was contracted in December 1906. Alonzo Bailey was an African American laborer hired to work for a term of one year on a cotton farm in Montgomery, Alabama. At the time of his hiring, he accepted a cash advance of $15 from his employer, the Riverside Company, to be gradually repaid from his monthly wages. When Bailey abandoned the farm and the job in late January with most of the debt unpaid, he ran afoul of Alabama Statute 4730, the state's false-pretense law. The measure classified borrowing money on the expectation of service and failing to perform or repay as a crime, and it identified the mere refusal to perform or repay as "*prima facie* evidence of the intent to injure or defraud." Along with a separate state evidentiary rule that denied the debtor the right to rebut the charge by testifying "as to his uncommunicated motives," the law endeavored to make the wage advance inescapable (in a way that would nominally respect earlier state court rulings that forbade the outright criminalization of default). Armed with such legal resources, the Riverside Company's case against Bailey was strong, and in short succession the debtor was arrested, convicted, and sent to jail, likely to await assignment to the chain gang or to have his labor purchased back by the employer through the Alabama surety law.[21]

Yet Bailey's wife made contact with a Montgomery attorney—Edward S. Watts—and filed a writ of habeas corpus in the courtroom of William H. Thomas, a city judge who was critical of false-pretense law. Thomas denied the writ, being bound by the state supreme court's toleration of Alabama Statute 4730. But he brought the case to the attention of Booker T. Washington, a friend and ally of Thomas's in some matters of regional reform, and Washington set about organizing an effort to appeal Bailey's conviction, with an eye toward invalidating the law on which it was based. The legal architecture of Black indebtedness was offensive to most race leaders of the era, but it was particularly troubling to Washington. In contrast to Du Bois, who hoped to chart a path for African Americans out of white supremacy through political and civil rights, Washington believed that Black progress would come through labor and moral improvement. "Our greatest danger," he cautioned at the Atlanta Exposition in 1895, "is that in the great leap of slavery to freedom, we may overlook the fact that masses of us are to live by the production of our hands." Instead of pursuing immediate legal equality, Washington recommended the steady accretion of wealth through work and the maintenance of peaceful relations with whites. Yet if people like Bailey could not own their wages and choose when and for whom to toil, then Washington's vision might never come to pass. African Americans might remain "at the bottom of life" rather than gradually ascending toward the top. It was in defense of a particular program of Black mobility that Washington seized on Bailey's conviction and used his social and financial resources to emancipate the beleaguered debtor.[22]

Washington was not alone in supporting Bailey's appeal. He was joined by several white businessmen from Montgomery and several progressive journalists from the North, including the newspaper editor Oswald Garrison Villard and the muckraking journalist Ray Stannard Baker. Watts and Fred Ball, another local lawyer, served as Bailey's counsel on the case's circuitous path: first, as an appeal to the Alabama Supreme Court, where it was denied in 1908; then on to the US Supreme Court, where it was remanded back to the state for a jury trial in 1909; and then, after Bailey was convicted by a jury and appealed again, back to Washington, DC, in 1911. The charge from Bailey's legal team—supplemented in federal Supreme Court proceedings by an amicus brief filed by the US attorney general— was that Alabama's false-pretense law transgressed against both the Thirteenth and Fourteenth Amendments, as well as the Peonage Act. While the language of the law did not name race, the petitioners conceded, there was not "a well-advised man in the State, lawyer or layman, that does not know that this act was passed in order to give the larger planters of the State absolute dominion over the negro laborer." Revisions to the law had trained it to apply only to debts contracted by farm tenants. "Are they less willing to pay their rent than the occupiers of dwellings or store houses?" the petitioners asked. By governing the contracts of just one class—and, upon observation, just African American class members—the measure had offended the Fourteenth Amendment's requirement that all persons enjoy "the equal protection of the laws." On these grounds—and for the fact that the law's alteration to the rules of evidence deprived the debtor of his liberty without due process—Bailey's legal team argued that the statute must fall and Bailey be emancipated.[23]

Additionally, and more substantially, Watts and Ball contended that the false-pretense law stood in violation of the Peonage Act of 1867 and the Thirteenth Amendment. The latter prohibited slavery and involuntary

servitude, except as punishment for a crime. The former clarified that labor compelled in liquidation of debt amounted to an illegal form of bondage, despite the view articulated by some in the nineteenth century that
indebted labor was a form of "voluntary and not involuntary servitude."
The architects of Alabama's false-pretense law had assured that by criminalizing fraud rather than default, they had placed the measure squarely inside
the Thirteenth Amendment's criminal-punishment exception. Bailey's legal
team argued that the state instead had merely attempted to "accomplish by
indirection what it could not do directly." The problem was not that, once
convicted, the debtor was subject to forced labor (which was acceptable under constitutional law). Instead, it was that the law used the debt as a pretext
to deny the borrower the choice to exit the employment relationship, by
penalizing that choice with arrest and incarceration. The law allowed "the
employer to keep the employee in involuntary servitude by the overhang-
ing menace of prosecution," for it was a near certainty that arrest would
lead to conviction because of the law's changes to the rules of evidence. The
statute was thus a part of a system that gave "a dominant class undue and
unequal powers over a great army of less fortunate citizens who eat their
daily bread [by] the sweat of their face." As Ball declared, "Negro slavery
has passed away, but if a system of peonage . . . shall arise in its stead, the last
estate shall be worse than the first, for the only limitation upon the masters
will be their want of wealth and power, both of which will be augmented
by the system they support." For Bailey, a $15 wage advance had been trans-
formed into a bond of compulsory service. His legal team demanded that
the law be struck down and the poor debtor freed, on the authority of the
Peonage Act and the Thirteenth Amendment.[24]

The Alabama law was defended before the Supreme Court by Alexander
Garber, the Alabama attorney general, and Thomas Martin, the assistant
attorney general. They built their case on three arguments. First, they explained that the law did not compel the specific performance of labor. It
did not deny the debtor the right to exit his contract with the Riverside
Company, and no Alabama court had ever commanded the debtor to return
to the farm and work off what he owed. Instead, the law simply defined
the act of accepting a loan with the intent of never repaying it as criminal
and established the evidence required to prove the offense. The "*essential*
ingredient of the offense is fraud," Garber insisted, and "if ulterior motives
and purposes of the Legislature had existed in fact, it is strange that up to
the present period such motives have failed of discovery." The debtor was
not denied the opportunity to offer evidence disputing the charge, and the
creditor was not relieved of the burden of proving that the fraud had occurred. If the case resulted in a conviction—as it did for Bailey—then the

state was permitted to assign a penalty that was consonant with constitutional law and conventional practice. If the false-pretense law was immoral or objectionable, then it was for the people of Alabama to change through their legislative power. Yet because the measure did not require one to labor in the service of the original wage advance itself, there was no trespass against the Peonage Act or the Thirteenth Amendment. "No element of a Federal question is involved," Garber insisted. The Supreme Court had no grounds on which to invalidate Bailey's conviction through the constitutional law of slavery and freedom.[25]

Garber also argued that the appellant's Fourteenth Amendment claims were misguided. The law applied equally to all persons in the state who entered into a specific type of contract—a wage advance issued to an individual entering into an agreement to perform farm labor. It was the "suggestion in brief of counsel for plaintiff in error, that the statute is void, for that it is applied to negro laborers and negro tenants and not to all classes of employees." Yet this claim was not borne out in the record. No evidence had been admitted in the original trial or in any of the appeals demonstrating that the law was used only against African American debtors, and the text of the law itself disclosed no special targeting of a particular racial group. Indeed, even if the Alabama legislature had been motivated by racial animosity—a desire, as the appellant maintained, "to give the larger planters of the State absolute dominion over the negro laborer"—this would not necessarily have given the court reason to invalidate the law. In *Soon Hing v. Crowley* (1885), the court had been presented with a San Francisco ordinance regulating the activities of public laundries. The charge had been made that the law was intended to discipline the Chinese men who primarily worked in the trade. The Supreme Court had considered an equal protection challenge and had found that "even if the motives of the supervisors were as alleged, the ordinance would not be thereby changed from a legitimate police regulation, unless in its enforcement it is made to operate only against the class mentioned; and of this there is no pretense." Just as such evidence had been wanting in *Crowley*, so too had "the diligent counsel for plaintiff in error . . . not seen fit to present" such evidence in *Bailey*, "and it is manifestly unfair to insist now that it is true." The Fourteenth Amendment case against the law was thus also insufficient, the attorney general insisted, and the debtor's conviction required to stand.[26]

Ribboned throughout Garber's statements—and commonly encountered in discussions of the peonage issue in the southern press—was also the suggestion that Bailey's challenge marked an attempt to excite sectional tension and to authorize the federal government's intrusion into regional affairs. This claim keyed into a political dilemma rather than a legal one, for in the decades since the withdrawal of federal troops and the end of Recon-struction, the nation had achieved a kind of peace premised on the South's relative autonomy to enact its white supremacist vision. The sources of the arrangement were many. A new liberalism in the North—cultured amid the rising class tension of the 1870s and 1880s—converged with southern con-servatism to see social legislation, popular democracy, and a strong central state as threats to the social order. The dawn of the nation's extraterritorial empire in the 1890s inspired a national investment in the myth of white superiority, even in places where racial difference was not a significant part of daily life. As South Carolina Senator Ben Tillman declared in 1900, "No Republican leader . . . will now dare to wave the bloody shirt and preach a crusade against the South's treatment of the negro," for after the conquest of the Philippines, "the North has a bloody shirt of its own." Ascendant strains of scientific racism provided intellectual resources for attributing African American poverty to inherent deficiency, and an emergent progressivism in the North came to see segregation as an efficient compromise that allowed for the peaceful management of social tension. Quietude on white suprem-acy became a precondition for national reconciliation, and the US Supreme Court was an active partner in this project, denying that the Reconstruction Amendments prohibited discrimination by private individuals (in the *Civil Rights Cases*), discrimination by the state (in *Plessy v. Ferguson*), or Black dis-enfranchisement (in *Williams v. Mississippi*). The gains of emancipation were thus narrowly defined, and the policies of the white supremacist South were made to fit into the category of acceptable regional distinction rather than constitutional offense. In this context, Garber encouraged the court to see the Bailey appeal as an impermissible challenge to a fragile national calm.[27]

Freedom for debtors was a clarion call of the late nineteenth century. Amid the high liberalism of the postbellum moment, an array of reform-ers had insisted that those who borrowed—and those who failed—were entitled to preserve their right to labor, to maintain a home, and to make independent moral choices. The Peonage Act, the Bankruptcy Act, and the state-level property exemption laws nationalized in 1867 gave institutional expression to this faith. In the South, debtor's rights entwined with the ef-forts of Black lawmakers to substantiate emancipation and ensure that Af-rican Americans would not be made the servants of their lenders. Yet the fall of Reconstruction was measured by the repeal of many of those state laws and the passage of opposing measures, as revanchist whites rolled back the protections for labor and property that Black and poor white debtors had briefly enjoyed. Tool and crop exemptions were rescinded, limitations on the duration of the lien were lifted, and surety and false-pretense laws criminalized default in order to impose an ostensibly constitutional form of servitude. Bailey's appeal challenged only one facet of the Jim Crow credit regime: he and his counsel held that his conviction under the Alabama false-pretense law violated the Thirteenth and Fourteenth Amendments and the Peonage Act. They asked for the promise of debtors' rights—at its most basic level—to be vindicated by the Supreme Court. Yet to do so would be to upset a national peace founded on sectional prerogative and race inequality. Would the Supreme Court deliver a portion of the freedom promised by emancipation? Or would it accommodate coercion to preserve the graded order of the age?[28]

For Justice Oliver Wendell Holmes Jr., Bailey's argument failed to convince. Holmes had been an abolitionist in his youth and was the only sitting member of the US Supreme Court to have served in the Union Army during the Civil War. In his career as a judge and legal theorist, he had developed a jurisprudence that often aligned with the rights of workers and the powers of the progressive state. Yet Holmes did not see in Alabama's false-pretense law a government illicitly conspiring to limit the debtor's freedom. Instead, he saw a legislature using ordinary means to accomplish ordinary ends. "Breach of a legal contract without excuse is wrong," Holmes wrote in response to the arguments of counsel. Individuals were morally responsible for keeping their promises, and the state had a legitimate interest in encouraging them to do so, for if contracts could not be trusted, then the business of the community would cease. All states engaged in this work by assigning civil penalties to nonperformance. If someone agreed to do something and did not keep their word, then the state allowed them to be sued. Alabama built on this foundation by attaching a criminal penalty to the breach. While this intensified "the legal motive for doing right," it did not create a condition of peonage, which Holmes defined as "service to a private master at which a man is kept by bodily compulsion against his will." He wrote: "I do not blink at the fact that the liability to imprisonment . . . may induce the laborer to keep on when he would like to leave," but "it does not strike me as an objection to a law that it is effective." Indeed, for Holmes, it might even recommend the Alabama legislation. At the least, it placed the false-pretense law in the same category as all the other state measures that took from the well of freedom in order to promote desirable behavior and order. These policies might encourage people to work if work was what they had promised to do, but encouragement was not the same as compulsion. Such laws did not, in the justice's view, "make the laborer a slave."[29]

In part, Holmes's opinion was rooted in a new modernist sensibility that rejected classical liberalism's belief in the sanctity of the autonomous individual. No man was an island in this emergent worldview. Instead, people were forever entangled in social relationships that pushed and pulled, compelled and coerced. By taking this interdependence as a starting point, individuals could discover new kinds of freedom in consumption and self-expression, and government could more fully wield its power to improve public life. In *Lochner v. New York* (1905), a test of a New York law regulating working conditions in bakeries, Holmes famously arrayed this philosophy against the Supreme Court's laissez-faire majority. To the rest of the court, the New York legislature had overstepped its bounds and trampled on the individual worker's right to agree to whatever working conditions he desired. To Holmes, on the other hand, the majority had erred twice: first, in presuming that the individual ever had the freedom of contract that the law supposedly trampled and, second, in denying society the right to experiment with different legal arrangements that might bring happiness and prosperity in the long run. "I think that the word liberty . . . is perverted," he wrote in dissent, "when it is held to prevent the natural outcome of a dominant opinion." Holmes's jurisprudence participated in a broad reevaluation of society and the self that took place across American life at the turn of the century: in the educational philosophy of John Dewey; in the institutional economics of Thorstein Veblen and Simon Patten; and in the social psychology of William James. While this outlook was often linked to progressive causes, it was not fundamentally anathema to exercises of state power that punished rather than protected. In *Bailey v. Alabama*, Holmes was presented with a borrower who claimed that Alabama had turned a loan into an unconstitutional obligation to serve. Not believing that the debtor was ever fully free or that courts should use individual rights to tame collective legislative action, Holmes rejected the borrower's appeal and sided with the state.[30]

Issues of high philosophy and selfhood thus informed the jurist's interpretation of the Constitution. Yet there were also social and historical concerns at play, for it could not be ignored that the case involved a Black man laboring for a white planter deep in the American South. While the court might wish to approach the case "in the same way as if it arose in Idaho or New York," Holmes did not imagine that such detachment was possible. Instead, he believed that the view that false-pretense law created a condition of slavery was premised on the "tacit assumption that this law is not administered as it would be in New York, and that juries [in the South] will act with prejudice against the laboring man." For Holmes, this meant that the case did not invite the court to evaluate the constitutionality of a particular law. Instead, it sought a judicial evaluation of the character of a particular region. As the Alabama attorney general had argued, *Bailey* urged the court to break the peace that had developed between the North and South and to place the social order of the latter under supervision and control. Holmes would not be the judge to unsteady the calm. He had come, in fact, to see abolitionism as a dangerous force. It demanded absolute victory, rejected compromise, and saw violence as an acceptable means of achieving moral goals. "When you know that you know," he would later write of the anti-slavery persuasion, "persecution comes easy." Thus was Holmes, the former Union soldier, specifically unwilling to emancipate the Black debtor—to tell the South that its social order was wrong and that the federal government was empowered to reform it. Between debtors' rights and the terrain of racial inequality, he would choose the latter. He was joined in his opinion by Justice Horace Lurton, another Civil War veteran, who had served in the army of the Confederacy.[31]

Yet Holmes's opinion was issued in dissent. The majority invalidated the Alabama law under which Bailey had been convicted for evasion of his debt. The seven judges who joined the ruling spanned the court's spectrum on matters of race, from Justice John Marshall Harlan on the left to Chief Justice Edward Douglass White—also a Confederate veteran—on the right. The shared majority opinion, authored by Justice Charles Evans Hughes, described a victory not for African Americans—and certainly not of North over South—but for the basic principle of freedom in debt. In contrast to Justice Holmes, Hughes declared that the case had nothing to do with place or person. "Opportunities for coercion and oppression, in varying circumstances, exist in all parts of the Union, and the citizens of all the states are interested in the maintenance of the constitutional guarantees." The facts that mattered to the court were simply that the laborer had borrowed money; that the contract had required the loan to be repaid from the laborer's wage; and that the Alabama law had denied the laborer the right to exit the relationship without committing a criminal act. The measure's "natural and inevitable effect is to expose to conviction for crime those who simply fail or refuse to perform contracts for personal service in liquidation of a debt." It thus created a form of "compulsory service," which was prohibited by the Peonage Act and the Thirteenth Amendment. Tending the precedent established in earlier cases like *Hodges v. United States* (1906), the majority opinion reminded that the Constitution offered no special protection for African Americans and did not authorize any unique supervision over the social relations of the South. The Thirteenth Amendment "was a charter of universal civil freedom for all persons, of whatever race, color, or estate, under the flag" and not a declaration in favor of a particular group. Indeed, Bailey's Fourteenth Amendment claim—that false-pretense statutes denied Black laborers the equal protection of the law—was completely ignored by the Hughes opinion. Instead, in deploying the language of racial and regional neutrality, the court used only the Thirteenth Amendment and the Peonage Act to emancipate Bailey and strike down a legal pillar of modern white supremacy.[32]

What did the judgment mean? What did it say about Black life and white power in the United States in the early twentieth century? At the least, *Bailey* invalidated a coercive law; it demonstrated that the Thirteenth Amendment was not a dead letter on the statute book. "Colored citizens generally are very often heard to complain bitterly that the federal government does not enforce the war amendments," a writer for the *Washington Bee* reported. The *Bailey* decision, however, indicated that the Constitution had some vitality. It was "a distinct triumph for the cause of freedom" and, for African Americans in the North, an important step in making "more secure the lives and liberty of their brethren in the South." Du Bois's *The Crisis* noted that "the record of the Negro in the courts this month [was] unusually encouraging," and Booker T. Washington, whose role in organizing the appeal was unknown to the public, declared the ruling a "great victory" and sent copies of the majority opinion to his allies in the North. The verdict was praised in the white progressive press too, but there a different narrative took hold: one that emphasized emancipatory themes as well as reconciliationist ones. Bailey's case had been argued by several "humane Southerners," the *Outlook* observed, whom "the whole country should hold in honor." A similar ruling had recently been reached by the South Carolina Supreme Court, the magazine continued, with the enlightened members of that tribunal declaring that "Liberty is better than Prosperity." On the US Supreme Court, "there were several justices whose sympathies undoubtedly would have dictated another ruling, being both Democrats and Southerners," the *Independent* informed, and yet "a disinterested love for justice" had overwhelmed provincial concerns and struck "a hard blow at such contracts all over the country." These reports built on the language of the majority opinion itself, with its denial of Bailey's Fourteenth Amendment claim and its emphasis on the racial and regional impartiality of the decision. They transformed the court's finding that slavery still existed in the South into a performance of reunion, nesting a ruling against the state of Alabama into the terms of the national peace.[33]

In so doing, they also told a story about freedom and inequality in the states of the former Confederacy. There was not one white South in this tale, but two. Each offered its own approach to the question of how African Americans were to live in a region that had fought to keep them enslaved. In "A Liberal Southerner's View of the Negro Problem" (1903), Edwin Mins, a literature professor from North Carolina, sketched opposing portraits of an extremist white southerner and a moderate. The extremist was "sectional in his ideas, passionate, prejudiced." He clung with all his might to the way of life he had enjoyed—or imagined he would have enjoyed—before the Civil War. The moderate liberal, on the other hand, was "open to new truths" and was "imbued with the modern spirit." He did "not believe in social equality, nor in universal suffrage; but he stands for legal justice and limited suffrage, impartially enforced." He rejected the lessons of Du Bois—"thoroughly sincere but an extremist" in his own right—and was sympathetic to "Booker Washington, who is pre-eminently sensible, fair-minded, and practical" and who acknowledged that "the Negro should not make much ado about certain social and political privileges" that he was not permitted to enjoy. The distinction between the liberal and the extremist was clearest, Mins proposed, on the subjects of peonage and lynching. The extremist "is the apologist of lynching on utterly illogical grounds, [and] if peonage is discovered, he falls to abusing those who attack it." The moderate liberal, on the other hand, spoke "from the pulpit and platform [against] the crime of lynching," and he "condemned and put down peonage" wherever it was found and was committed to "exposing and punishing [the] white men engaged in it." He raged not against the ordinary rituals of Black submission—expressed in the crop lien, the reckoning, segregation, and disenfranchisement—but in Jim Crow's violent excesses. These were the values that defined his "modern spirit."[34]

It was as much the liberal white southerner's plea as the Black debtor's that the Supreme Court answered in *Bailey v. Alabama*. The case had been developed by Washington, the preferred race leader of the southern moderate. The expenses for Bailey's legal representation were cofinanced by a group of local white businessmen—perhaps motivated, like the white businessmen who had funded other Thirteenth Amendment challenges, like *Hodges*, by a desire to free Black laborers from illicit captivity so that they could become more available to them. Bailey's attorneys offered both a Thirteenth Amendment challenge to their client's conviction—premised on false-pretense law's indiscriminate coercion of labor—and a Fourteenth Amendment challenge—rooted in the fact, known to every "well-advised man in the State . . . that this act was passed in order to give the larger planters . . . absolute dominion over the negro laborer." The Supreme Court chose to engage only the former, discounting the notion that compulsion through finance in the South was related to racial control. Instead, in a show of national unity, justices of both parties and sections joined to free the debtor using the law of emancipation. To do so, in the context of the failed Thirteenth Amendment challenges in *Hodges*, *Plessy*, and other tests of Jim Crow, was to include Bailey's plight in the category of slavery and yet also to exclude from that category the abuses of segregation, disenfranchisement, the perpetual crop lien, and private violence. These indignities, the ruling suggested, did not involve the question of freedom itself. *Bailey* confirmed that the Thirteenth Amendment was not forgotten or abandoned. The Supreme Court was not unwilling to enforce it. Instead, to much of the emerging racial order of the era, it simply did not apply.[35]

Bailey v. Alabama affirmed the illegality of using debt to compel the specific performance of labor. It did so on behalf of an African American debtor, yet at a time when peonage could be cast as a vulgar excess of white supremacy, which was more safely and modestly preserved by other means. The majority's legal thinking was a bridge too far for Holmes, but three years later he would rejoin the fold in *U.S. v. Reynolds* (1914). The case tested Alabama's surety law, which allowed private parties to purchase the fines of convicted criminals in exchange for their mandatory labor. Citing *Bailey*, the court affirmed that debt and the criminal law could not conspire to create a condition of servitude. Holmes, in a short concurring assent, again insisted that there was "nothing in the Thirteenth Amendment or the Revised Statutes that prevents a state from making a breach of contract . . . a crime and punishing it as such." Yet, he wrote, the Black farmworker at the center of *Reynolds* had become unfree, owing less to the law itself than to his membership in a group of "impulsive people with little intelligence or foresight" who "may be expected to lay hold of anything that affords a relief from present pain, even though it will cause greater trouble by and by." His was a form of bondage rooted not in state action, the coercions of employers, or the nature of debt, but in the deficiencies of the enslaved. The logic, for Holmes, was that "the tyrant harms those only that he can reach." Thus, in *Reynolds*, with recourse to the classical discourse of the natural slave and the new language of race traits and tendencies, Holmes modified his conclusion in *Bailey*. The basic premise of that dissent, however—that all law coerced and all debts compelled—remained intact.[36]

Holmes's journey between the two cases suggested important themes in the modernist culture of the era and the ambivalence with which his fellow travelers—pragmatists, progressives, and realists—greeted the moral problems of domination and control. Ambivalence characterized the response to *Bailey* in other domains as well. Many southern states simply ignored the Supreme Court's ruling. Alabama reinscribed its discredited false-pretense statute in the Code of 1916, while Mississippi included an identical law in its Code of 1917. North Carolina's false-pretense statute had applied only to certain counties when it was first passed in 1905; the legislature not only left it on the books after the *Bailey* case but expanded its territorial reach. Whether these laws were used and enforced (or preserved simply as a defiant gesture) became harder to discern with the election of Woodrow Wilson to the presidency in 1912. The Department of Justice would pass into

Democratic hands for the next eight years, and investigations of southern labor abuses would fade as a federal priority. As the problem of Black peonage in the South retreated from public discourse, indebted labor in another part of the world claimed greater attention. Two years after *Bailey* and one before *Reynolds*, Secretary of the Interior Dean Worcester published *Slavery and Peonage in the Philippine Islands* (1913). The Philippines had been a foreign possession of the United States since the Spanish–American War, and Worcester was an advocate for the long-term retention of the islands. *Slavery and Peonage* yoked the imperial cause to the antislavery impulse by documenting Indigenous practices of debt bondage and casting American tutelage as a force for emancipation. Worcester did not cite the *Bailey* ruling, but his argument was tacitly bolstered by the court's recent determination that the Constitution stood opposed to indebted labor. Thus was *Bailey* positively implicated in two profoundly conservative projects: the legitimation of "moderate" Jim Crow at home and the projection of imperial power abroad.[37]

In the South, the direct impact of the case was limited. There, the Black scholar Carter Woodson wrote in 1918, "the planters [were] still a law unto themselves." In the "sequestered districts, where public opinion against peonage [was] too weak to support federal authorities in exterminating it," the "actual slavery" of indebtedness persisted. For many African Americans the freedoms threatened by credit were best pursued—and perhaps achieved—using the same tactic that had appealed since the 1870s: exodus. Beginning at the turn of the century and accelerating after 1910, African Americans decamped from the rural South en masse, leaving for the region's larger industrial cities and, most especially, for the North. For those who remained, the captivity of wage advances and the crop lien persisted. When H. C. Tinney toured the region in the 1930s during the Great Depression, interviewing freedpeople under the auspices of the Federal Writers' Project, he encountered one tale told time and again. A white man and a Black man had been traveling a road together and came upon two boxes. The Black man seized the larger box and opened it to find the instruments of agriculture: picks, shovels, and hoes.

> He then turned around to see how the white man had fared. "Well the White man, he got the little box and when he opened it there were pens and pencils and paper and a big account book where he can keep what the n——s owe him. And that's the way it's been ever since. The N—— just can't outfigure the White man, for he's sure to cut you down."[38]

4

THE WAGES OF CREDIT

In December 1900, a short column in *Harper's Bazaar* reported on a new government study of bankruptcy filings in the United States. The study was meant to cast light on the functioning of the Bankruptcy Act of 1898, a successor to the measure of 1867 that its architects hoped would transcend the administrative difficulties that had frustrated the older law. Per the government's tally, 21,938 petitions in insolvency had been filed in the federal courts the previous year. Nearly all had been voluntary on the part of the debtor, with only a small percentage representing actions initiated by creditors against the debtor's will. Surprisingly, the report noted, "the greatest number . . . stigmatized by debt were wage-earners." The reason that this alarmed was that the wage earner was not the figure traditionally expected to make use of bankruptcy. He was not a farmer relying on credit to survive between planting and harvest, nor was he a merchant purchasing goods on the margin and expected to resell them at a profit. Ambition was not supposed to draw the wage worker into the financial market, and he was not supposed to be vulnerable to sudden reversals. Forestalling such risks was the expected stability of the wage, with the cost of the worker's business being "nothing except the cost of his living." That the wage earner was, in fact, so often found insolvent suggested an asymmetry between earnings and needs. It indicated that the laborer's income was too often inadequate to "the cost of his living" and thus that the industrial order might be incompatible with freedom and dignity. The indebted wage earner was not a self-possessing subject, emancipated from the status dependencies of old. Instead, he appeared to be held "in slavery" by debt, the column concluded, beset by "the wretched, dogging sense that [his] labor belongs not to himself or yet to his employer, but in truth to the credit house to which his wages . . . are pledged."[1]

The wage earner's debts had been interpreted as a social and moral problem since the mid-nineteenth century. An important part of the republican accommodation to wage labor had been the belief that such work might represent a transitory stage on the way to independent proprietorship. While the hireling was not an autonomous subject in liberal thought, it was hoped that the "prudent, penniless beginner" who "labor[ed] for wages awhile" would eventually "save a surplus with which to buy tools or land . . . and then labor on his [own] account." But if many wage earners struggled merely to break even—with most ending each year with belongings in pawn or back rent owed to the landlord—then those tools and land would never arrive. The hireling's poverty would be permanent and class division would calcify into a fact of social life. Even as the ideology of contract provided resources for recasting wage earning as a type of autonomy, debt continued to signal deep problems in the unfolding industrial era. There was the question, for one, of how much debt the worker could be in before his laboring power was effectively owned by someone else. Common law had long accepted the assignment of wages as a legitimate expression of the hireling's will. Was there a point, however, at which too much of one's unearned income had been sold for the exchange to accord with the free-labor ideal? There were also questions about the ability of the wage to support a household and family. Domestic goods put up for pawn or seized by chattel mortgage lenders keyed into concerns about the collapse of the public and private spheres and the decay of the working-class home. Finally, reformers and charity workers drew connections between the desperation of the indebted wage earner and social unrest. As class division gave rise to strikes, sabotage, and violence in the late nineteenth and early twentieth centuries, many wondered whether the debts that pressed on workers and sapped their meager incomes were not a significant source of labor's discontent.[2]

Conservative critics who observed these trends looked for solutions in the patterns of working-class consumption. If wages and wants were out of balance, then harmony lay in persuading workers to discipline their desires. The antigambling and temperance movements of the era gave form to these ideas, seeking to steer workers away from profligacy, as did a renewed discourse of domestic economy. Indeed, in the estimation of the *Harper's Bazaar* columnist, "the remedy for the evil" of working-class debt rested entirely on the spending habits of working-class women. "Individual wives should shun the credit house as they would a pest house," the editorial advised, "and bodies of women organized to the end of bettering the conditions of labor should recognize the harm wrought by these credit institutions and proceed against them." In this telling, the wage earner's enemy was not capital but rather his own wife, with whom lay the power to spend within the family's means—or exceed them and upset the fragile industrial peace. On the left, labor activists and radicals placed the blame on industrialism itself, seeing in "the ruinous resort of the pawn" the inequity of the system of waged employment. Proposals for revising the system ranged from granting labor a greater share of earnings to cooperatizing firm ownership or abolishing private property altogether. Debt was not a primary social problem for such figures. Their target was the broader economic architecture that made the mass of working people dependent on the sale of labor. Yet borrowing and defaulting helped index the injustice of that order. It gave lie to the notion that wage labor accorded with the liberal subject's right to independence, self-ownership, and a private family. The worker's captivity to debt thus tested the moral progress of the age.[3]

In the early twentieth century, a new cohort of urban reformers reconsidered the problem of the wage earner's debts through a different lens. These figures were not of the working class, and they did not identify with radical or conservative persuasions. Instead, their faith lay in the concept of improvement. The financial actor on which they focused was not the employer, the employee, or the wage earner's wife. It was the high-interest, small-sum financier—the loan shark—who cut into the borrower's modest earnings and terrorized him with the threat of dispossession. The loan shark was not singularly responsible for labor unrest and domestic discord, but he was one reason the social order appeared to be perennially imperiled. Reforming the wage earner's access to credit and freeing him from this lender became, for these progressives, a way of addressing the social question without asking more of labor or capital.[4]

The promise of financial freedom had been challenged by the plight of the debtor's wife in the late nineteenth century and the Black debtor at the turn of the twentieth century. What did it mean for these persons to be saddled with debts that threatened their rights to free labor and an inviolate home? Could they be made independent from debt without also making them independent in those domains—the family, the workplace, and society at large—that the law was loath to upset? In the state of the indebted wage earner and the campaign to emancipate him from high-interest lenders in the 1910s and 1920s, this tension again took shape, for it was the poverty of the wage and the resulting dependency that drove the urban worker to the pawnshop, the installment house (where home goods were sold on credit), and the loan shark. Would the law challenge this foundational inequality by raising wages or provisioning social goods? Or would it accept that the industrial order destined the working class to debt? Initially, reformers sought to protect the poor borrower by enhancing the enforcement of usury laws and promoting the establishment of philanthropic banks, which would address working-class demands for credit outside the market. Over the 1910s, these strategies lost support, and some progressives drifted toward alternative remedies, like the expansion of the welfare state or the movement for the living wage. Yet many reformers remained fixed on the high-interest lender and gradually migrated to an unexpected solution. They identified usury laws as the reason that wage earners were forced to borrow from a lower, more predatory class of financier. They argued that by lifting such laws and allowing for a freer financial market, the wage earner would be able to borrow from a less predatory class of banker, who would merge the philanthropist's values with the dictates of business. Debt was defined in this reformist discourse not as a sign of industrialism's failings or as a source of social discord, but as a tool that, in the hands of reputable lenders, could help the worker stave off want without becoming reliant on charity or the state. In the deregulatory battle these progressives waged, the interests of lenders and workers were cast as positively conjoined.[5]

Turn-of-the-century newspapers brimmed with tales of wage earners consigned to desperation by high-interest, small-sum loans. There was the case of Harry H. Tower, a department store clerk from Chicago, who in 1902 assigned his salary as collateral for a $15 loan contracted by a friend. The friend defaulted on the note, and fees and interest began to mount for Tower. The birth of a child put additional strain on Tower's income, and soon he was borrowing from three different loan agents to make payments on the debt. When Tower contacted the Chicago Legal Aid Society in 1912, hoping to put a stop to the endless cycle of borrowing and repaying, his advisers found that the $15 pledge had cost him more than a thousand dollars over the intervening decade. There were also cases like the anonymous San Francisco railway employee, who lost his job and took out an emergency loan at 20 percent monthly interest to cover his basic living expenses. Several weeks later, the worker had secured another job, but the interest on the note made it difficult to pay down the principle. When the lender began to send intimidating letters to the borrower's new employer, demanding that a portion of his weekly wages be set aside to service the debt, the worker was promptly fired, and further counseled by management to "disappear from sight" so as to evade the usurer in the future. There were also the countless of women of Detroit, reported on by the *Free Press*, whose beds, irons, and ovens were seized by installment companies when their husbands took ill and failed to make their regular loan payments. "Had it not been for the kindness of Sergt. Hicks and the poor commission," a neighbor wrote of one household dispossessed of its cookstove by an installment lender, "mother and child would have perished."[6]

Such stories described the labor of survival in the modern industrial city. Most wage earners—those who worked in factories, offices, or retail spaces—balanced on the edge of solvency. The $70 that a railway clerk could expect to make in a month, for example, might be just enough to pay for rent, food, and clothing for a family of five in Boston, Philadelphia, or New York. A tradesman who earned a good wage but on a sporadic schedule could make ends meet if his wife took in laundry or cleaned houses on the side. Children could be put to work to supplement the household budget, and second and third jobs for the primary breadwinner were never out of the question. Working families were unlikely to have significant savings, but many could find a way to earn the $1,000 per year that charity studies indicated was required to maintain the majority of working households. Yet misfortune could always strike on either side of the domestic economy equation. An income could unexpectedly cease, owing to workplace closure, termination, an injury, or a labor strike. New expenses could appear as well. The most common were medical bills to treat injuries or illnesses, but moving costs, burial expenses, and the needs of family members and friends also ranked as frequent sources of financial exigency. Married women were also vulnerable to spousal desertion. When a husband left town, even for a short time, two-income households were forced to subsist on one, and one-income households became destitute. One woman, whose partner fled from New York to Baltimore, was hesitant about pursuing a reconciliation. She did not trust her husband to not abscond again, even if he could be persuaded to return home. She also, however, was "very much discouraged trying to support herself and the three children [while] working at Macy's earning $7. a week," and eventually elected to reunite with her spouse (who deserted her again the following year).[7]

To weather such disruptions, working people looked to several sources of financial assistance. The most immediate were short-term loans from friends and family. Mutual aid societies, into which members paid regular dues in order to have support when times were hard, were another option. Churches, synagogues, and private charities distributed relief funds as well. Government assistance largely took the form of service provision, such as hospitals and clinics for the ill, rather than direct cash aid. The gaps in this institutional patchwork that could not be addressed through savings were papered over with debt. Book credits with grocers and rent delays from landlords could help households survive small disruptions to income. Pawnshops offered one of the oldest forms of financing for the urban working class. Such establishments allowed borrowers to pledge a piece of personal property as collateral in exchange for cash. "If the borrower failed to repay the loan after a certain period of time, the lender could sell the item," but the dispossession stopped there, with the lender having no claim to the debtor's wages or other belongings. At the installment house—the institution decried by the *Harper's* column—the wage earner could buy necessary household goods on a payment plan, with the goods themselves serving as security. Finally, there were salary and chattel mortgage lenders, who loaned cash in larger amounts than pawnbrokers on the assignment of unearned wages or a mortgage on household furnishings. These figures—the "loan sharks" of popular parlance—operated at the margins of the law, but they did not always do so in secret. While some financiers acted through local intermediaries, such as barbers and saloonkeepers, others, like Buell & Company, Wells & Company, and the Household Finance Corporation, were incorporated businesses that advertised in newspapers and maintained offices in major city centers.[8]

Social surveys reported on the frequency with which urban wage earners turned to pawnshops and lending firms in the early twentieth century. One study, conducted by the New York State Conference of Charities and Correction, found that nearly a third of families earning less than $700 annually turned to the loan sharks at some point during the year to weather an unexpected expense. Robert Coit Chapin, in *The Standard of Living among Workingmen's Families* (1909), put the number at closer to half. In Homestead, Pennsylvania, one report found that nearly a sixth of working-class purchases were made on credit of one form or another, while a single industrial lender in Boston was found to have made an average of 1,600 small loans per year at the median amount of $90. Those in need of money might find a lender through a classified listing in a newspaper. "I HAVE $75,000 that I desire to loan out in sums of from $10 to $500 on household goods, pianos, etc.," one notice in the *Pittsburgh Dispatch* read. The prospective borrower would journey to the published address, where he would often by received a female cashier (many lenders believing a female cashier "reduced the risk of physical violence from angered clients"). The borrower would submit an application that included a range of personal information, including the names of employers, family members, and friends. He would then sign a promissory note, secured either by a mortgage on household property or an assignment of wages, and "a form giving a representative of the loaning company a power of attorney by which to confess judgment" in case the sum was not repaid. Interest rates varied, but it was not an unusual for a borrower to pay $1 per month on a $10 loan—an amount that annualized to 120 percent. Until the debt was retired, the borrower would be subject

Articles.	Washington.			Boston.			Chicago.		
	Number.	Total value.	Average value.	Number.	Amount loaned.	Average loan.	Number.	Amount loaned.	Average loan.
Gold watches	809	$10,761.25	$13.30	1,430	$12,325.34	$8.62	5,160	$40,242.35	$7.80
Silver watches	542	1,179.75	2.18	2,546	2,698.18	1.06	2,980	5,270.55	1.77
Rings	1,294	12,523.50	9.69	2,592	10,525.44	4.06	4,822	34,141.10	7.08
Jewelry	562	6,070.10	10.80	597	3,324.64	5.57	2,276	25,841.34	11.35
Clothing	555	1,051.25	1.90	6,938	7,263.00	1.05	6,543	11,344.45	1.73
Musical instruments ...	38	176.25	4.64	247	401.22	1.62	356	768.46	2.16
Firearms................	53	221.50	4.18	141	234.22	1.66	596	1,225.50	2.06
Miscellaneous	228	322.10	1.41	1,622	1,848.00	1.14	1,724	5,415.55	3.14
Total..............	4,081	32,305.70	7.92	16,113	38,620.04	2.40	24,457	124,249.30	5.08

FIGURE 4.1. "Number of Articles, Amount Loaned, and Average Loan on Articles Pledged in Several Cities of the United States during One Month," from W. R. Patterson, "Pawnbroking in Europe and the United States," in US Department of Labor, *Bulletin* 4 (March 1899): 274.

to surveillance ("tracers" were routinely hired by lenders to locate clients who moved around) and the harassment of "bawling out," wherein the collection agent "would confront the debtor while he was in the presence of others, and level abuse at him."[9]

Progressive observers of high-interest lending worried about the practice's implications for public and private life. They feared that the indebted worker was a poor employee. Despondency would wear him down until he would "lost all efficiency" and became "a danger to the business." Desperate for more money to pay the extortionary interest charges, he would likely be tempted by crime and might embezzle from the firm or steal from neighbors. He could also become a convert to radicalism, demanding deep changes to the system that enriched capital at the expense of labor. "The social unrest of the non-propertied classes" could in many instances be traced directly to insolvency, one charity leader suggested. It would "steady the electorate" to channel such people away from the usurious loan companies and toward more wholesome means of financial aid. Compounding the problem of the debt itself was the policy of many large employers to terminate employees whose wages had been assigned or were under garnishment. This was a rule meant to discourage borrowing while saving the employer the administrative labor of dividing each paycheck in two. It had the effect, however, of giving the lender an additional weapon with which to menace the debtor. When enforced, these firings prevented the worker from marketing his labor, robbing him of self-ownership and furthering his drift into crime and desperation.[10]

The private damage wrought by the loans could be even more troubling. "Men of family are really the pillars of usury," it was held, for those with dependent children most felt the bite of necessity and thus would borrow on the most iniquitous terms. As the interest charges grew, the loan would press on those foundational family relationships. "We believe that much marital infelicity, and not a few disrupted homes, are directly traceable to the discouragement caused by the endless chain of debt," R. W. Sharp affirmed in *The Chattel Mortgage Loan Business* (1910). Husbands would turn to drink, and wives would seek affection elsewhere. "Love and tender care cannot survive in such a home," reformers believed. The suffering that husband and wife endured was not reserved for adults. "Almost before he can walk," one journalist found, "the child of the unfortunate or the profligate begins to pay tribute to the shark. His body is weakened, his home surroundings are ruined by the brooding air of apprehension." At the earliest age, he would be forced to leave school and earn a wage, "giv[ing] up his own future to pay for the [father's] usurious past." For the head of household who witnessed these tragedies, despair beckoned. "A case of suicide is reported from St. Louis," one newspaper disclosed, "as John F. Fahey, a bridegroom of six months, killed himself on account of debts contracted before his marriage and of which his bride knew nothing." Another debtor, working for a Midwestern railroad company, was said to have declared as he sat in a hospital bed, "They cannot collect now!"—having taken poison to escape the loan sharks who each month claimed "every penny of his salary." The journalist James Collins wrote in *McClure's*: "Driven to desperation in the same way twenty-two borrowers from one New York loan company committed suicide in three years, according to a statement by the manager." In the wake of these deaths were orphaned children and impoverished widows. Plainly, reformers affirmed, "the loan shark is a home breaker."[11]

Industrialization had given rise to a class of permanent wage earners. Labor was the chief property such men and women possessed; none could expect to rise to the rank of owning their own farm or factory. In lieu of independence, they received the stability of the wage, yet earnings were insufficient to survive the myriad challenges of modern life: injury, sickness, desertion, and unemployment. The recourse to indebtedness both signified these dilemmas and amplified them, adding to the worker's sense that he was not the owner of his labor and the master of his home. Wrote one borrower, "I cannot understand what has become of my wages. I know I am so seriously involved that even if I secure a new position I can never hope to pay the different companies all they demand and at the same time support my family. I have had no money and my wife had barely enough to pay our living expenses." Such statements indexed a crisis of public order and private home life that crystallized as a moral problem for progressive reformers in the early twentieth century.[12]

The organization that became most invested in the struggle against high-interest lending was the Russell Sage Foundation. Founded in New York City in 1907 by Margaret Olivia Sage, the widow of the Gilded Age rail-

road financier Russell Sage, the foundation's earliest concerns lay in the
field of working-class housing. It was a charter contributor to the model
community movement, underwriting construction of the Forest Hills Gardens neighborhood for wage-earning families in suburban Queens in 1909.
Among Sage's most trusted philanthropic advisers were W. Frank Persons,
an officer with the New York Charity Organization Society, and Robert W.
de Forest, the president of the National Conference of Charities and Correction. In 1893, de Forest had helped organize a remedial lending agency in
Manhattan intended to aid working families in weathering the depression
of the 1890s. Persons, in his role with the Charity Organization Society,
received thousands of letters each year from indigent individuals who often
cited extortionary debts as their most pressing economic concerns. The two
advisers persuaded Sage to place a small portion of the foundation's endow-
ment in de Forest's remedial bank in 1907. By 1909 they had decided that
the problem of working-class credit merited a deeper commitment on the
part of the organization. That year, the foundation's board of trustees voted
to fund a fellowship program at Columbia University that would support
two dissertations on small-sum finance: one on wage assignments, by Clarence Wassam, and another on chattel loans, by Arthur Ham. The following
year, Persons pressed Sage and the trustees to expand the foundation's in-
volvement in the loansharking issue, and the leadership agreed, hiring the
twenty-six-year-old Ham to direct its Division of Remedial Loans in 1910.[13]

Property exemptions and limitations on garnishment were not considered meaningful solutions to the problem. Wage earners might have little
property to shield and, in their desperation for credit, they might waive
whatever protections they enjoyed. The release of bankruptcy was also not
thought to be genuinely emancipatory, as poverty would inevitably return
the worker to debt. Instead, the first tool that Ham and his colleagues took
up to discipline the small-sum-credit business was usury law, the regulations which in most states fixed the maximum allowable interest rate at between 6 and 10 percent per year. Such measures traced a lineage back to
the Founding era and, in Europe, far earlier. In the mid-nineteenth century,
interest restrictions had been repealed in England (1854), Belgium (1865),
and Germany (1867), but they had been retained—and, in some instances,
strengthened—in the United States by civic leaders who saw them as necessary guards against the market's exploitative urgings. Their "true spirit," declared one observer in 1874, was to prohibit anyone from "taking an unjust
advantage of the necessities of the borrower." Let them be rescinded, advocates warned, and both mechanic and merchant would find himself "more
and more fleeced by Shylock." But the implementation of usury limits had
always been a challenge. They relied in large part on the debtor's choice to

initiate litigation, which in turn depended on his awareness of the law. In the South and West, where capital was scarcer, legislatures had permitted higher interest charges than in the East, in order to draw investment to the periphery and cultivate the land. Yet the moral suspicion of interest—often articulated through the supposed Jewishness of moneylending—endured and was shared by the reformers in Ham's circle, who decried the "crucifying" interest rates of the "loan brethren" compared to whom "Shylock [was] a monument to charity." Like their Gilded Age forebearers, the progressives invoked the law of usury, pressuring city police and district attorneys to enforce the interest rate restrictions already on the books and encouraging legislators to criminalize the transgressions as well.[14]

In New York, for example, Ham researched the interest rates demanded by the city's licensed lenders and convinced the authorities to revoke the licenses of four credit houses and press charges against another two. He partnered with the Legal Aid Society to provide inexpensive counsel to borrowers who wanted to contest exploitative financial contracts, and he persuaded the district attorney to appoint a special prosecutor expressly devoted to usury prosecution. In 1913, the salary lender Daniel Tolman, who maintained a sprawling personal finance empire with storefronts and offices in sixty-three cities, was convicted of usury in New York and sentenced to six months in prison and the forfeiture of $500,000 in uncollected debts. The following year, at Ham's suggestion, the city hired Walter Hilborn, an attorney experienced in private usury litigation, to head a new anti-loansharking operation, and wage assignments against municipal employees soon fell by a third. Similar efforts were undertaken in other cities and states. In Pittsburgh, city officials collaborated with the chamber of commerce and the Legal Aid Committee of Allegheny County to defend eighty-one debtors saddled with usurious loans. In Ohio, a "so-called insurance company" was found endorsing small notes for wage earners at "exorbitant prices" and was forced to forgive more than $100,000 owed by 1,500 borrowers. In Kansas, the courts compelled one lender to pay damages of $6,000 to a debtor "to compensate him for the loss of his position and the annoyance and embarrassment caused by the shark's Persecution in his efforts to extort his illegal profits." Progressives welcomed these developments as meaningful achievements in the fight to aid poor borrowers, both as positive correction for the personal finance industry and a public reminder that interest rates were the legitimate purview of the law.[15]

Ham and his colleagues believed that the enforcement of usury laws was a necessary part of the struggle against the loan shark. The prosecution of extortionary lenders certainly rooted out some of the worst abuses in the popular financial system. Such actions promised, however, only a partial solution. Usury laws could often be evaded on technicalities—by classing certain charges as administrative fees rather than interest, for example. They also did nothing to address the demand for small-sum credit among the working classes. So long as needs for emergency funding existed, lenders would inevitably arise to profit from them, legally or otherwise. Indeed, reformers acknowledged that lenders would likely offset the risk of prosecution by simply extracting higher interest payments from their customers. Progressives were unwilling to move in the direction recommended by many liberal political economists—repealing interest rate restrictions altogether and trusting the competitive market to lower rates and discipline the business on its own. Unchecked by law, Ham and his allies believed, lenders would follow the lure of profit to whatever objectionable ends it might lead. Of the Morris Plan banks—a chain of small-sum-lending institutions touted as a viable alternative to the loan shark—they were dismissive, doubting that "a cold-blooded business proposition," led by men with "no motive in the work except that of personal profit," could resolve the moral problems of wage-earner debt. Instead, in the early years of the anti-usury campaign, the Russell Sage Foundation elected to invest its energies in promoting philanthropic banks that would be legally barred from pursuing profit, partially or entirely. Like Odysseus's deafened crew in the land of the Sirens, lenders who nested themselves in the non- and limited-profit corporate form would be trusted by reformers to ignore the market's urging to exploit.[16]

A model of this type of institution was found in the Provident Loan Society of New York, a "remedial" bank established in Manhattan in 1893. The bank was capitalized by investments from wealthy individuals, and it operated under a special legislative charter requiring it to lend to indigent borrowers in any amount, even unprofitably small sums. Interest rates were permitted to rise higher than New York's legal limit of 12 percent per year, but the dividends that could be distributed to investors were capped at 6 percent. If the society found that it was earning more than it could legally disburse to investors, then it was obliged to lower its interest rates until the balance was restored. The bank could not discriminate among borrowers based on their likely ability to repay, and it was bound by law to lend only for such necessities as food, rent, or medical expenses. Thanks to "the society's semi-philanthropic capital fund, its unpaid directorate, its very large volume of business, and its efficient management," the Provident Loan Society was able to charge customers as little as 1 percent interest per month on loans that typically ranged from $10 and $50. Barred from maximizing self-interest by its semi-philanthropic charter, the society pursued what reformers understood to be the higher moral imperative of delivering dignified service at a reasonable fee. During the first decade of the twentieth century, this model of social provision was adopted by civic leaders in fifteen other cities, and in 1909, the heads of those organizations met in Buffalo, New York, to form the National Federation of Remedial Loan Associations (NFRLA), with the goal of standardizing industry practices and attracting new investors to the field.[17]

Between 1910 and 1915, Ham made it the mission of the Russell Sage Foundation to encourage the growth of the philanthropic lending sector. He served as the secretary of the NFRLA while holding his position with Russell Sage, a dual appointment that illustrated the reform movement's philanthropic orientation. In progressive magazines and newspapers, Ham celebrated the ability of the remedial lenders to occupy an important middle ground between charity, with its objectionable air of paternalism, and the open financial market, with its threat to the family and the laboring self. "Agencies of this character, by limiting their dividends," he explained, were able to loan money at reasonable rates of interest and "satisfy the needs of small borrowers." Other reformers agreed, maintaining that "competition based on philanthropic interest" was one of "the chief means by which the evils of loaning money . . . may be decreased if not entirely eliminated." It was a blessing, they declared, that necessitous wage earners were no longer forced to do business with "agencies of the purely commercial type." Over the first five years of Ham and the philanthropists' partnership, twenty-one additional lending societies were founded in cities across the nation, and the NFRLA provided each with vital access to its storehouse of operational information. The spread of these institutions—all of which were insulated from the lure of "mere commercial profit" by the legal requirements of their charters—constituted for Ham "the most important phase" of the foundation's early work.[18]

Ham also directed foundation resources toward the creation of credit unions, a model of cooperative enterprise imported to the United States in the first decade of the twentieth century. The first credit unions had been organized by socialist reformers in Germany in the 1840s, and then had spread to Italy, in the form of the Luzzatti banks, in the 1870s and 1880s and to French Canada in the 1890s. Like cooperative farms and factories, these institutions were owned and operated by a working-class membership that disposed of their product—credit—to themselves and "divided up among themselves what the net earnings may be." Credit unions charged modest interest rates that covered their operating costs and served to absolve their lending "from the taint of paternalism" and to "inculcate the habits of thrift" in the borrowers. The credit union was thus conceived as an engine of moral economy, connecting wage earners with emergency finance while promoting independence and strengthening the bonds of mutuality. In 1909, the progressive Boston businessman Edward A. Filene toured the credit unions in Italy and Quebec and soon after persuaded the Massachusetts legislature to pass an enabling law to permit the creation of the nation's first such establishment in his home state. The institution opened the following year in Boston under the leadership of Felix Vorenberg, Henry Dennison, Filene, and "several other public-spirited citizens." In a frequently repeated phrase, it was "an association of men, not of capital"—a model to which Ham devoted himself to promoting in New York and elsewhere in the early 1910s.[19]

The credit cooperative and the philanthropic bank reflected an essential progressive ambivalence toward modern economic society. Reformers like Ham did not advocate for ending the wage system that consigned workers to precarity. They did not interpret small-sum debts as evidence of the failures of the industrial age—the wage's inability to sustain a family and furnish labor with a just reward. Instead, they believed that the moral problems of indebtedness were principally financial and that by targeting the loan sharks themselves, many of the perils of working-class economic life could be eased. In seeking the enforcement of usury laws, they summoned the state to police the boundary between legal commerce and exploitation. As the movement matured, progressives increasingly sought to remove indebtedness from the market environment altogether, disconnecting lending from the pursuit of private gain. As one reformer explained, "Rope has its commercial value, and it is entirely within the province of business and ethics to manufacture and sell it at a profit. But if a man is drowning, it becomes the duty of the man who has a rope to throw it out." The desire to turn need into advantage was the source of the poor borrower's suffering. The usury prohibition had aimed to forbid lenders from succumbing to temptation. If it could not, then the reformers preferred to use the law in a different way—to create institutions that addressed financial need outside the traditional market. In the early years of the Russell Sage Foundation's campaign against loansharking, the philanthropic bank and cooperative credit association assumed a strategic pride of place because, like the usury law of old, they promised to shield both lender and borrower from the market's urging to exploit.[20]

In 1912, the journalist Irwin Ellis declared that "the most successful weapons developed against the loan sharks are the semi-philanthropic loan associations." Along with the enhanced enforcement of existing usury laws, the remedial banks appeared poised to root out the traffic in high-interest finance. Four years later, such confidence was much rarer. After an initial burst of additions, growth of the NFRLA had stalled, owing, Ham surmised, to "the lack of wealthy people in most communities willing to invest in the loan society on the basis of a definitely limited dividend." Credit unions were faring little better, struggling to establish themselves outside the Northeast and lacking a bureaucratic infrastructure to coordinate their national expansion. The campaign to prosecute loan sharks on criminal charges had run aground as well. Instead of arresting the industry's chief proprietors, the police often settled for cashiers and clerks. "The big fellows escape," Ham observed, "but the little ones, who have to work for a living, suffer the consequences." Letters from impoverished borrowers addressed to the Russell Sage Foundation indicated that a large illegal trade in high-interest money was still thriving in many industrial cities, with the demand absorbed into philanthropic alternatives being more than replaced by raw growth in the population of precarious wage earners. By the mid-1910s, the anti-loansharking campaign thus found itself at a crossroads, returned by operational setbacks to the original problem of small-sum-lending reform.[21]

Some progressives reconsidered the very framing of working-class indebtedness as a financial issue in the main. The ascendant movement for the living minimum wage, for example, argued that the answer to "the social question"—including its expression in debt—was simply higher pay. "What is the use of wages, and therefore what is the use of working, unless thereby one gets enough to live?" asked Samuel Crowther, one of the living-wage movement's acolytes. Many economists, religious authorities, middle-class reformers, and labor leaders shared this concern and converged at the belief that workers were entitled to a sustainable income. Justice in compensation stemmed not from the market rate for labor or from the value added by work but from the wage earner's right to be free from want. Gendered notions of household headship were woven into this faith, as male workers dismissed low salaries as "girls' wages" and called for an income sufficient to keep their dependents from working. Race and nationality were marshaled to define just earnings as well, with the American standard of living (and the wage required to enjoy it) contrasted with the needs of immigrant laborers, who would work for less because their "wants [were] simple." Working-class and middle-class advocates offered competing definitions of what labor needed and deserved, but points of transitory consensus could be achieved, and over the 1910s and early 1920s many states enacted minimum-wage laws for both working women and men. The weakening of organized labor after World War I enervated a chief means for securing wage raises privately, through collective action and bargaining. Adverse court decisions—none more significant than *Adkins v. Children's Hospital* (1923)—hampered progress as well. Yet the struggle for higher wages did offer disillusioned veterans of the anti-usury crusade an opportunity to punish the loan shark by addressing, through earnings rather than credit, the working-class needs that nourished financial demand.[22]

Another alternative approach also existed in the nascent welfare state. What debt allowed workers to purchase on installment, and what minimum wage laws allowed them to purchase with their income, the welfare state proposed to take out of the market partially or entirely and make available as an entitlement of citizenship. Many workers borrowed money to pay for necessities during periods of unemployment. Organizations like the American Association for Labor Legislation (AALL) advocated in the 1910s and 1920s for the creation of state unemployment reserve funds, into which labor and capital would both pay so that out-of-work individuals could receive support as they searched for new jobs. Workplace injuries were another common source of indebtedness, as men and women borrowed to pay for medical treatment and to supplement lost wages as they recovered. Many progressives sought to socialize those risks through public injury–compensation funds and laws requiring employers to furnish workers with private injury insurance. In both scenarios, a safety net would hang between the wage earner and the disabling accident. Relatedly, the AALL and other reformist organizations also battled against employers, the commercial insurance industry, and doctor and hospital groups over proposals to create a system of public health insurance. With illness and medical expenses ranking among the primary reasons why the working classes borrowed money, such proposals promised not only to enshrine the right to health in American public policy but also to save the American worker from the hazards of debt and default. Borrowing was a function of need, and need could be addressed in myriad ways. For those who believed that the puzzle of small-sum-lending reform was truly unsolvable—that credit for the working poor could never be made safe for the borrower and sustainable for the lender—the living-wage movement and the welfare state suggested a more promising option for emancipating the wage earner from high-interest finance.[23]

The Russell Sage Foundation was active in many of these battles and invested its resources in a range of progressive causes. Yet it also continued to devote itself to the project of small-sum-lending reform itself. After the initial failings of the campaign, those figures who did not gravitate toward other social movements began to reevaluate their analysis of markets and profit. In 1915, Ham reported an argument at the annual meeting of the NFRLA between those who remained committed to the non- and limited-profit model and those who believed that such "straight-laced" moralism was hampering "the growth and influence of the Federation." An insurgent view was offered by F. E. Stroup of Grand Rapids, Michigan, who invited the convention to imagine two lending agencies, one semi-philanthropic and one purely commercial. They each managed to "charge exactly the same rate to the borrower, loan money only for legitimate purposes, protect the borrower from the usurious money lenders, and give all such good service that they are well regarded by all social service organizations in their respective cities," Stroup proposed. "Will you tell me why the companies that pay 4 and 6 percent dividends are regarded as philanthropists and the other is regarded with suspicion?" The NFRLA was composed of firms that defined themselves by their relationship to profit. These agencies were capable of balancing personal finance with public good, the association believed, precisely because they were shielded from market forces by the dividend-limiting requirements of their charters. "It is, of course, desirable . . . to reduce the rates [charged] to the borrower," Stroup countered, "but it occurs to me that [it is] the real social service performed by the company [and] its attitude toward [the borrower] that should determine membership in the federation, and when we recognize this fact it will then be easier to interest capital."[24]

This argument challenged the moral categorization that had organized reformers' approach to working-class debt. Ham and his allies had privileged the philanthropic and cooperative forms because they believed that the tendency of market lenders was to charge as much and provide as little to the borrowing public as it would bear. They accepted the classical political economists' claim that interest rates, like water, eventually found their natural level, but they worried that the level they reached might be high enough to "wreck happy homes" and "turn honest men into embezzlers." Their solution had been to take the small loan as far out of the market as possible, if not through the usury prohibition then through limited-dividend corporations, which were legally barred from pursuing their full self-interest. Stroup, on the other hand, offered a vision of the market in which profit-seeking lenders retained the autonomy to set prices, deliver dignified service, and look after the well-being of the borrower, even when it ran contrary to their economic aims. He suggested that the relevant moral line ran not between nonprofit and for-profit lenders but between ethical and predatory ones. This was not a faith in the market's power to produce fair and socially desirable outcomes, as later generations of market enthusiasts would propose. Instead, it was a claim that ethical lenders could temper market forces without the restraint of the law.[25]

Stroup's vision aligned with broader changes in the popular perception of finance underway in the 1910s. The ascendant field of consumer economics, for example, preached a new gospel of credit, insisting that the deflationary cycles that had tormented borrowers in the past had been replaced by a modern economy of steady growth. These figures urged Americans to set aside their moral aversion to indebtedness and to recognize finance as a vital instrument of sound, efficient spending. The creation of the Federal Reserve in 1913 appeared to resolve the longstanding issue of currency control, assuring that the money supply—and thus the value of debts—would be managed by experts with an eye toward stability and justice. The mass financing of the nation's military mobilization during World War I provided perhaps the strongest grounds for reappraisal. State actors promoted small-denomination war bonds—loans made by ordinary people to the federal government—as expressions of patriotism and public-spiritedness. As one scholar observes, the publicity materials dispersed by state agencies "identified the practice of investment with the process of democracy, urged Americans to recognize investment as a distinguishing feature of the nation's culture, and equated the figure of the investor with that of the citizen." Lending was constructed in this discourse as an act that braided selfish and selfless aims. It was a way of doing service to others while also making money for oneself. When the United States emerged after the war as a net creditor to a shattered Europe, popular narratives similarly naturalized the new relationship, assuring that there was no inherent tension between financial profit and traditional ethics. There was not the "slightest analogy" between Uncle Sam and that "hard-fisted miserly rascal, best typified by the character of Shylock." The debt relation did not require the lender to behave in any certain way. It did not mandate acquisitiveness, abuse, or domination. Its edges could be softened by the sensibilities of the parties it drew together. The American creditor was sympathetic and caring, easily satisfied by fair terms and a reasonable repayment effort. Shylock, in contrast, "was a Jew."[26]

Narratives such as these joined with the doubts sowed at the NFRLA meeting in 1915 to point toward a new strategy in the struggle to emancipate wage earners from high-interest debts. Reformers such as Ham continued to encourage the growth of philanthropic banks and the cooperative movement. They urged law enforcement to persist in policing the traffic in usurious loans. Yet they also gradually embraced the view that certain commercial lenders, thoroughly immersed in the market, could be trusted to deliver the fair credit that the working classes required. The belief was that the moral tragedies of small-sum lending were not natural to the trade but a result of the character of the lenders in question. Instead of protecting poor borrowers from the market, reformers needed to build a bridge between necessitous wage earners and the purveyors of "reputable capital." The problem, Ham reasoned, was how to extend aid to struggling families while avoiding demoralization: "There is in most people a wholesome dread of becoming dependent [and] a pride in being able to support one's self and family." Debt furnished by the reputable lender would sustain that pride, providing a pathway for bringing morals, markets, and the industrial order together. The Russell Sage Foundation would set itself increasingly on loosening interest rate regulations and assuring commercial lenders of greater, legal profits. Reformers would no longer seek to guard borrowers from the exploitative market. Instead, they sought to make it possible for reputable capitalists to take root in the field of personal finance and thrive.[27]

"In the open market," William Jevons wrote in *The Theory of Political Economy* (1871), "there cannot be two prices for the same kind of article." In the early twentieth century, the law of indifference continued to reign as the first principle of competition, predicting that profit-maximizing actors in a market environment would inevitably converge at identical prices for identical goods. In 1916, the anti-loansharking movement entered into an alliance with the American Association of Small Loan Brokers that was premised on an opposing view. The association, soon to be renamed the American Industrial Lenders Association (AILA), was a professional organization of three hundred small-sum lenders spread out across the nation, then operating at the margins of profitability and the law. Working with the Russell Sage Foundation, the lenders' trade association agreed to collaborate on a state-level Uniform Small Loan Law (USLL) that would raise the permissible interest rate from the standard ½ to 1 percent per month to 3½ percent per month—the amount that the AILA claimed was necessary for its membership to realize an adequate profit. Those who lent under the provisions of the USLL would not be required to limit their dividends. They would not be compelled to loan in the smallest amounts, to refuse service to improvident borrowers, to forgive debts once they became damaging to the home, or to lower interest rates if they found they could subsist on more modest returns. Instead, after submitting to a short investigation by a licensing board and posting a public bond, small-sum lenders would be largely free to meet their customers as equals in the competitive market and sell them money for up to 42 percent interest per year.[28]

The collaboration between the Russell Sage Foundation and the AILA marked a break with the reform movement's philanthropic roots. The basis of the accord, Ham explained to his colleagues, was the foundation's new belief that the small-sum lender was "a necessary element" in working-class life and that "the importance of attracting reputable capital in the business [required] the allowance of somewhat higher charges than are required by the remedial loan societies whose return upon capital is definitely limited."

Abandoning the prohibitive regime of strict usury laws and the philanthropic regime of limited dividends was the only way to draw reputable capital—also called "legitimate capital," "honest capital," and "responsible capital"—into the personal finance market. The higher class of lender would not enter a field where the assumption of risk was not duly rewarded, and it was only by pairing necessitous borrowers with "men of character" that the moral tone of the trade could be improved. Reputable capital would treat the wage earner with the same dignity as the salaried professional. It would put the good of the family and the interests of the community above a singular concern for the bottom line. It would carry personal finance "out into the open" and cleanse the industry of the infamy "which for a great many years has surrounded it." Reputable capital, reformers insisted, would respond to the promise of profit while also deferring to the highest "standards of ethics and practice." It would reconcile morals and markets.[29]

In part, this vision rested on the presentation of the licensed lenders as an essentially different type of market actor than the loan sharks they would replace. Distinctions specific and internal to each type were important because of the sameness that characterized the legal environments in which both would work. Neither group would be substantially restrained by law—the latter because they had long ignored it, and the former because of the permissive provisions of USLL. Neither would temper themselves via the non- or limited-profit corporate form. Instead, different values were said to animate the licensed lenders, guiding them toward a more agreeable peace with their working-class clientele. Reformers emphasized the familial character of the new lenders. They were not the "heartless despoilers" of old who would allow "husbands [to] secure loans unknown to the wife." Indeed, "married people go to the loan offices to borrow money" together, the advocates of the industry insisted, suggesting that even when spousal consent was not legally required, it would be encouraged. The reputable capitalists envisioned themselves as aiding the family like "a friend or relative who [could] tide [them] over [their] difficulty." Compassion underwrote their credit and assured that it would not become the basis of abuse. The word that captured this ethic, lenders and reformers declared, was *service*. It was the cornerstone of the industry and its primary commodity. In "that one word, *service*," one banker wrote, "anyone's success in business is measured." The reputable capitalists did not concern themselves exclusively with "the question of dollars and cents." Instead, their "first and uppermost thought [was] service to the customer." Their "sympathy, interest, and sincerity" lay in "providing a service" which was "vital to the life of [their] community." The true object of their trade was not "the making of money." Rather, it was to serve "one to another, and always above the self."[30]

Ethnic difference was also an important part of this narrative. It was the Jewish moneylender, industry advocates suggested, whose lust for gain had consigned so many wage earners to desperation and dependency. The reputable capitalists, on the other hand, were "in general, a fine type of business man, drawn usually from the older American stocks." They knew little of the grasping practices common among "the gyp automobile lenders and the real Shylock pawnbrokers," who "were predominantly of Jewish stock." Natural selection had once left only the most "exacting" and "thick-skinned" individuals standing in the field of personal finance, industry allies explained—men willing to suffer the risk of arrest and certain they could ex-tract enough from borrowers to make illicit lending profitable.[31] The reform-ers, however, working "with the art of the chemist almost," had discarded "the elements that were unworthy" from the small-sum-credit market and preserved only those who would adhere to a "higher standard of principles." The rising ranks of "faithful and friendly servants" in the banking industry embraced "the principles of Americanism in the conduct of business" and were "satisfied with fair profit."[32] As Ham announced at a meeting of lend-ers in 1921, while reputable capitalists might not "yet deserve a place in the roll of fame beside the Christian martyrs," they were charting an ethical course that to the older "lending fraternity generally was anathema." The days when "persons endowed with a shrewd business sense for profitable opportunities [subjected] the public to oppressive and illegal interest exac-tions" were ending, reformers explained. Borrowers would soon discover the dignities of doing business with the "men of standing in their own com-munities." They would learn that finance could be compassionate and family affirming when it was transacted with "capital of a less greedy nature."[33]

The discourse of reputable capital served to contain some of the moral anxieties that had long stalked working-class indebtedness. It taught that violence, intimidation, and high-interest extortion were natural not to small-sum credit but only to the class of lender who traditionally populated the market. "New men with new traditions and new ideals have come into the loan business," one progressive assured. A break had been effected be-tween the industry's illicit past and its moral present. Alongside—and even superseding—this claim was the belief that debt could enhance the wage earner's experience of the modern, liberal era. It was not only "a neces-sary element" in working-class life but, in fact, a beneficent one that would resolve the dilemmas of the industrial age rather than typify or exacerbate them. The wage earner had both a duty and a right to borrow money, one reformist pamphlet explained: "The home may be large or it may be small, in a separate house or in a flat, in two rooms or in one, but it is YOUR home and in that home must be the thought that is destined to make you rise or fall in this world." Rather than assailing the boundary between public and private, small-sum credit provided the means to maintain it, "to keep up your home [and] to keep life going." Additionally, "if there is a real need of immediate money in your home affairs, and you have a reasonable prospect of paying it back when due, then you have a right to borrow that sum . . . on strictly business principles." Debt, in this narrative, provided a way for the wage earner to navigate the vicissitudes of urban life while maintaining his "self-respect, independence, self-reliance, and . . . sense of responsibility." It promised to prevent the worker from slipping into poverty, losing his home, or having to choose some necessities over others.[34]

This was a far cry from the meaning assigned to working-class debt in the late nineteenth century, when the hireling's recourse to the loan shark and the pawnshop indicated the inadequacy of the wage system—its production of dependency and want. "Every competent adult laborer should receive enough as wages . . . to enable him to get along without debt," an 1875 report by the Massachusetts Bureau of Statistics of Labor had insisted. That he did not—that for many debt was not a choice but a "necessity"—stood as a troubling indictment of the ascendant industrial age. Ham, at the beginning of the anti-usury campaign, shared an element of this view, reading debt as a symptom of the "low wages in force in certain industries" and the "systems of monthly pay to workmen in many states." The decision to nevertheless focus reformist energies on the problem of debt, rather than that of the wage, had always been an accommodation to the industrial order—a retreat from the kind of searching moral inquiry exampled by the Bureau of Statistics of Labor and other investigatory bodies. Yet in advancing the USLL, reformers pressed further, reiterating that the relations between capital and labor were not the primary source of the hireling's discontent and further concluding that the moral crises of the industrial era could be salved by the business of finance. To achieve a reasonable standard of living, the working-class family did not require a radical revision to the industrial order, nor did it require the expansion of the welfare state—the other device summoned in the early twentieth century to resolve the problems of need. The worker simply needed credit, provided by individuals who, while not philanthropists, were content to make profits "by financial service at reasonable cost to the borrower."[35]

These arguments did not always convince. As reformers campaigned to pass the USLL, they faced opposition of two sorts. First, there were traditionalist and populist voices who refused the narrative of reputable capital. "Both classes charge all the traffic will bear," an Atlanta editorialist wrote of the licensed lenders and the older loan sharks. "It is a matter of the pot calling the kettle black." One reformer reported: "Yesterday I had a very long talk with a lady whose name I did not catch, but who called me on the telephone. The basis of her argument was that we were 'bargaining with criminals.' She did not think very much of the idea of reputable small loan dealers charging 42 percent a year driving out the disreputable group." Such objections challenged the framework of the foundation alliance with the AILA—disputing the very existence of bankers who were not solely motivated by profit. For such critics, there was no reason to believe that new lenders would behave any differently than the old. There were also progressive voices who viewed the USLL as a trespass on the territory claimed by the emergent welfare state. For these advocates, it was wrong for the poor and working class to have to borrow for necessities that ought to be entitlements of citizenship. "These 'remedial' loan shark laws . . . are a back thrust of the Russell Sage foundation at the mothers' pension laws," one activist announced, describing a tension between the foundation's work and one of the earliest forms of modern social provision. Let the welfare programs, "honestly administered, do the work," the activist implored, and keep the poor and the working class out of the hands of those who aimed to "make money out of charity."[36]

Organized labor, however, supported the USLL, as did business groups. Backed by the traditional ideological opponents of price controls and an added column of progressive reformers, the USLL advanced through state legislatures with impressive speed. It was enacted in Illinois, Indiana, and Maine in 1917 and in nineteenth other states by 1925. In New Hampshire, its passage was guided by the agricultural constituency, which hoped that replacing the old usury law would draw money into the state and make credit more affordable for farmers. Borrowers in all the states that enacted the law—a grouping that held three-fifths of the nation's population—quickly found a range of institutions willing to profit from their financial needs. Of the several hundred members of the AILA, most were independent brokers who lent on wage assignments or chattel pledges of furniture and other household valuables. Many others belonged to nationwide lending chains like the Household Finance Corporation, which had evolved out of Frank J. Mackey's usurious firms founded in the Midwest in the 1880s. In 1924, small commercial banks began to enter the industry as well, opening personal loan departments that took advantage of the new, more generous interest rate allowances to extend credit to the salaried middle class. The movement was given "a strong stimulus in 1928," two reformers later recalled, "by the organization of a personal loan department of the National City Bank of New York," one of the largest and most influential banks in the nation. "Within a few months some 50 additional banks announced the opening of similar departments," in a development that foreshadowed the migration of personal credit from the margins of the American finance industry to the center in the succeeding years.[37]

As the Russell Sage Foundation devoted more of its attention to the promotion of the USLL, its ties to the philanthropic and cooperative community frayed. In the early 1920s, Ham left the foundation and joined the NFRLA full time. His replacement, Leon Henderson, a former deputy in the administration of Pennsylvania Governor Gifford Pinchot, was hired under a strikingly different mandate than his predecessor, being told to "give nearly all your time to the work relating to the enactment of the uniform law" and to treat the credit unions and the philanthropic banks as "a secondary matter." The cooperatives were especially resentful of the shift in reformist strategy. Under the aegis of Edward Filene and Roy Bergengren, the Credit Union National Extension Bureau, founded in 1921, grew to be one of the USLL's chief rivals, campaigning against the law's passage in Massachusetts and denouncing the commercial lenders in progressive magazines. In 1922, Ham had urged Bergengren to acknowledge the inevitability of commercialization, writing that it would take "twenty, thirty or forty times as many credit unions as are now in existence" to rival the loan shark without the USLL's "allowance of a sufficient rate of interest." The Extension Bureau resisted the point, and by the end of the decade, Henderson's frustration with the combative organization had reached its limit. "I cannot see that we can do anything but definitely break with Bergengren," he confided to foundation director John M. Glenn in 1928.[38]

The leadership of the NFRLA was more willing to accept a diminished role in the anti-loansharking movement. It even considered merging with the AILA, so as to help the for-profit lenders "maintain good standards of ethics and practice." The federation's rank and file, however, was less sanguine. When federation president John Ryan censured the managers of the nonprofit Newark Provident Loan Association for lobbying against the passage of the USLL in New Jersey, the NFRLA's membership was incredulous. "Has the national federation gone over bag and baggage to the commercial brokers in support of the uniform small loan law and everything else that they advocate?" demanded George Upson of Utica Provident. Such objections, while forceful, represented the last gasps of a dying vision. By that point, most of the nation lived in the liberal lending environment created by the USLL, and the membership of the NFRLA had dropped from forty philanthropic agencies in 1915 to only twenty-six. Significantly, in 1925, the Russell Sage Foundation had sold its own experiment in philanthropic lending, the Chattel Loan Society of New York City, to Mackey's Household Finance Corporation. There was no future, the foundation reformers seemed to believe, in philanthropic finance.[39]

Despite the broad adoption of the Uniform Small Loan Law by the late 1920s, reformers approached the end of the decade unsure of the legacy of their efforts. The discourse of reputable capital had suggested that certain borrowers and certain lenders could meet in the market and agree to financial contracts that would not exploit the debtor or endanger his home. The role of this narrative, observed one small-sum banker, had been "to justify the profit" that lenders were able to claim to under the permissive framework of the USLL. Yet time and again, the membership of the American Industrial Lenders Association had demonstrated that the promise of reputable capital was an empty one. The honest brokers had refused to lower interest rates when returns were strong, and had repeatedly lobbied for more permissive laws without the Russell Sage Foundation's approval. They had even fought progressives on the issue of hidden fees—the last demand of a rudderless reform movement. To many, the reputable capitalists seemed scarcely distinguishable from the covetous loan sharks they had replaced. "As we have realized, almost from the start," Ham reflected in 1927, "the alliance of the Foundation and the lenders is an unusual one." It had been forged on the expectation that the promise of profit would operate differently on the "big, clean fellows" of the AILA than it had on their predecessors. Unlike their underworld analogs, they would pursue a reasonable income but not an excessive one, settling for less in order to preserve the dignity of the debtor and his family. This had been the reform community's expectation, but experience had revealed its mistake. "The lenders are essentially selfish," Ham concluded. They could not be trusted to behave any differently than other profit-seeking actors. In order to preserve its progressive reputation, the Russell Sage Foundation needed to distance itself from its partners. Soon, the foundation's Department of Remedial Loans was renamed and its charge narrowed to merely studying working-class credit rather than seeking to solve it. In the 1940s, the office would close entirely.[40]

The work of the anti-usury reform movement could not be easily undone, however. At the level of law and economics, the passage of the USLL in most of the nation opened up a new frontier in American personal finance. With the opportunity to earn higher profits, banking institutions entered into a trade they had long avoided. They developed more efficient methods for evaluating borrowers and processing loans, and they formed relationships with other industries at the vanguard of consumer capitalism, such as automobile dealers. Installment selling and charge accounts would permeate the American economy over the coming decades as usury laws continued their retreat. In the soil tilled by the interwar campaign against the loan shark, a new political economy would take root. The United States was becoming, in one observer's words, "a credit nation."[41]

Alongside these material changes was a moral one. The advent of wage labor in the nineteenth century had inspired concerns about republican virtue and liberal self-possession. Was the hireling an autonomous person?

Could he be the bedrock of a democratic polity? Did his sale of labor represent an expression of the modern ideal, or augur its demise? Abstract issues of political and moral philosophy acquired practical meaning as charity workers documented urban crime and household squalor. The wage earner's indebtedness was seen as a measure of this crisis. It proved that industrial earnings were insufficient to pay for the "cost of [the worker's] living," raising questions about the sustainability of the industrial order. For an important cohort of progressive reformers, debt gradually became a primary source of the social problem. The loan shark was *why* the wage was insufficient, as high interest and violent collection practices upset the fragile balance between income and expenditure, labor and capital. From its inception, the anti-usury movement provided a way to center the wage earner's plight on relationships other than that of employment, in his ties to local lenders. Yet by the end of the movement, with the philanthropic fix swapped for usury deregulation under the auspices of reputable capital, a new moral narrative had taken form. Small-sum credit did not index or amplify the dilemma of labor but rectified it. It provided a way for the worker to maintain the central privileges of the modern age—"independence, self-reliance and the sense of responsibility for those dependent"—without challenging the foundational inequalities of the industrial order. With credit, the worker could manage his household needs on his own while accepting the hegemony of the wage.[42]

5

A NEW DEAL FOR DEBT

When the city marshal arrived at the home of Mrs. Toni Maxwell on July 27, 1936, he encountered a scene "reminiscent of war-torn France." Sunnyside Gardens, in Queens, New York, had been transformed by its residents into a defensive outpost. "Sandbags, barbed wire, [and] barricades" stood between the marshal and the homes. When three of the marshal's assistants approached the encampment, they were pelted with pepper and flour until their faces "were white as ghosts" and they were forced to retreat. Theatrical resistance had become a commonplace at Sunnyside in the battle between homeowners, the city, and the holders of the residents' mortgages, who had driven more than half of the community's households into foreclosure since 1931. Movers sent to evict the foreclosed often found that furniture had been bolted to the floor or weighed down with cement. Children regularly picketed the neighborhood carrying signs that read "6% more sacred than the home," in reference to the rate of interest charged by their parents' lenders.[1] At one foreclosure hearing, a group of women showed up in Victorian dress and sang, to the tune of "John Brown's Body,"

> Glory for the 6-per-centers,
> Who are out to make us renters,
> What a pity we're dissenters
> We'll stay in Sunnyside.[2]

The eviction protests were an unexpected denouement for a settlement that a decade earlier had been praised as bringing to its fullest expression the promise of progressivism in housing. Inspired by the English garden city movement and priced to be within reach of the urban working class,

Sunnyside had been celebrated as an example of the harmony that was achievable through rational planning and modernist design. Yet the onset of the Great Depression had devastated the neighborhood. Forty percent of working residents lost their jobs, and 60 percent of households were forced to draw upon their savings. Many took out second or third mortgages to release some of the equity they had stored in their property, but gradually most of the neighborhood's borrowers slid into default, and the lenders began to seize their homes. The crisis of debt and foreclosure that unfolded in Sunnyside was one illustration of the financial suffering wrought throughout the nation. As the boom of the 1920s broke into the bust of the 1930s—with high unemployment, low commodity prices, the collapse of the stock market, and the failures of savings banks—borrowers at all levels of society were faced with failure and dispossession. Over one million farmers in the South and the Great Plains teetered on the edge of insolvency, with many abandoning their land and debts and moving to the West to make a fresh start. Wage earners in the industrial cities fell behind on rent and struggled against forced evictions initiated by landlord-creditors. The progressive press again turned its attention to the Black worker in the rural South, whose perennial indebtedness gave "plenty of reason for wondering just what the Emancipation Proclamation may have accomplished." From all corners of the country, begging letters poured forth as insolvent Americans asked elected officials for protection and relief. "Please let me have $600.00 dollars just to pay my back debts," a North Carolina woman wrote to President Franklin Roosevelt in 1935. "I am in debt needing help," a distraught Texan similarly implored. "It is coming nearer toward colder weather and I have nothing for my body to keep me warm and can't see where I will be able to get it out of my husband's small earnings as we have debts to pay," a woman from Jamestown, New Jersey, explained. The problem of debt had been a diffuse theme in moral and political discourse for decades. It crested in certain contexts and retreated in others. In the crucible of the Great Depression, it took on new urgency across the United States at once, keying into ideas both old and emergent about the power of credit in American life.[3]

Lawmakers responded to the financial crisis in a variety of ways. Models of debtor protection last used in the late nineteenth century were revived. Many state legislatures returned to the politics of foreclosure moratoria, passing laws that suspended executions on property or extended the period in which the debtor could reacquire his belongings by paying off the debt. The Supreme Court had disallowed such measures in *Edwards v. Kearzey* (1877), but in 1934, in a test of the Minnesota Mortgage Moratorium Act, *Kearzey* was reversed and the stay laws that had been enacted in Minnesota and thirty-two other states were permitted to stand. At the federal level, the prevailing bankruptcy law was rewritten to make voluntary discharge more accessible and the foreclosure of agricultural property more difficult. The Emergency Farm Mortgage Act loaned money directly to insolvent farmers at discounted rates, and the Farm Credit Act established a system of government banks that would manage agricultural finance outside the market permanently. Struggling lenders were invited to seek relief from the Reconstruction Finance Corporation, and struggling residential debtors could apply to have their mortgages purchased by the Home Owners' Loan Corporation and refinanced on more manageable terms. On the edges of liberalism, proposals circulated for the expansion of credit cooperatives and the introduction of public banking facilities for small businesses—calls that were partially answered by the federal government's promotion of savings and loan associations. Beyond the compass of the New Deal, dissidents and radicals pressed further, demanding the prohibition of installment selling and an end to the legal processes of foreclosure and repossession. The first point of Senator Huey Long's Share Our Wealth campaign was for "every family to be furnished by the Government [with] a homestead allowance, free of debt," and the Reverend Charles Coughlin, a vocal foe of the "money-lenders and changers," clamored for the "establishing of a Government Bank of Control" and the "complete nationalization of all credit." The idea that borrowing presented hazards anathema to private freedom and the public good proved compelling in the 1930s, and it animated calls for dramatic revisions to the financial order.[4]

Yet a new generation of reformers did not draw from the well of rights and protections as they contemplated the crises at Sunnyside and elsewhere. Instead of privileging the person of the debtor and looking to guard his home and labor, many federal policymakers in Roosevelt's New Deal administration focused on the health of the residential mortgage itself and asked how it could be immunized against risk and failure in the future. In part, they envisioned a revival of the national economy founded on the mortgaged home. If families could borrow more easily, then more houses would be built, which in turn would animate a cycle of virtuous consumption throughout the country. Residential finance could be "the wheel within the wheel to move the whole economic engine." Liberal reformers were not insensitive to the problems that borrowing had long posed to the embattled debtor—captured with poignancy in the begging letters from insolvents and the theatrics in suburban Queens. Yet they believed that the indignities of indebtedness were rooted in poor lending practices and that by rationalizing the marketplace through law, the mortgage could be made harmless. It did not have to engender profound moral questions because it could be relocated from the realm of chance to that of predictable order. New Deal liberals would not seek to protect the borrower from the creditor and the vagaries of fortune. Instead, they would set out to protect the mortgage itself from volatility and risk.[5]

The nineteenth century gave rise to the conviction that debtors should be protected in their labor, domestic property, and personhood. That conviction was instantiated in law and tested, across the Age of Capital, in contexts in which to secure the debtor's freedom was also to challenge social inequalities that the law was reluctant to upset. The onset of the Great Depression marked the dawn of a new era, and the keynote of American political economy shifted from governing the reach of a turbulent market to governing the market itself. "The primary goal," writes one scholar, "was control: to de-volatilize capitalism and to employ breadwinning men." That transformation had profound implications for the cause of debtor's rights. The change began before the 1930s, as a diverse array of economic experts advanced a vision of the market as something patterned and knowable. It did not, "like Providence, move in a mysterious way," but instead was predictable, and when lenders and borrowers were equipped with knowledge of its impending twists and turns, debt could be decoupled from the possibility of loss. For some forecasters, this project entailed refining tools for anticipating the ups and downs of economic time. For others, it meant identifying islands of certain value—from people and firms to neighborhoods and nations—that were less vulnerable to fortune than others. In both frameworks, indebtedness was not to be instinctually feared but carefully—even scientifically—contracted. In the depths of the Great Depression, many New Deal policymakers embraced this teaching. Unlike the dissidents of Sunnyside, who built up barriers between the debtor, the creditor, and the market, these reformers sought to bring borrowers and lenders together while excluding vulnerable actors from the market entirely. The guiding light of financial law in the emerging Age of Control—most especially in the National Housing Act of 1934—was the belief that to make indebtedness moral and modern, "more discrimination is necessary."[6]

In the letters sent to President Roosevelt by insolvent men and women, one theme was paramount: the debtors were not to blame. Again and again, embattled writers insisted that they had failed "through no fault of mine" and had always "worked hard" and had "saved money." They had not been improvident—borrowing recklessly for items they should do without—and they had not chosen to speculate in land or stocks. Instead, they had become indebted for necessities, like housing, medical care, or sustenance during a period of unemployment, and they had been overwhelmed by vast economic forces that no one could have predicted or controlled. It was as the victims of misfortune and as persons who deserved more—as an entitlement of citizenship or, very often, as a privilege of patriarchy or whiteness—that they pled their case for relief. These narratives recalled the appeals that had been sent to bankruptcy advocates in the late nineteenth century. They also echoed the language of inevitable uncertainty that had propelled the state-level exemption laws. One could no more calm the economic seas than legislate "the temperature of the globe," reformers of an earlier era believed. While this conviction endured in popular interpretations of the Depression, a new vision had taken form in the field of economic science and financial forecasting over the first decades of the twentieth century. The acolytes of this new view did not, in opposing the discourse of random chance, retreat into the individualization of economic fate—the notion that every person was wholly responsible for his or her financial rise and fall. Instead, a range of emergent experts contended that the twists of the market were knowable and that one could rationally manage one's exposure to chance. The sailor could not pilot the vessel through each and every storm, but by using the predictions of the meteorologist, he could determine when it was safe to venture out and when it was best to remain at shore.[7]

For Roger W. Babson, the discovery of the knowable economy came from the problem of paperwork. Babson was born in Gloucester, Massachusetts, in 1875 and graduated from the Massachusetts Institute of Technology in 1898. Shortly after, he was hired by a New York investment house to perform the tedious labor of cataloging bond circulars. The market for corporate securities had expanded amid the great merger movement of the late nineteenth century, and with each new bond issue came a new parcel of data about the firm seeking financial support. Pages of documentation detailing the operations of railways in New Mexico, mining concerns in Colorado, and steelworks in Indiana were deposited on Babson's desk each day. The young clerk was tasked with sorting the paperwork into appropriate files so that it could be easily located by traders. What impressed Babson more than the volume of information he was asked to order was the fact that his labor was being duplicated in the offices of all the neighboring Wall Street firms. Every bank and investment house received the same daily circulars, and most employed a clerk to dutifully file them. Those that were too small to maintain a records department wished that they could, with many bond prospectuses left unopened and unconsulted. As Babson moved from job to job in the early phase of his career, taking similar positions with other companies and briefly venturing directly into bond trading himself, his interest in the problem of paperwork grew. In 1904 he founded a business designed to address the torrent of information. In the Babson

Card System, the inaugural product of the Babson Statistical Organization (BSO), the young entrepreneur offered investors the opportunity to out-source the work of the circulars office to a single, dedicated enterprise. Each week, Babson's clerks would compress the latest bond information onto small, readable filing cards and mail them out to subscribers.[8]

The Babson Card System was not the only such service available in the early twentieth century, and the efficiency of centralized data management was not a discovery unique to Babson or his historical moment. Since the 1860s, the thick volumes of Henry Varnum Poor's annual railway surveys had been a familiar sight in the libraries of most major financial institutions. Like Babson's filing cards, the *Poor's Manual* was a compilation of public in-formation on companies seeking to borrow money from the public to fund their expansion. The manual did not rate the quality of railway bond issues or predict how the borrowing firms were likely to fare in the future. Instead of analysis, it offered disinterested reportage, leaving the work of evaluation to the volume's readers. Another antecedent was the mercantile credit sur-vey, gathered and distributed by firms like R. G. Dun & Company, founded originally as the Mercantile Agency in 1841. These texts furnished informa-tion on the creditworthiness of small proprietors, such as shopkeepers and manufacturers, rather than large corporations. Befitting their focus on in-dividual borrowers, agencies like R. G. Dun gathered data of a personal and intimate nature. They sought to discern their subject's attitude toward debt and repayment as much as his objective financial position. Whereas Poor amassed public and neutral information, the mercantile surveys were pry-ing and evaluative. Their animating premise was the belief that solvency was a matter of choice and character rather than chance or the actions of others. "There is always a reason, *in the man*," one scholar writes of the ideology of the early credit reports, "for his good or bad fortune."[9]

Babson's statistical service built on these older models. All were alike in supplying valuable information to help investors navigate the financial marketplace. Yet Babson differed from his predecessors in two important ways. He departed from Poor in seeing his customer as requiring not just data but expert guidance. "If you are a business man, you are also a busy man," he explained in one advertisement. "You certainly have no time for extra reading or studying." Whereas Poor had fixated on the problem of data scarcity, Babson saw a crisis of data surplus, with the investor strug-gling to interpret the wealth of "government investigations, corporation returns, banking statistics, [and] crop and market reports." Accordingly, after gaining a client base with his disinterested index cards, Babson began to tailor his operation toward analysis, adopting the goal not just of print-ing information but of telling his readers what it meant. He also diverged in discounting the individual or corporate borrower's ability to be the master of its destiny. There was not always a reason *"in the man"* for a firm's success or failure. Instead, most economic actors were subject to trends and forces over which they had little control. The task of the investor was to prevision those trends and to determine how different borrowers would likely be affected by them. The sailors of old had left port with only "a prayer for luck" to guard them against misfortune, Babson explained. Modern mariners, on the other hand, "first consult the indications of the Weather Bureau, and so far as possible govern themselves accordingly." Babson believed that a similar approach could inform the project of investing. In 1911, he published the first edition of the *Babson's Report*, a monthly document that promised to transform the data the BSO gathered into a market meteorology.[10]

Babson's financial forecast was based on the concept of the business cycle—the belief that economic life was ordered by a regular rhythm of expansion and contraction. The origins of this faith lay in the nineteenth century, in texts like Samuel Benner's *Prophecies of Ups and Downs in Prices* (1878) and William Stanley Jevons's "Commercial Crisis and Sun-Spots" (1878), which explored the causal links between weather, agriculture, and the temper of the larger economy. In the early twentieth century, a range of economic experts seized on the concept and enhanced it, by incorporating the reams of data that had previously been unavailable to scholars. The country was always "passing through a period of improvement, prosperity, decline, or depression," Babson insisted. A century of history suggested that such movements transpired not at random but instead occurred "with reasonable regularity." Forecasting the tip from one to another could be accomplished by analyzing certain "fundamental statistics," such as bank clearings, business failures, immigration rates, and crop conditions, and using them to construct a "barometric index of the conditions of trade" at any given moment. "Of course, the captain of an ocean liner wants to know what the weather is today, but primarily he is interested in what the weather will be tomorrow." By charting subtle shifts in fundamental data and interpreting them in accordance with the "laws of nature, commerce, and industry," Babson suggested that the line of current business could be extended into a reasonable prediction of the approaching future. On the basis of such knowledge, stock could be purchased, money could be borrowed, and one could avoid the pain of being saddled with outstanding obligations amid a period of panic or decline.[11]

Babson's forecasts were distributed widely. In 1913, he sold his card system to another statistical bureau and invested all his resources in the monthly *Report* and an array of newsletters that trained on more specific realms of economic life, like the commodities trade or the currency market.

A sales force of several dozen agents spread out across the country to sell the products, and by 1920 Babson was reaching twelve thousand individual and institutional subscribers each week. Others encountered his counsel in the columns he regularly published in the *New York Times* and the *Saturday Evening Post*. Many investors who did not follow Babson took advice from the growing field of like-minded prognosticators. James H. Brookmire, founder of the Brookmire Economic Chart Company, published a popular weekly circular offering a similar "barometric" reading of the nation's financial environment. Irving Fisher, the Yale University economist, launched a syndicated forecasting column in 1923, based on his research on the quantity theory of money. C. J. Bullock and Warren M. Persons of the Harvard Economic Service marketed a set of regular predictions to corporate clients and government agencies, while scholarly volumes, like Wesley Clair Mitchell's *Business Cycles and Their Causes* (1913) and *Business Cycles: The Problem and Its Setting* (1927), advanced the scientific basis for economic projection in the academic realm. Important distinctions separated these figures and their predictive products. They had roots in different intellectual traditions, hewed to different political programs, and pitched themselves to different audiences. Yet they were united in advancing a vision of the market as coherent and knowable, and the public took note. "The rise of the business forecaster," one editorialist observed in 1927, was one of the most notable developments of the early twentieth century. "The obvious presence and importance of cycles . . . in business prosperity" was making it possible to escape financial disaster "by knowing where we [are] as to the crest and trough of the wave."[12]

The predictive economy was cast as a discovery of science. It reflected an accumulation of evidence about how the nation's financial system worked. "Nobody is surprised that engineers can foretell whether a bridge or building will sustain the future strains and stresses to which it will be exposed," Babson insisted. For him and his peers, the economic forecaster deserved a similar respect. In an era of eugenics, intellectual aptitude testing, scientific management, and administrative statistics—foremost in the field of life insurance—the prognosticator's confidence was familiar and plausible. Yet forecasting also carried ideological implications. It was an argument about how the economy and its various inequalities worked. For one, prediction represented an economic order that was large and complex. It was a field of activity governed not by any one factor—by bank clearings or interest rates, for example—but instead by a diverse combination of forces. Accordingly, in the predictive imagination, the robber barons of old could be afforded only minor roles. Forecasting drew a necessarily abstracted portrait of the aggregate economy, made up of countless small and interrelated forces that were too numerous to be controlled or swayed by any singular actor or class. The power of the elite was dampened in this discourse; so, too, was the state cast as less relevant to the project of economic governance than many progressive reformers imagined. The future "depends not on tariffs or ship-subsidies, not on Sherman Laws nor on any other such legislation," Babson declared in 1912. It was not reliant on "political happenings or court decisions," another prognosticator averred. Instead, it rested "on educating our bankers, manufacturers, and merchants in the fundamentals of . . . economics." Properly trained, these actors would render the regulatory state unnecessary by adjusting their businesses to the temporary economic conditions that often drove social discontent. Industrial disharmony was not rooted in competing class interests for Babson. Instead, it was inspired by the unexpected disruptions that occurred in economic time. By making those disruptions more predictable, financial forecasters would help business leaders curb loss, promote prosperity, and calm the social seas more effectively than the interventionist state.[13]

At the heart of this assurance was the concept of the natural economy—a cyclical and balanced realm of activity in which human history unfolded. Its ups and downs were like the steady rhythms of respiration, and panics and busts owed to the tendency of excitable traders to overreact to regular shifts in business life. Within this logic, risk attended all types of investments, from the buying of stock to the borrowing of money. Its basis, however, was not in the financial tie itself but in the amount of uncertainty courted by the individual, in choosing to research or not to research the approaching economic future. By discerning the natural ebb and flow of the economy and timing one's commitments accordingly, forecasters suggested that all people could guard themselves against failure and dispossession. Moral considerations need not enter into discussions of indebtedness. It was, in the logic of economic forecasting, a matter that was "practical rather than ethical."[14]

Economic authorities like Babson helped promote the concept of the natural and knowable economy in the early twentieth century. Yet within the field of economic forecasting, an alternative vision existed, with different beliefs about how that financial future should be studied and conceived. For Babson, forecasting was based on the business cycle. Competing analysts might use different indicators to gauge where in the cycle the nation's commerce was, but they agreed that prediction consisted of evaluating the character of present and future blocks of time. To others, however, the unfolding of economic history remained mysterious. The most desirable information—what was about to happen next—was forever hidden just over the horizon. Patterns from the past were irrelevant. The market could "repeat the same series of movements for fifty years and then suddenly stop doing so," the economist Paul Clay declared in 1924. Yet this did not mean that important facts about the future could not be known. Clay was a forecaster too, employed by Moody's Investors Service to analyze data and publish predictions in an annual guide to securities investing. Rather than trying to determine whether the economy was in the midst of an upswing or a downturn, Clay and his colleagues accepted the premise of an anarchic market and then sought to identify which investments were most dependent on arbitrary forces and which were most secure. Their vision of the forecaster's task was not meteorological. They did not believe that the storms of economic life were signaled in advance by subtle movements in one indicator or another. Instead, their assumption was that boom and bust took shape at a level beyond prediction but that the degree to which different actors were exposed to them could be appraised. Analysis of each investment object's economic and institutional moorings would not produce the same sweeping prognostications as Babson's *Report*. It could, however, tell investors where their money would be safer in the twists of economic time.[15]

This approach to prediction reflected the ideas of Clay's employer, John Moody. Born in New Jersey in 1868, Moody was the son of a shipping agent who had lost most of his savings in the depression of the 1870s. As a result, Moody was forced to leave school at an early age and earn a living in Manhattan, first as a clerk for a woodenware wholesaler and then as an assistant at a small investment house. He was determined to avoid the speculative entanglements that had bankrupted his family, always seeing Wall Street "as something of a casino." Yet his early experiences in investment convinced him that the randomness of the market was, in fact, patterned in two important ways. First, he observed that certain businesses consistently weathered misfortune better than others. Second, he reasoned that among the advantages that accrued to these enduring entities was access to superior information. Firms that had been around for a long time and had the resources to employ financial analysts could use their accumulated data to detect strengths and weaknesses in the market that were beyond the view of less established traders. Taken together, these observations pointed toward a nuanced investment philosophy. Moody came to identify the packaging and selling of financial facts as a democratic gesture, leveling imbalances among investors and promoting a more equitable marketplace. He also, however, saw the purpose of financial data as allowing investors to make comparative evaluations between different securities and helping them determine which were more subject to chance. Moody thus aspired to lessen the inequalities of information while making more visible the inequalities of business strength, talent, and stability.[16]

His first efforts to turn this commitment into a profitable enterprise was the *Moody's Manual of Industrial and Miscellaneous Securities*, launched in 1900. Like the Babson Card System, the *Moody's Manual* was a collection of disinterested business statistics, compiled by Moody himself and centralized in one volume for the benefit of traders. Unlike Babson with his newsletter model, Moody did not promise to provide his subscribers with weekly or monthly updates. Instead of receiving new filing cards with revised information on a regular basis, investors were expected to rely on one *Moody's Manual* throughout the year. The *Manual*, in turn, was expected to contain data that was timeless. Rather than tracking trading prices or other ephemeral developments, Moody sought to identify commercial facts that were invulnerable to change and thus would remain meaningful regardless of how the broader economy turned. How a bond was legally constructed, what rights it afforded its holder, and what assets a firm owned outright were perennially suggestive of the strength of the security in question. This represented an alternative approach to the problem of information management in an inundated age. Whereas Babson and others prioritized technologies of conveyance, seeking to communicate new information to investors as efficiently as possible, Moody emphasized technologies of distillation, seeking to parse out those facts that were most elemental and least likely to require revision over time.[17]

This approach would characterize Moody's approach to financial forecasting as well—a field he entered at the same time as Babson. Bankrupted by the Panic of 1907 and forced to start his business anew, Moody launched a predictive volume in 1909 devoted to previsioning activity in the railway industry. The *Analyses of Railroad Investments* aspired to help investors navigate an economic landscape that was constantly in flux. Again, it was an annual publication. Moody stamped each surveyed security with a rating, ranging from Aaa down to C, that indicated how "affected by market conditions" the underlying firm was likely to be. The highest ratings suggested that the corporation was likely to be solvent in any economic context. The lowest ratings signaled that the corporation's "future [was] not so well established" and could be substantially shifted by boom and bust. These evaluations were intended to be stable and settled over the longue durée. If they were ever revised, it would not represent an adjustment to changed conditions but rather the discovery that "an error as to . . . the proper rating" had been made in the original analysis. Whereas business cycle forecasters prided their ability to track market developments, Moody's impulse was the opposite. It was a selling point for him to advertise that "market action has no effect on the rating agency's deliberations."[18]

The goal of permanency led Moody to privilege facts about borrowing institutions that he believed were firmly rooted in the social and natural world. The bonds of a railroad corporation would be rated according to the territory served, the current freight and passenger density, and the amount of local competition. The debts of a manufacturing firm would be evaluated based on the company's access to raw materials, the availability of reliable transportation, and its larger organizational structure, rather than transitory data like the current demand for its product. Whether the public would continue to purchase a particular good lay beyond the prognosticator's horizon. What could be discerned was which securities would "show changes in price more readily" based on their level of dependence on the economic environment. By taking into consideration "the long-term outlook for the industry, the position of the enterprise within the industry, the probable effects of legislative treatment or regulation," and other fundamental factors, Moody believed he could identify those features of the economic landscape that were most likely to persist in good times and bad.[19]

When evaluating business securities, Moody's analysis was institutional. He did not consider the individuals who led a company—who could always be replaced—but instead focused on organization and structure. After World War I, Moody's attention shifted to the landscape of public debts, and his method of evaluation altered as well. "In these days of world changes, when American investment capital is going more and more into foreign obligations," he wrote in the introduction to the inaugural *Municipal & Government Manual* in 1920, "the value of a publication of this kind can hardly be minimized." American investors had traditionally confined themselves to the local and national markets. They had placed their money in American companies and US states and municipalities. In the physical and financial wreckage of global war, however, many saw new opportunities for their funds abroad. With the average man facing tremendous promise and terrific risk, Moody believed it was "more important than ever . . . whether he be an investor or not, to have some convenient sources to which he may turn for authoritative information" on the character of the foreign countries that sought to borrow his money. The international bond market was the leading edge of American financial experimentation at the dawn of the interwar period. Its unique challenges inspired forecasters like Moody to develop different techniques for evaluating change and stability over time. As such, his predictions began to incorporate information that had never appeared in the analysis of conventional business securities, concerning environments, cultures, and people.[20]

Geography was an important part of Moody's evaluation of foreign securities. Lakes, rivers, fertile lands, and arid regions were all accounted as contributing to or detracting from a nation's vulnerability to reversals. Similarly important were natural resources and permanent infrastructure installations, such as railroads and seaports. These features indicated a capacity for commerce that would endure through boom and bust. The legal status of a country also mattered. "A state which depends, like Poland or some of the new Balkan states, upon international alliances and agreements, is manifestly not as good an investment as a state like Switzerland," Moody observed, "whose existence is almost assured by physical geography itself." One could call the former an "artificial" state and the latter a "natural state," the forecaster explained, with the natural always offering greater security to the investor than the dependent or the contrived. Most important in gauging the nation's future, however, was what Moody termed "the moral history of governments." By this, he meant the formal structure of a nation's political institutions and the traits and tendencies of its population. These social characteristics in particular were "about the slowest things in the world to undergo change" and hence among the best predictors of how a country would behave in varying times. They helped one to forecast whether a people would progress or founder and whether they would repudiate their debts or work to retire them honestly. There was, in fact, "no road which leads to success" in the international securities market, Moody explained, other than amassing a "general knowledge of the government in which [one] is investing [and] of the people behind it."[21]

Sound bonds were those backed by communities that were unlikely to abandon their commitments during times of recession. In all the "nations of the world where a reasonably high standard of intelligence and education has prevailed, external obligations . . . have always been considered prior charges against revenue and have always been taken care of." Behind the public debt of the United Kingdom, for example, lay the "marvelous history [and] character of British civilization," which had inspired "a quality of confidence which is not easily accorded any other nation." At a deep level, Moody insisted, "the American investor instinctively feels that racial qualities are especially important and would rather have his money in the hands of Anglo-Saxons . . . than in the hands of other peoples." In this "he is probably justified." Similarly, the investor could responsibly lend to Australia, "an almost purely Anglo-Saxon country [whose] people have shown exceptional qualities for self-government." Those traits assured that the Australians would work and deal fairly with their creditors even when the nation or the world was struck by panic or recession. It was why, though Australia's "financial and economic position . . . may not really be any better than Argentina," their bonds earned a consistently higher rating in the *Municipal & Government Manual* than the South American nation.[22]

The compass of creditworthy people was not limited to British settler states. Other populations which possessed the "mental character and cultural standards" required to issue well-regarded debt included the French, Dutch, Germans, and Japanese. Through the vector of imperialism, such traits could also be found in less familiar locations. El Salvador had long been associated with the primitive and the backward, Moody informed his readers, but at present there were "practically no aborigines or full-blooded Indians left" in power, with the nation's obligations primarily backed by a majority "said to be of Spanish-Italian blood, with a very heavy Caucasian strain." Likewise, the natives of Guam, "although preserving many of their ancient characteristics and customs, have through their affiliation with their Spanish and American suzerains . . . undergone marked changes in their racial and social life." Tutored in the value of hard work and the ethics of repayment, inhabitants of the colonial periphery could be trusted to fulfill their financial promises in a wide range of economic contexts.[23]

What made these nations acceptable risks was the fact that their financial identities were deeply seated. "If, for example, every official in Great Britain suddenly perished," one of Moody's manuals explained, "a whole new government would be established the next day by virtue of the British universal conceptions of common law and constitutional rights." These values were an essential part of Englishness and were likely to persist regardless of passing fortune. The forecaster could predict with reasonable certainty that British debt would always be respected and retired because of these essential qualities. "If, on the other hand, officialdom in Mexico [suddenly] perished," Moody claimed, "government itself would almost perish with it," for the civilizational heights that the Mexican state had reached were owed to the labors of "mere persons" and did not rest on the population's fundamental characteristics. Racial and national traits thus marked the country's securities as unreliable. Similarly, Brazil, despite its expansive territory and plentiful resources, comprised mostly "illiterate natives, being Indians, negroes, and half breeds" and had developed little "European civilization." This was not the basis for a public bond that could be trusted to weather adversity; hence Brazil's debts earned a trepidatious rating of B. Peru and Bolivia were noted as enjoying "stable governments" and "great natural resources in the shape of minerals," but they were burdened with "comparatively sparse populations, only about 50 percent of which are white or of European descent." Moody assessed the blood lineage of many other central American nations similarly, while for the free states of Africa, such as Liberia, it was observed that only a small fraction of the citizenry "may be considered civilized, using the English language and being Christian in religion." These facts mattered for Moody because they suggested exposure to chance. They pointed to the conclusion that the public debts of these countries should be regarded as "extremely risky." These nations were not destined to fail, but they were more likely to be the servants of circumstance than its master.[24]

Moody's international securities analysis did not traffic in a single theory of historical determinism, racial or otherwise. Indeed, race did not carry one meaning for the forecaster but several, signifying an axis of biological distinction, a measure of social achievements (such as high literacy rates and constitutional government), and a diffuse set of attitudes toward work, obligations, and order. These facts mattered in a discourse that presumed the market was in some sense patterned or knowable, if not strictly predictable. It was not, as many nineteenth-century voices had insisted, a realm of unrelenting hazard, in which even "angels . . . as well as feeble mortals" might be menaced by misfortune and "fail to comply with their engagements." Instead, it was like an ocean on which some traveled on rafts, others on rowboats, and others on freighters and frigates. The task of the forecaster was to discriminate between these vessels and determine where an investment would be most secure when the storm inevitably struck. Race joined with other categories of social difference to narrate the vulnerability of some debtors to misfortune and the sturdiness of others. This way of seeing the market and the actors within it was clearest in the field of international investment, where lenders were furthest from their borrowers and most deprived of the familiar security furnished by local law. Yet what Moody and other like-minded forecasters practiced was an approach to financial analysis that was mirrored elsewhere in economic life, as isolated transactions were conceived in aggregate terms and as large financial institutions searched for devices for governing individual investments and loans. In these domains, the older image of the embattled debtor and even the endangered lender receded and a new vision took form, in which financial obligations could be experienced as safe, rational, and even scientific bonds.[25]

The collapse of the stock market in 1929 and the onset of the Great Depression in the 1930s came as a surprise to the financial forecasters. Some claimed to have predicted it, but most had not. All saw their investments suffer, as the Brookmire Chart Company failed, the Babson Statistical Organization shrank, and many of the securities raters, such as Moody's, managed to survive only through layoffs, mergers, and the benevolence of fortune. While the business of forecasting was profoundly unsettled by a collapse that halved the nation's industrial production, drove bank failures up tenfold, and sent the unemployment rate to more than 20 percent, the principles of forecasting were not. Instead, they were embraced by a new generation of liberal policymakers who would give form to Roosevelt's New Deal. As the nation's economy was rebuilt, the belief that risk could be removed from debt joined with the belief that consumer credit could spur commercial revival to authorize an ambitious federal law. The National Housing Act of 1934 marked an important break with the protective legal priorities of the late nineteenth century and sowed the seeds of a new American political economy.

The incorporation of predictive principles into federal policy preceded the ascent of New Deal liberalism. In 1931, William Pole, the comptroller of the currency in the Herbert Hoover administration, issued a memorandum instructing federal bank examiners to appraise highly rated securities on bank balance sheets at their (higher) purchase price rather than their (lower) current market price. The change was made to keep banks from falling out of compliance with their reserve requirements simply by consequence of their investment portfolio having cratered with the stock market crash. Yet it had the effect of incorporating *Moody's Manual* and other predictive publications into federal law. Federal regulations would apply differently to investments that forecasters believed rested on firm foundations (and thus had been given high ratings). Two years later, Congress followed the comptroller in deputizing the forecasters as adjunct regulators in the Banking Act of 1933. The act sought to stabilize the financial sector by, among other interventions, guaranteeing the deposits at most savings institutions through the Federal Deposit Insurance Corporation. Banks could apply for insurance protection, and if their application was approved, they could advertise to customers that their deposits were secure. Within the act was the stipulation, however, that applications for coverage would only be approved for institutions that stored the vast majority of their reserves in highly rated stocks and bonds. In effect, this prerequisite delegated to Moody and his competitors much of the responsibility for determining whether a bank was investing prudently or not. It also gave the forecasters the power to shape investment choices into the future, as banks that deviated from the forecaster's recommendations would lose their deposit insurance. Private prognostication was thus given public regulatory power—a testament to the faith that market entanglements could be made stable and safe.[26]

The Banking Act and the bank examiner's memorandum introduced the principle of predictive evaluation into federal law. To build a new financial regime, policymakers would embrace the view that the market was not random but deeply patterned. Risk could be identified, isolated, and minimized. The key was to recognize that in a complex economic environment, "more discrimination is necessary." Yet it was not only volumes of stock and bond analysis that policymakers considered as they endeavored to make American finance modern. Prognostication was also ascendant in real estate economics, and for New Deal liberals the revival of real estate was paramount. As for civic leaders of earlier eras, the home stood as a privileged site of gender hierarchy and democratic pedagogy. "Adequate housing goes to the very roots of the well-being of the family," the Harvard ethicist James Ford declared, "and the family is the social unit of the nation." The home was where husbands felt the pride of independence, wives assumed their customary duties as mothers and caregivers, and children enjoyed the freedom to "develop into normal healthy men and women." All these figures realized their natural role within the four walls of the private residence. Further and perhaps paradoxically, the home served to train its inhabitants (especially men) in the duties of democratic citizenship. Where republican theorists had once preached on the virtues of disinterestedness, with the home providing a refuge from the public realm of partiality and acquisitiveness, modern liberals now envisioned housing (and the debt that was serviced to keep it) as an ennobling source of discipline. "Democracy is not a privilege but a responsibility," one policymaker announced, "and human nature rarely volunteers to shoulder responsibility [without being] driven by the whip of necessity. The need to protect and guard the home is the whip that has proved, beyond all others, efficacious in driving men to discharge the duties of self-government." As the reformer Catherine Bauer concluded in 1931: "Although it is not true that any social-economic order which could produce good housing would be ispo facto a good system, it is certainly true that any arrangement which cannot do so is a reactionary and anti-social one."[27]

A deep moral significance was thus read into the single-family home. It was joined by an interpretation of its deep economic significance. In the mid-1920s, builders were beginning construction on nearly a million new residences each year. By the early 1930s, the number had fallen to a hundred thousand. One-sixth of the nation's unemployed were in the building trades, and one-third of the households receiving government aid were in some way connected to the construction industry. The physical home, apart from its capacity to cultivate order and virtue, sat at the center of an economic collapse that, in the mid-1930s, was stretching into its fifth year. If construction could be restarted, it would mean the reemployment of a meaningful amount of the nation's idle and poor. Yet it might also spread beyond the housing industry and animate activity in corners of the economy only tangentially related to the home. Spur the construction and purchase of dwellings, Marriner Eccles, one of Roosevelt's economic advisers and his appointee to chairman of the Federal Reserve, would later write, and "it would affect everyone, from the manufacturer of lace curtains to the manufacturers of lumber, bricks, furniture, cement, and electrical appliances. The mere shipment of these supplies would affect the railroads, which in turn would need the produce of steel mills for rails, freight cars, and so on." Coal would be needed by the mills; tools and chemicals would be needed for the extraction of the coal; and wage workers would be needed for the manufacturing of tools. A cohort of economists inspired by the rise of business-cycle theory believed "that certain industries, often described as durable good or fixed capital industries, were most likely to lead both recessions and recoveries." By supporting these industries, "of which housing was the largest and most sensitive," government could "smooth or eliminate the business cycle" and deliver a new prosperity.[28]

Housing drew the interest of policy advisers across the New Deal spectrum. Many of them proposed different methods for encouraging residential construction. Members of the New Deal's left wing discussed a system of direct grants to homebuilders or government entry into the construction market itself, perhaps under the authority of the National Industrial Recovery Act of 1933 and the Public Works Administration. The mass forgiveness of residential debts, through Congress's power under the Contract Clause, was suggested as a means of freeing up moribund capital for building investment too. On the New Deal's conservative wing, the solution lay in making residential finance more affordable and accessible for individual borrowers. Advocates of this view, such as the former banker Eccles, believed that mortgage issuance should be kept in the hands of private lenders, who already possessed operational capacity in the field of personal finance. Instead of participating directly in the market, government could work to reduce the rate of interest that lenders needed to charge to secure a profit. It could restructure the mortgage, for example, to extend it over a longer period of time. Monthly payments would be lower for borrowers, but banks would earn more total profit. It could also create secondary markets for mortgages, in which banks could sell the debts they were owed to larger entities—including insurance companies and the state—in a trade of risk for cash. Finally, government could reduce the risk of lending itself by tutoring lenders in the science of prognostication. Through the law of mortgage insurance—a system akin to that of deposit insurance—the state could encourage private finance to pilot capital away from vulnerable borrowers and toward those who, like the established corporation and the civilized country, were independent, responsible, and secure.[29]

Mortgage risk evaluation invoked the discourse of the patterned, knowable economy promoted by figures like Babson and Moody. In the realm of residential finance, those ideas found expression in the work of land-use economists like Frederick Babcock and Homer Hoyt. Like the forecasters of stocks and bonds, these experts took as their subject a market long plagued by speculation and collapse. They sought to make it rational—or to discover its inherent rationality—not by hemming investment to the rhythm of the business cycle, like Babson and the financial meteorologists, but by discerning the spaces of stability, like Moody and the financial cartographers. The judicious lender, Babcock wrote in *The Appraisal of Real Estate* (1927), would "obtain information concerning the trend of development of the district in which the property is located." He would consider "public improvements in progress or contemplation, zoning restrictions . . . [and] contemplated and existing local transportation facilities." Schools, parks, and highways were relevant, as was the distance to places of work, commerce, and entertainment. Ponds, rivers, landfills, and swamps affected a site's underlying worth, as did factors having to do with the "inherent capacity of the parcel itself," such as size, soil quality, and the presence of natural resources. All this data spoke to the true value of the property pledged to back the mortgage and thus indicated whether the lender was likely to face loss in the future. Land that was desirable for many reasons would be a sound investment in many markets, whereas land that was desirable for only one reason could be subject to dramatic swings in price.[30]

"In the final analysis," however, "the values of real estate are dependent upon people." It was residents—and prospective residents—who made the mortgage and the property chancy or secure. People earned the wage that serviced the debt. People performed the maintenance and improvements that kept the dwelling viable. They supplied the tax dollars and neighborly culture that kept the area appealing. It was people, too, who would one day buy the property, whether it was sold by the residents or auctioned in foreclosure by the bank. The judicious lender needed to know what kind of debtor would stand behind the mortgage. Thus did many categories of human and social difference acquire meaning in the discourse of residential risk. It was the individual borrower's "habits [and] character" as well as the community's composition that allowed the lender to evaluate "the neighborhood and its future." Class mattered as a measure of the stability of income. Professionals, "such as doctors, dentists, and lawyers," were less likely to see their earnings drop "in the event of a depression" than ordinary wage workers, who were more likely to experience reduced hours or termination. Women presented more risks as borrowers than men. As single workers, their incomes were less and their employment more tenuous, and in marriage their property in wages and wealth more compromised by the lingering law of coverture.[31]

Yet it was race and ethnicity—with religion often included as an adjacent identity—that carried the most predictive weight for land-use economists as an efficient indicator of exposure to financial hazard. As Hoyt explained in *One Hundred Years of Land Values in Chicago* (1933), there was an unmistakable relationship between the presence of African Americans, Latin Americans, and southern European immigrants and the decline of residential real estate. The link might owe to biological and cultural traits. Perhaps those accustomed to precarious living would be unmotivated to remedy a crumbling roof or repair a collapsing porch. Race no doubt entwined with economic status, with disfavored groups earning lower wages and being more vulnerable to unemployment than others. Prejudice mattered too. Hoyt conceded that while it might be unethical and "have no reasonable basis" that "the entrance of a colored family into a white neighborhood causes a general exodus [that is] reflected in property values," it nevertheless warranted consideration by the lender as a source of risk. Mortgagees did not have to approve of residential segregation. They were advised, however, to respect and anticipate it in order to guard themselves against hazard and loss. Often, the meaning of racial and ethnic difference could not be reduced to a single explanatory factor. "In many cases," Hoyt observed, "the undesirable racial factor is so merged with other unattractive features, such as proximity to factories, poor transportation, old and obsolete buildings, poor street improvements, and the presence of criminal or vice elements, that the separate effect of race cannot be disentangled." But the end result was that race had implications for the security of the residential loan in the eyes of land-use prognosticators. It was an efficient technology of financial prediction and "one of the factors in which risk lurks."[32]

It was to this discourse that New Deal liberals turned as they drafted and defended the National Housing Act of 1934. The law would create a system of federal mortgage insurance indemnifying lenders against loss when they lent to borrowers whom the government considered to be reasonably insulated from chance. As with federal deposit insurance, the program would divide the labor of risk management between business and the state, with the former mitigating a portion of their vulnerability through judicious investment and the latter pledging public funds to offset the rest. The act, its advocates believed, would have three effects. First, it would lower the cost of debt—realized in the interest rate—by limiting the likelihood of default. Second, it would trigger a cycle of borrowing, buying, and building that would animate the economy. Third, it would strengthen the financial system by steering capital away from people and places most exposed to the turns of fortune. Although the measure was concerned with housing, the name was "really a misnomer," Representative John Hollister of Ohio observed when the bill was brought to Congress. The true purpose of the law was to reform the circuitry of finance pertaining to consumer debt. It was most properly understood as a "banking act"—one that contemplated profound changes to American political economy as a whole.[33]

The bill would place personal indebtedness at the center of the American experience as it had not been in earlier eras. One would not borrow to weather a period of difficulty or to achieve productive independence. Instead, debt would finance consumption and become normative and long term. What protections were introduced by the Housing Act would mainly apply to lenders, incentivizing their investments by shielding them against loss. Indeed, the architects of the law believed that state-level protections for borrowers—foremost, the stay laws—should be rescinded, in order to "remove the obstructions that now impede a free movement of mortgage funds."[34] When the bill was considered by Congress, several elected leaders noted the moral departure that it would represent. "In most foreign countries," Representative Phillips Goldsborough of Maryland objected, the wealthy "see to it that their peasant class is under debt from the time they are born until the time they die." Their labor was never truly their own and their families were never secure. "I think we all will agree that independent home ownership is fundamentally essential to the welfare of society," seconded Representative Henry Steagall, chair of the House Committee on Banking and Currency and cosponsor of the Glass–Steagall Act of 1933. "Insofar as home owners are in position to improve their homes, it means the elevation of the standard of living, and it touches the very heart of all that means most to society. . . . But if we go beyond a safe line and invite home owners to mortgage away their independence, we shall have brought about an aggravation of the difficulties" that presently beset the nation. Marie L. Obenauer, joint chair of the Home Owners' Protective Enterprise, testified as to the law's double expense for borrowers, who would carry the mortgage on their house and carry the bankers' losses as taxpayers: "If you want any other evidence of it, I will call your attention to the fact that every one of the nongovernmental witnesses who have appeared before this committee are either money-lending brokers . . . or they are the business men who make money out of home owners."[35]

Representative Robert Luce of Massachusetts also spoke against the bill. He observed that "one of the unfortunate features of our social structure today is the tremendous amount of debt. Half of the public is in debt, half of the farms are mortgaged, half of the homes in the cities are mortgaged . . . [and] they now come to us and ask a measure [that will] increase the debt." Luce considered the proposal from within an older moral idiom. "It happens that I am a New Englander and that in my day I have read something of Ben Franklin's Poor Richard's Almanac, and was brought up in the philosophy that happiness ends when one gets in debt." Indeed, for Franklin, as for the agrarians, abolitionists, labor leaders, and feminists of the nineteenth century, debt bred not only misery but dependency, for it was a fact, as he had quoted from Proverbs, that "the borrower is slave to the lender." Luce was "reluctant to see the agencies of the Federal Government used to incite men to add to their troubles . . . for debt involves a period of time in which there is grave chance of illness, deaths in the family, [and] other changes, accidents of one sort or another, which make the burden of debt the most serious blow to happiness that one can find." It was thus the uncertainty of finance that troubled the Massachusetts congressman, as well as the relation of power. When one borrowed, one tethered oneself to the creditor and to an unknown future, and if misfortune came to pass, the debtor would be squeezed by the "mill-stone" of outstanding obligations. The individual's right to freely labor, to maintain a family, and to make independent moral choices would be compromised. It was better, Luce suggested, to use the facilities of the law differently. They should not encourage debt but wall it off from person and property, perhaps as "sandbags, barbed wire, [and] barricades" arrayed against the creditor, like the Sunnyside dissidents had raised, or, as the nineteenth-century advocates of exemption law had envisioned, like a "sea-wall uplifted against the tide."[36]

Against these objections, New Deal policymakers—and, indeed, representatives from the banking industry—offered several arguments. They emphasized that the insurance system was intended to benefit homeowners by lowering interest rates, and would only incidentally assist financiers. They assured that the program's administrators would give priority to local lenders over distant metropolitan ones, easing the unequal concentration of capital that advantaged bankers in the urban Northeast. They explained that the interconnectedness of credit meant that concerns about the power dynamics between borrowers and lenders were misplaced, for the true owners of the community's mortgages were the depositors at the bank—the members of the community themselves. In a competitive market environment, creditors were merely intermediaries, helping to circulate funds that were, in fact, the property of all. They also argued that many of the moral problems long attached to the practice of borrowing and lending arose not from debt itself but from failure—the point at which the borrower could not repay. It was then that coercion, dispossession, and dependency crept into the frame. Failure was precisely what modern risk management promised to reduce to a minimum. "Debt is not serious," said Frances Perkins, Roosevelt's secretary of labor, "provided that you can establish stability of income." "High appraisal standards" would do just that, explained Morton Bodfish of the US Building and Loan League, with evaluators being "so scientific that it is known that a family is going to break up from domestic troubles in 3 years." The housing bill would "revise our whole conception of appraisals and undertake to do so on a highly scientific basis," Orrin Lester of the Bowery Savings Bank assured anxious lawmakers. Lending officers would take into consideration "all the factors that tend to destroy or to enhance" the value of a piece of property, including those specific to the prospective owner and "the entire influences of the community." Absent a catastrophe far worse than the Great Depression, the proposal's advocates insisted, the borrower's independence and the lender's investment would be secure. For the federal government—which would insure the loan—the arrangement was "absolutely riskless."[37]

Such exhortations did not address all of Congress's concerns. But the urgency of the crisis, the ostensibly private character of the intervention, and the assurance that modern predictive practices would channel debt only to where it could be mastered did suffice to summon a large majority. In the House of Representatives, the act was approved by a vote of 176 to 19. In the Senate, its margin was 71 to 12. On June 27, 1934, President Roosevelt signed the bill into law, and state legislatures across the country promptly set to work drafting enabling measures that would allow lenders to enjoy the full privileges of the act. Chief among the obstacles razed by local lawmakers were nineteenth-century proscriptions on who could issue mortgages and how many residential loans a bank or insurance company could make. Such laws had reflected beliefs about what was best for the banking system and best for the community of borrowers—as laborers, householders, and independent moral agents. In the 1930s, policymakers embraced a new vision of law and political economy, in which the modern was defined through scientific appraisal, purposeful discrimination, and the economic growth catalyzed by loans. The Depression would only be eased "by the releasing of private credit through some appropriate channels and appropriate means," Harry Hopkins, head of the Federal Emergency Relief Administration, explained, and there was perhaps no sounder site of investment than the American family dwelling. It was "altogether a desirable thing," the New Deal liberal insisted, "to go into debt to buy a home."[38]

Responsibility for realizing the promise of the National Housing Act was delegated to the Federal Housing Administration, led by James A. Moffett, a former Standard Oil executive, and a leadership team drawn from private finance, advertising, and sales. Among the administration's first tasks was publicizing a program of small home-modernization loans, which would be issued by banks but insured by the FHA. "At a time when the country was just beginning a slow climb out of its worst depression," one official recalled, the job of the agency "was to sell property owners on the idea of spending money for repairs and improvements, even if they had to borrow it; and to sell lending institutions on making consumer credit loans . . . without collateral, co-makers, or endorsers." That salesmanship was pursued under the auspices of the Better-Housing Campaign, a nationwide publicity drive intended to encourage small indebtedness. The campaign enlisted the services of tens of thousands of volunteers, as civic leaders in small communities mobilized businesses, banks, neighborhood groups, and trade workers to tout the merits of the Housing Act. Promotional materials listed the kinds of improvements that homeowners might make to a residence, from the repointing of the foundation to the finishing of an attic. They emphasized that small loans could be paid off over a period of years and that government insurance allowed the interest rates to be kept low—no higher than 6 percent. They also countered many of the conventional narratives of household indebtedness as reckless, indulgent, or wasteful. Instead, the literature suggested that the residential debtor was a kind of investor, with the home a valuable security that, "[when] neglected[,] . . . pays no dividends." Those who contracted loans to maintain and improve their dwelling did so not to enjoy pleasure in the present but to realize profits in the future. They were more akin to the banker than to the borrower of traditional thought.[39]

Women were doubly impressed into the Better-Housing drive. FHA instructional materials indicated that many canvassers would likely be greeted by the wives of the head of household rather than the head himself. This was not a difficulty but a gift, the literature explained, for it was the wife who truly knew the home: "She has lived in it. She knows what is needed in the way of new floors, freshly papered walls, and modern bathroom and kitchen equipment. . . . She knows if the roof leaks or if the heating plant is not functioning properly." The wife was not cast as a vector of frivolity in this narrative—in fact, to do so would have suggested that the housing drive endorsed unnecessary debts rather than responsible ones. Instead, the wife's counsel assured prudence, as she could be persuaded to borrow

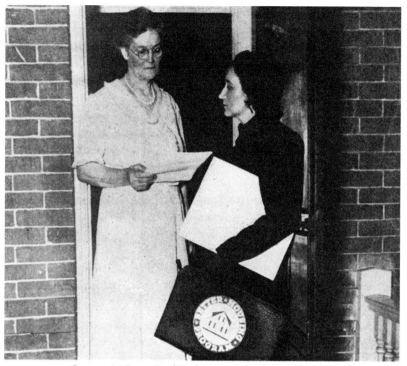

FIGURE 5.1. *Community Campaign* (Washington, DC: Federal Housing Administration, c. 1935), 29, Printed Materials Box 136, FDR Presidential Library and Museum.

only for "the conveniences that spell comforts to her family, and efficiency
for herself." Local campaign centers were also advised to hire women as
door-to-door canvassers. "You will be amazed at the volume of new business that will come to you if you go after it, and at the volume of business
an intelligent, energetic woman can bring in," one publicity pamphlet explained. In part, it was held that housewives would not trust the appeals
of a man; women would sell better to women. Yet women could also market to men, bringing to the encounter their unique knowledge of domestic
beautification and the calm of their selfless guidance. How many women
were so deputized was not recorded, but the success of the Better-Housing
Campaign was clear. The first modernization loan was issued by the First
National Bank of Cloquet, Minnesota, which provided John H. Powers with
$125 to use for painting his home, completing a roof repair, and installing a
hot-water tank. By the end of 1934, more than seventy thousand such loans
had been contracted across the country, with homeowners borrowing at a
rate of nearly $400,000 a day.[40]

As the Better-Housing Campaign unfolded, officials with the FHA set to work on implementing the more ambitious feature of the National Housing Act—the system of mutual mortgage insurance. One administrator recalled the challenges: "A system of risk rating had to be developed, based on new and untried principles. A sound transaction involved sound properties and neighborhoods. Standards for these had to be established. The mortgagor's willingness and ability to repay the debt were probably the most important elements in the transaction. A basis had to be found for making sure he was not taking on more than he could. The mortgage was to be within a fixed percentage of appraised value, and there was no national system of appraisal to be used as a standard. The word 'value' itself had to be defined." The work of resolving these dilemmas fell to a staff of appointees drawn from business, banking, government, and residential economics. Ernest M. Fisher of the University of Michigan was made the economic adviser to the endeavor, and Babcock was hired as the chief appraiser and assistant administrator in charge of underwriting. It was his department that drafted the *FHA Underwriting Manual*, which would invest the principles of residential economic forecasting with the power of law. Loans that complied with the *Manual*'s instructions were eligible for federal mortgage insurance. Borrowers themselves would receive no protection, but the lenders would be indemnified against loss. Loans that were noncompliant—because they channeled credit to people and property suspected of carrying too much risk—would be ineligible for insurance and, as much as possible, excluded from the market.[41]

Prospective mortgages were analyzed by underwriters at three discrete levels. First, there were the qualities of the mortgage contract itself. Was the debt constructed in such a way as to maximize the chance of full repayment? Loans were required to be scheduled across fifteen years, and annualized interest charges could not exceed 5 or 6 percent (depending on local financial conditions.) The loan was also required to be self-amortizing, meaning that the borrower would service both interest and principle each month and steadily chip away at the total obligation. This stood in contrast to conventional home mortgages, which were scheduled for five years and in which the borrower serviced only the interest and then was expected to pay the entire principle at the end. These debts often led to second mortgages to cover the large final payment, which were more likely to terminate in default. "Unquestionably there are certain ills or diseases to which mortgages are susceptible," one underwriter observed, "and it is equally true that here, as in matters of public health, an ounce of prevention is worth a pound of cure." Making the debt as serviceable as possible—realized in a reasonable and predictable monthly payment—was the first step in "immunizing" both borrower and lender against failure and dispossession.[42]

Underwriters secondly considered the individual at the center of the contract. Was the debtor a person likely to repay what was owed? Could he be trusted to make good on the obligation? Objective data and subjective impressions were solicited by the FHA in order to produce a composite portrait of the borrower's financial identity. Employment status, annual income, life insurance coverage, net savings, and existing debt obligations (for automobiles, furniture, and household goods) ranked as the most important facts to be learned in the personal examination. Indeed, it was only this information that the FHA required lenders to furnish in their application for federal insurance, along with the names of two persons with whom the borrower had had "business dealings for a considerable period of time." Lenders were encouraged, however, to evaluate the borrower's personality as well—his "character" and his "attitude toward obligations." Here lay the legacy of the faith that there was always "a reason, *in the man*," for the debtor's good and bad fortune. It was an echo of the belief that the ability to promise marked the emergence of the modern individual—the person who could take responsibility for his actions both in the present and in the uncertain future. Yet in many respects these instructions merely paid homage to the older liberal creed, performing fealty to an idea that, at least to financial law, no longer convinced. The FHA assigned the borrower's character no weight in gauging his impact on the mortgage's exposure to risk. It was as a nexus of capital flows—earnings in, debits out—that the individual mattered. Choice was made within context, and, in the aggregate, people's decision to honor their debts simply reflected their capacity to repay.[43]

Finally, underwriters summoned knowledge of the property that secured the mortgage and its place in the slipstream of economic change. There was the home itself and its fitness, function, and durability. Had it been well built? Was it suitable to the climate and resistant to the elements? Did it have new features that were likely to appeal to potential buyers? Or was it old, small, poorly designed, or otherwise out of step with the needs of the modern consumer? Next came the environment and social topography of the neighborhood where the home was located. Was it serviced by good schools and close to places of work, shopping, and entertainment? Was there adequate transportation and sites of scenic beauty and play? Did any nuisances intrude into the homeowner's experience of comfort and repose, such as industrial development, rising crime rates, or onerous tax burdens? Underwriters further considered the apparent trajectory of the community—its capacity for maintenance and growth or its tendency toward deconcentration and decline. Was the neighborhood located in a city that relied on one industry for employment or several? Could the local economy weather a recession, or was it sensitive to shifts in consumer tastes or the broader financial environment? Even family formation and reproduction became privileged pieces of knowledge in risk analysis, with underwriters tracking rates of marriage and birth in different areas and using them to gauge whether housing demand was likely to change in the coming years. This suggested to analysts whether a loan on a property would be a sound investment, with excellence in these categories indicating that the lending institution—and the federal insurer—would unlikely be left with a worthless home that could be sold only at a loss.[44]

Included in this endeavor was knowledge about the racial composition of borrowing families and the nearby neighborhoods. "If any member of the household is negro or of a race other than white," an agency memorandum explained, "consider the whole household as belonging to that race." This information was significant because race was identified as a reliable indicator of the borrower's exposure to risk. White borrowers in white neighborhoods were said to enjoy "a higher degree of economic stability" than any other group. Their incomes were higher, their employment was more secure, they were less likely use their dwelling to house extended family or tenants, and they were more likely to have wealth with which to weather an inauspicious development. The presence of African Americans, Latin Americans, and certain European groups, on the other hand, tended to "forecast several grave problems for the community." Whether those problems owed to those people's "economic instability" or to their "inherent characteristics" was irrelevant, housing officials maintained. The fact—evidenced by the statistical analysis of prognosticators like Hoyt—was that home values in markets consisting of nonwhite persons were "subject to wider swings than ones in which native-white persons predominate." Over the 1930s, the language that federal underwriters used to describe that phenomenon subtly shifted, from nonwhite groups predicting risk to actively embodying it. The "Negroes of Baltimore," a 1939 market survey advised, "constitute a *particular hazard* with which the underwriting office must deal." So entwined were race and risk in the predictive imagination that they became synonymous, with the exclusion of African Americans from the credit nexus signifying the exclusion of risk and the triumph of rational lending.[45]

In this way, debt was transformed by difference. A landscape of borrowing and lending was promoted in the United States by new laws presuming that "debt [was] not serious" when one eliminated "the element of risk" from the exchange. That transformation was achieved—or defined as achieved—by the act of excluding from finance those people whose unequal lot left them more endangered by economic volatility. That vulnerability conveyed a truth about them, rather than about debt or the market. The task of the law was to steer credit away from the risk they embodied, rather than building them up with rights and protections. This marked a departure from the law and language of the nineteenth century, in which difference served to express the dislocation wrought by debt, with the white borrower feminized by his obligations or captivated like the Black slave. "It's a dog's life to live—this running from store to store to scrape together money enough to keep your concern in decent credit," one antebellum writer had declared. "Better to be a day-laborer, hand-cartman, hod-carrier, or a plantation negro, than lead such a miserable, truckling, dependent, precarious existence." The new law also inspired a different political economy of knowledge, with information about the borrower's identity and status being used to qualify him for credit, whereas in the past such information had been used to exempt land, tools, and personal possessions from seizure and forced sale. Prior to this turn, to be indebted was to be Othered—to lose (or risk losing) the freedom and independence natural to the normative liberal subject. Now it was to be accepted as Same—to enjoy a form of citizenship expressed through access to debt that others were denied.[46]

Yet difference was also transformed by debt. What justified the unequal distribution of rights and privileges effected by the FHA? How could private actors and the public state countenance discrimination, both morally and legally? The age of race science was receding. "Separate but equal" endured but faced mounting constitutional challenges. On what grounds could the federal government compel, encourage, or permit finance capital to be piloted away from African Americans and other minority constituencies? The National Association for the Advancement of Colored People asked this of the FHA in the early 1940s as the pattern of discriminatory underwriting practices became clearer. The answer it received was that, first, residential finance remained a private practice, and the federal government did not make decisions that directly touched prospective borrowers. "The FHA does not lend money," a memorandum from the agency insisted. "The FHA does not build houses." But it was staffed by "specialists in determining mortgage risk," the agency continued, and in accordance with the responsibility placed on the administration by the National Housing Act, "FHA underwriting personnel are required to analyze communities, neighborhoods, [and] individual sites . . . in order to determine the degree of risk which will be present in assuming the contingent liability of mortgage capital." One factor that was uniformly correlated with dramatic swings in home values—and thus the security of residential loans—was the location and movement of African Americans. The cause of those swings was irrelevant to the FHA. The agency did not "encourage or discourage [the] seg-regation of the races." But it did have to honor and give regulatory authority to the prejudices of others if these added to or subtracted from the potential risk of a loan. And it was there, "in the market's mind," that discrimination could subsist without the soil and sunlight of a modern rationale and yet retain the power and force of law.[47]

CONCLUSION

Personal debt emerged from the New Deal era as a vital instrument of social provision and state power. The home-loan programs created by the federal government during the Great Depression not only persisted but expanded in the postwar period. They allowed certain persons, buying homes in certain neighborhoods, to borrow money easily, with the risk that remained in the debt absorbed by the liberal state. Close to half the houses built in the United States in the 1940s were financed with federally guaranteed loans, and by the 1950s, banks were issuing mortgages to homebuyers at roughly the same volume as mortgages contracted by commercial borrowers like private businesses and large corporations. By 1960, American consumers had over $162 billion in outstanding home debt, up from $23 billion in 1940. Those who borrowed to buy homes were more likely to borrow for other items, such as cars, refrigerators, and televisions. Automobile debt grew from $346 million in 1944 to $16 billion in 1960, while consumer credit generally—including installment debts for home repairs, charge accounts at department stores, and personal bank loans—swelled from $4 billion to $50 billion. Often, lenders issuing these kinds of debts drew on the processing efficiencies refined in the 1930s, when federal indemnification had allowed creditors to experiment with small loans at high volume in ways they had previously avoided. Always, they took advantage of the higher interest rates permitted by the Uniform Small Loan Law and its various successors. During the 1940s, the federal government attempted to place some limits on consumer borrowing via the Federal Reserve's Regulation W, in order to hold back inflation. But by the 1950s, organized business interests had defeated the effort, marking the state's "last attempt to fully restrain consumer credit."[1]

Debt was not only deployed in the service of mass consumption. In agriculture, a range of federal agencies, including the Farm Credit Administration and the Farmers Home Administration, brought ordered and more-affordable finance to rural America. Some of those programs mirrored the approach taken with consumer debt, with the federal government insuring loans to reduce the risk of loss for private lenders, while in other instances the state participated directly in the business of making loans. The Small Business Administration, chartered in 1953, extended the principle of loan insurance to entrepreneurial finance, and in higher education a range of programs—launched by the GI Bill (1944), the National Defense Education Act (1958), and the Higher Education Act (1965)—furnished loan funds to schools and students and federal insurance to private education lenders. The Education Amendments of 1972 would even create a new public entity—the Student Loan Marketing Association—to allow creditors to sell student debts on a secondary market, as a means of further reducing their risk. A 1963 report by the US House of Representatives found seventy-four federal programs either extending credit directly or facilitating debt through insurance and securitization. The extensiveness of those activities was belied—and thus perhaps encouraged—by their invisibility. The traditional arsenal of governmental power included "the authority to tax, the ability to spend the proceeds of that taxation, and the capability of issuing rules and regulations determining or influencing private behavior," one postwar economist observed. The fulcrum of modern politics was in fact the question of how much those traditional weapons should be used. In contrast, "most of the [government's] credit activities . . . [did] not appear in the federal budget" and were not even regarded by many as formal state behavior; "hence, they seem[ed] to be a rather painless way of achieving national objectives." They did not invite grand debates about the size and power of government because it seemed that the state was barely acting. In the main, it was "'merely' guaranteeing private borrowing or sponsoring ostensibly private institutions."[2]

A new age of credit thus blossomed in the mid- and late twentieth century, propelled by policies that offered discounted finance as a means of purchasing social goods. Debt was not uncontroversial in this period. Efforts to shield the vulnerable borrower from abuse endured, animating the jurisprudence of unconscionability, for example, and legislation like the Fair Debt Collection Practices Act of 1977. Yet the dominant moral questions of the age centered on the problems of access and discrimination. What social differences were lenders permitted to include in their evaluation of risk? What kinds of appraisals offended the principle of equality and ought to be forbidden? How was the spirit of antidiscrimination—embodied in mid-century achievements like *Brown v. Board of Education* (1954) and the Civil Rights Act of 1964—to be carried into the realm of personal finance? Those who sought to rid the credit market of illicit prejudice encountered myriad challenges. There was the question of whether discrimination was rational or irrational—and thus whether eliminating it made the market stronger or more unstable. There were questions about how discrimination was to be identified. Did race or sex need to be named as a category on a loan application for discrimination to exist? Or could discrimination be known by its effects? In the case of married women seeking credit, did it constitute gender discrimination for the wife to be treated differently on account of her diminished legal capacity? "If an applicant does not . . . control his or her income or assets," the Senate Committee on Banking, Housing, and Urban Affairs explained in its commentary on the Equal Credit Opportunity Act (ECOA) of 1974, "denial of credit would be based on proper credit criteria and the concept of discrimination would be inapplicable." The ECOA represented one of the era's most direct engagements with these dilemmas, along with the Fair Housing Act of 1968. Both acts prohibited discrimination in lending on the basis of race, religion, sex, marital status, age, or ability. Yet federal legislation (and its state-level counterparts) marked not a resolution of these questions but the beginning of their migration into the courts, where the problems of discrimination and antidiscrimination would continue to unfold.[3]

These problems were not wholly disconnected from the issues of freedom, coercion, and dispossession that predominated in the Age of Capital. African Americans who sought the legal end to redlining did so in order to escape the more exploitative forms of lending that thrived on their financial exclusion, such as rent-to-own arrangements. For women, equal access to credit meant achieving economic agency and loosening some of the bonds that might hold them in abusive relationships. For all, antidiscrimination law represented a path to fuller participation in the social and economic life of a nation that made the ability to borrow (on the most favorable terms) a primary method of building wealth and achieving power. Laws that created a substantive right to enter the credit market were important additions to modern American citizenship. Yet they were different from the reforms undertaken in the late nineteenth and early twentieth centuries, which emphasized protection from credit and the right to exit the market with one's freedom and personhood intact. The iconography of injustice in the post–World War II era centered on the lender who would not lend, and the scene of rectitude came when the prospective borrower was evaluated fairly as an individual and given the loan. In this vision, moral finance came by way of inclusion, with many of the classical hazards of indebtedness cabined from view.[4]

In the period bounded by the Civil War and the Great Depression, a different narrative had prevailed. The iconic victim of injustice in this era was not the individual who could not secure a loan but the destitute debtor who regretted that he had. A line of analogy ran from the borrower who was imprisoned for debt—a deprivation long compared to slavery—to more quotidian experiences of indebtedness, such as the loss of land and labor, the invasion of the private sphere, and the inability to make independent moral choices. Even as imprisonment was gradually abolished, proponents of this view believed that "the hands of the debtor [remained] effectually bound, because even his daily wages were declared to belong to his creditor, and when night came he found his bed, pillow, and blanket in the hands of the bailiff, and his wife and children houseless, homeless beggars." Liberal moral theory identified this figure as an unfree subject. The hardening of the debt contract, and the postbellum economy's recurrent booms and busts, brought the borrower to the fore of legal and social thought. Several overlapping social contexts—the sagas of westward expansion, industrialization, and slave emancipation—imbued the problem of the debtor's liberty with additional significance. Personal tragedies were transformed into public and national ones. In keeping with "the progressive spirit of the age," a range of reformers converged on the project of investing the debtor with rights, assuring his ability to exit oppressive contracts through bankruptcy law and exempting land, tools, family possessions, and labor power from seizure or execution. The borrower would not be left vulnerable to creditors or to the chaotic market. Instead, he would be shielded against dispossession by the "strong arms of the state." Some reformers pushed further and called for an end to the legal enforcement of debt contracts entirely and the placing of credit squarely on the grounds of mutuality and trust.[5]

Legal improvements to the debtor's condition defined the boundaries of the market. They rendered certain possessions liable to the twists of fortune, and they marked others—above all, the possession of the self—as inviolable. Debtor's rights were also pedagogical. They taught that credit relations had progressed from the time when the lender might "not only reduce the debtor himself to slavery, but . . . may even violate the chastity of the wife." The lesson was that in the modern and moral United States, the tension between finance and freedom had been resolved. And yet counterexamples abounded in the late nineteenth and early twentieth centuries that challenged that claim. Reformers encountered the plight of married women who were burdened by the debts of their husbands; African Americans whose labor was coerced by wage advances and crop liens in the rural South; and industrial workers who were harassed and abused by high-interest-loan sharks. Each of these was a figure whom the revolution in debtors' rights had not fully touched. Yet to include them in that emergent moral and legal order was to push up against larger inequalities of which debt was only one part: the hierarchy of marriage, the architecture of white supremacy, and the poverty of the industrial wage. A shortfall thus opened between the promise of debtors' rights and its delivery. The sum was paid in two currencies. First, real reforms were enacted that gave wives, African Americans, and industrial wage earners more financial protection than they once had had. But second, and more so, new narratives took shape—new ways of seeing and unseeing—that obscured the coercions to which these groups remained exposed. These struggles and their ambivalent resolutions contributed to a profound moral shift across the Age of Capital, as debt lost its power to measure unfreedom and to articulate the social questions of the day.[6]

Today, an element of the older moral discourse has been revived. Amid the twenty-first century's overlapping crises of housing, medical, and student debt, as well as the ascendance of darker entanglements like criminal justice debt, activists have converged on the debtor as perhaps the quintessential basis for a new progressive—even revolutionary—politics. They have called for the formation of debtors' unions, the organization of debt repayment strikes, and the political achievement of mass debt forgiveness—a modern jubilee. Opponents from across the political spectrum have in turn revived familiar counterarguments against the renunciation of debt. They have suggested that finance is ultimately beneficial—that even towering student debt represents a fair trade for a highly valuable degree. They have claimed that debt forgiveness is excessively legalistic and politically immature, particularly when it prioritizes the work of judges and executive actions over grassroots struggle. Most of all, they have intimated that debt repayment is moral—it is the right thing to do—and that one of the burdens of freedom is the responsibility to honor one's promises. The history set out in this book does not convey a single lesson for these contemporary battles. In part, it reveals the conservatism of debtors' rights—the ready alignment of financial activism with a politics of status and order, and its use as a distraction from deeper structures of domination, such as white supremacy or the wage. Yet the story told here also insists that one of the central priorities of the modern era has been deciding what (and who) should be left vulnerable to debt and what (and who) should be protected. Freedom has not only meant the power to self-bind; it has also meant the right to decide what debt and failure should entail, what indignities should never touch the person. Activists today are engaged in a profoundly modern and moral task: that of drawing the boundaries between the market and what exists outside it. This, like promise keeping, constitutes a burden of freedom, too.[7]

Acknowledgments

One throughline of this study is the importance of good fortune, and I am thankful for the opportunity to acknowledge my own. The research for this book began in the Department of American Studies at Brown University. Robert Self, Seth Rockman, and Samuel Zipp provided unparalleled mentorship. Each inspired me to think critically about markets, power, inequality, and the law. As teachers and scholars, they set a standard to which I will forever aspire. I thank them for their guidance and support.

Three universities provided me with a home while researching and writing this book. At Brown, I thank the faculty and staff of the Department of American Studies, the Department of History, and the Center for the Study of Slavery and Justice, particularly Anthony Bogues, Jeffrey Cabral, Matthew Guterl, Tracy Steffes, Michael Vorenberg, Shana Weinberg, and Debbie Weinstein. At the State University of New York at Buffalo, I thank the faculty of the School of Law and the staff of the Baldy Center for Law and Social Policy, particularly Samantha Barbas, Guyora Binder, Caroline Funk, Martha McCluskey, Errol Meidinger, John Schlegel, Matt Steilen, Matteo Taussig, and Laura Wirth. At the University of Illinois at Springfield, I thank Deborah Anthony, Brooke Depenbusch, Amanda Hughett, and the members and leadership of UIS United Faculty.

I am grateful for the financial assistance provided by the following institutions: the Institute for Citizens and Scholars, the Center for the Study of Slavery and Justice at Brown, the Baldy Center for Law and Social Policy at Buffalo, the Joint Center for History and Economics at Harvard University and the University of Cambridge, the American Society for Legal History, the American Historical Association, the University of Illinois Foundation, the Franklin D. Roosevelt Library and Museum, and the Rockefeller

Archive Center. It is also a pleasure to thank the librarians and archivists at the Library of Congress, the National Archives, the Franklin D. Roosevelt Library and Museum, the Rockefeller Archive Center, the Illinois State Archives, the Horn Library at Babson College, and the Rockefeller and John Hay Libraries at Brown, as well as Pete Beatty, Catherine Osborne, Lily Roberts, and Amy Sherman for their research and editorial assistance.

The Baldy Center generously convened a workshop at which several scholars commented on this manuscript in its entirety. For their incisive feedback, I thank Guyora Binder, Lawrence Glickman, K-Sue Park, Jamie Pietruska, Gail Radford, and Amy Dru Stanley. Portions of the manuscript were also read by Deborah Anthony, Susanna Blumenthal, Rosanne Currarino, Nate Holdren, Benjamin Holtzman, Alicia Maggard, Seth Rockman, Sylvia Schaefer, Tamara Plakins Thornton, Michael Zakim, and Samuel Zipp, as well as by the editors, anonymous reviewers, and prize committee members at two journals, *History of the Present* and the *Journal of American History*, where parts of the second and fourth chapters appeared as articles. I am grateful to all these readers for their time, guidance, and encouragement. Conversations at workshops and conferences also enriched the manuscript. It is a pleasure to thank Evelyn Atkinson, Dan Bouk, Cornelia Dayton, Carole Emberton, the late Anne Fleming, and Barbara Young Welke. At University of Chicago Press, Timothy Mennel, the editorial staff, and the anonymous reviewers expertly guided this project in its journey from proposal to finished book. They improved it at every step of the way, and I thank them for their patience, vision, and support.

My interest in history was nurtured by excellent teachers and mentors at Adlai Stevenson High School, Loyola University Chicago, and the University of Connecticut. I thank Peter Baldwin, John Bolger, Eduardo Canedo, Christopher Clark, Terry Fife, Robert Gross, Suzanne Kaufman, Micki McElya, John McManamon, Sylvia Schaefer, Nancy Shoemaker, and Jason Stacy. I hope they see their influence in these pages, as I do.

The best fortune is to have spent the years that I have worked on this book surrounded by friends and family. For their care, humor, and inspiration, I thank Don Brown, Sarah Brown, Eleanor Catton, Brian Cleary, Ellen Cleary, Colleen Cundiff, John Cundiff, Adam Drici, Jeffrey Egan, Adam Fagel, Anne Gray Fischer, Mark Foss, Samuel Franklin, Noreen Hernan, Katrina Hudy, Michael Goldberg, Benjamin Holtzman, Amanda Hughett, Jim Hultquist-Todd, Taylor Hultquist-Todd, Henk Isom, Will Klein, Rachel Knecht, Brooke Lamperd, Jonathan Lande, Kate Lande, Sarah Ludin, Alicia Maggard, Sara Matthiesen, Will Myers, Emily Olsen, Katherine Robinson, Louisa Rockwell, Zachary Sell, Joel Simundich, Benjamin Spies, Emma

Tavares, Emmanuel Tavares, Steve Toussaint, and Brendan Vincent, as well as my cats, Koji and Lupita.

Scholarship rests on a combination of curiosity and persistence. What I possess of each I owe to my parents, Charles and Angela Platt. I would not have started or finished this project without them. For their wisdom, encouragement, and example—and that of my godparents, James and Audrey Quinn, and my grandparents, Joseph and Evonne Weyhaupt and Milton and Elaine Platt—I am truly grateful.

While writing this book, I became a father. The greatest joy in completing it is that I can spend more time with my daughters, Zadie and Elaina.

I dedicate the book to Grace. I never knew I could be so happy making our life together.

Notes

INTRODUCTION

1 Lori Teresa Yearwood, "The Bill for My Homelessness Was $54,000," *New York Times*, December 29, 2021; Connolly quoted in Rachel Hampton, "Debt Nation: The Faces and Lives Behind America's Student Loan Crisis," *Slate*, July 16, 2020, https://slate.com/business/2020/07/debt-nation-the-faces-of-americas-student-loan-crisis.html; Steve McQueen, dir., *Widows* (20th Century Fox, 2018); Catherine Lacey, *The Answers: A Novel* (New York: Farrar, Straus and Giroux, 2017), 67.

2 On contemporary crises of debt, see Howard Karger, *Shortchanged: Life and Debt in the Fringe Economy* (Oakland: Berrett-Koehler, 2005); Allan Collinge, *The Student Loan Scam: The Most Oppressive Debt in U.S. History and How We Can Fight Back* (Boston: Beacon, 2010); Donna Murch, "Paying for Punishment: The New Debtors' Prison," *Boston Review*, August 1, 2016; Raymond Kluender, Neale Mahoney, Francis Wong, and Wesley Yin, "Medical Debt in the U.S., 2009–2020," *Journal of the American Medical Association* 326 (July 20, 2021): 250–56; Ruquaiyah Zarook, "Abolish the Debt Sentence," *Nation*, March 22, 2022; and Eleni Schirmer, "The Aging Student Debtors of America," *New Yorker*, July 27, 2022. On debt in the developing world—identified as a crisis well before the twenty-first century—see Cheryl Payer, *The Debt Trap: The International Monetary Fund and the Third World* (New York: Monthly Review Press, 1974); and Eric Toussaint, *The Debt System: A History of Sovereign Debts and their Repudiation* (Chicago: Haymarket Books, 2019).

3 "The Exemptions," *Wisconsin Democrat* (August 22, 1846) in *The Movement for Statehood, 1845–1846*, ed. Milo M. Quaife (Madison: State Historical Society of Wisconsin, 1918), 163–64. This book adopts the Age of Capital periodization from Jonathan Levy, *Ages of American Capitalism: A History of the United States* (New York: Random House, 2021). Levy characterizes the period of 1860 to 1932 as defined by the twin dynamics of "a linear rise in productivity unleashed by the multiplying effects of greater industrial investment, and a repeating, speculative boom-and-bust credit cycle" (190). On contemporary debt radicalism, see Strike Debt, *The Debt Resisters' Operations Manual* (Oakland: PM Press, 2014); and Debt Collective, *Can't Pay, Won't Pay: The Case for Economic Disobedience and Debt Abolition* (Chicago: Haymarket Books, 2020).

4 Uriah W. Oblinger to Laura I. Oblinger, Maggie Oblinger, and Stella Oblinger, May 31, 1882, in *Prairie Settlement: Nebraska Photographs and Family Letters, 1862–1912,* http://memory.loc.gov/ammem/award98/nbhihtml. On debt politics in early America, see Charles Sellers, *The Market Revolution: Jacksonian America, 1815–1846* (New York: Oxford University Press, 1991); Robert A. Gross, ed., *In Debt to Shay's: The Bicentennial of an Agrarian Rebellion* (Charlottesville: University Press of Virginia, 1993); Terry Bouton, "A Road Closed: Rural Insurgency in Post-independence Pennsylvania," *Journal of American History* 87 (December 2000): 855–87; Marjoleine Kars, *Breaking Loose Together: The Regulator Rebellion in Pre-Revolutionary North Carolina* (Chapel Hill: University of North Carolina Press, 2002); Tamara Plakins Thornton, "'A Great Machine' or a 'Beast of Prey': A Boston Corporation and Its Rural Debtors in an Age of Capitalist Transformation," *Journal of the Early Republic* 27 (Winter 2007): 567–97; Bruce H. Mann, *Republic of Debtors: Bankruptcy in the Age of American Independence* (Cambridge, MA: Harvard University Press, 2009); and Jeffrey Sklansky, *Sovereign of the Market: The Money Question in Early America* (Chicago: University of Chicago Press, 2017).

5 *Herald* (Jackson, Georgia), February 26, 1892, quoted in Steven Hahn, *The Roots of Southern Populism: Yeoman Farmers and the Transformation of the Georgia Upcountry, 1850–1890* (New York: Oxford University Press, 1983), 202. See also Allan G. Bogue, *Money at Interest: The Farm Mortgage on the Middle Border* (Ithaca, NY: Cornell University Press, 1955); Irwin Unger, *The Greenback Era: A Social and Political History of American Finance, 1865–1879* (Princeton, NJ: Princeton University Press, 1964); Hahn, *Roots of Southern Populism*; James Livingston, *Pragmatism and the Political Economy of Cultural Revolution, 1850–1940* (Chapel Hill: University of North Carolina Press, 1994); Stephen Mihm, *A Nation of Counterfeiters: Capitalists, Con Men, and the Making of the United States* (Cambridge, MA: Harvard University Press, 2009); and Levy, *Ages of American Capitalism.*

6 Hahn, *Roots of Southern Populism*, 202; Jonathan Levy, "The Mortgage Worked the Hardest: The Fate of Landed Independence in Nineteenth-Century America," in *Capitalism Takes Command: The Social Transformation of Nineteenth-Century America*, ed. Michael Zakim and Gary J. Kornblith (Chicago: University of Chicago Press, 2012), 40; Walt Whitman (1860) quoted in David M. Scobey, *Empire City: The Making and Meaning of the New York City Landscape* (Philadelphia: Temple University Press, 2002), 47. On the ideology of western expansion, see Drew R. McCoy, *The Elusive Republic: Political Economy in Jeffersonian America* (Chapel Hill: University of North Carolina Press, 1980); Patricia Nelson Limerick, *The Legacy of Conquest: The Unbroken Past of the American West* (New York: W. W. Norton, 1987); Amy Kaplan, "Manifest Domesticity," in *No More Separate Spheres! A Next Wave American Studies Reader*, ed. Cathy N. Davidson and Jessamyn Hatcher (Durham: Duke University Press, 2002), 183–208; and Anne F. Hyde, *Empires, Nations, and Families: A New History of the North American West, 1800–1860* (Lincoln: University of Nebraska Press, 2011).

7 Massachusetts Bureau of Statistics of Labor, *First Annual Report* (1870), quoted in Amy Dru Stanley, *From Bondage to Contract: Wage Labor, Marriage, and the Market in the Age of Slave Emancipation* (Cambridge: Cambridge University Press, 1998), 150; Abraham Lincoln, "Address before the Wisconsin State Agricultural Society, Milwaukee, Wisconsin," in *The Collected Works of Abraham Lincoln*, ed.

Roy P. Basler (9 vols., New Brunswick: Rutgers University Press, 1953), 3:478; US Congress, *Report on the Committee of the Senate upon the Relations between Labor and Capital* (4 vols., Washington, DC, 1885), 3:535. On the meanings of work and class in the nineteenth century, see Daniel T. Rodgers, *The Work Ethic in Industrial America, 1850–1920* (Chicago: University of Chicago Press, 1978); Sean Wilentz, *Chants Democratic: New York City and the Rise of the American Working Class, 1788–1850* (New York: Oxford University Press, 1984); Leon Fink, *Workingman's Democracy: The Knights of Labor and American Politics* (Champaign: University of Illinois Press, 1985); David Montgomery, *The Fall of the House of Labor: The Workplace, the State, and American Labor Activism, 1865–1925* (New York: Cambridge University Press, 1987); Lawrence B. Glickman, *A Living Wage: American Workers and the Making of Consumer Society* (Ithaca, NY: Cornell University Press, 1997); Stanley, *From Bondage to Contract*; and Rosanne Currarino, *The Labor Question in America: Economic Democracy in the Gilded Age* (Champagne: University of Illinois Press, 2011).

8 Clinton Bowen Fisk, *Plain Counsels for Freedmen, in Sixteen Brief Lectures* (Boston, 1866), 57; "Gettysburg Address" in *Abraham Lincoln, Slavery, and the Civil War: Selected Writings and Speeches*, ed. Michael P. Johnson (New York: St. Martin's Press, 2001), 263. On slave emancipation as a moral, legal, and social experience, see Eric Foner, "The Meaning of Freedom in the Age of Emancipation," *Journal of American History* 81 (September 1994): 435–60; Thomas C. Holt, *The Problem of Freedom: Race, Labor, and Politics in Jamaica and Britain, 1832–1938* (Baltimore: Johns Hopkins University Press, 1992); Julie Saville, *The Work of Reconstruction: From Slave to Wage Labor in South Carolina, 1860–1870* (New York: Cambridge University Press, 1996); Stanley, *From Bondage to Contract*; Michael Vorenberg, *Final Freedom: The Civil War, the Abolition of Slavery, and the Thirteenth Amendment* (New York: Cambridge University Press, 2001); Steven Hahn, *A Nation under Our Feet: Black Political Struggles in the Rural South from Slavery to the Great Migration* (Cambridge, MA: Harvard University Press, 2005); David Brion Davis, *The Problem of Slavery in the Age of Emancipation* (New York: Knopf, 2014); and Manisha Sinha, *The Slave's Cause: A History of Abolition* (New Haven, CT: Yale University Press, 2016).

9 Deuteronomy 23:20; Adam Smith, *The Theory of Moral Sentiments* (London, 1892 [1759]), 62; Schroeppel v. Corning, 5 Denio 239 (1848), at 240 (a case affirming the debtor's exemption from liability for contracting a criminally usurious debt). On classic critiques of debt, see Benjamin N. Nelson, *The Idea of Usury: From Tribal Brotherhood to Universal Otherhood* (Princeton, NJ: Princeton University Press, 1949); and Charles R. Geisst, *Beggar Thy Neighbor: A History of Usury and Debt* (Philadelphia: University of Pennsylvania Press, 2013).

10 *Speech of Col. Richard M. Johnson of Kentucky, on a Proposition to Abolish Imprisonment for Debt* (Boston, 1822), 3; "The Exemptions"; W. G. Maxwell, "The Rights of Debtors," *Albany Law Journal*, March 20, 1889, 311; H. Teichmueller, "The Homestead Law," *American Law Review*, May 1901, 414; Marshall van Winkle, "Imprisonment for Debt," *Albany Law Journal*, May 15, 1897, 20.

11 *Moody's Analysis of Investments* (New York: Moody Investor Service, 1923), xiii.

12 On corporate finance, see Richard White, *Railroaded: The Transcontinentals and the Making of Modern America* (New York: W. W. Norton, 2011); Julia Ott, *When Wall Street Met Main Street: The Quest for an Investor's Democracy* (Cambridge,

MA: Harvard University Press, 2011); and Noam Maggor, *Brahmin Capitalism: Frontiers of Wealth and Populism in America's First Gilded Age* (Cambridge, MA: Harvard University Press, 2017). On public finance, see Robin L. Einhorn, *Property Rules: Political Economy in Chicago, 1833–1872* (Chicago: University of Chicago Press, 1991); Sandy Brian Hager, *Public Debt, Inequality, and Power: The Making of a Modern Debt State* (Berkeley: University of California Press, 2016); Destin Jenkins, *The Bonds of Inequality: Debt and the Making of the Modern American City* (Chicago: University of Chicago Press, 2021); and Michael R. Glass and Sean H. Vanatta, "Frail Bonds of Liberalism: Pensions, Schools, and the Unraveling of Fiscal Mutualism in Postwar New York," *Capitalism* 2 (Summer 2021): 427–72. On credit and mass consumption, see Lendol Calder, *Financing the American Dream: A Cultural History of Consumer Credit* (Princeton, NJ: Princeton University Press, 1999).

13   "Notes and Comments," *National Citizen*, April 1881; Erika Vause, "Disciplining the Market: Debt Imprisonment, Public Credit, and the Construction of Commercial Personhood in Revolutionary France," *Law and History Review* 32 (August 2014): 648. Particularly illuminating studies of the morality of credit in different national contexts include Craig Muldrew, *The Economic of Obligation: The Culture of Credit and Social Relations in Early Modern England* (New York: St. Martin's Press, 1998); Amanda Bailey, *Of Bondage: Debt, Property, and Personhood in Early Modern England* (Philadelphia: University of Pennsylvania Press, 2013); Chia Yin Hsu, Thomas M. Luckett, and Erika Vause, eds., *The Cultural History of Money and Credit: A Global Perspective* (London: Lexington Books, 2016); Vause, *In the Red and In the Black: Debt, Dishonor, and the Law in France between the Revolutions* (Charlottesville: University of Virginia Press, 2018); and Mishal Khan, "The Indebted among the 'Free': Producing Indian Labor through the Layers of Racial Capitalism," in *Histories of Racial Capitalism*, ed. Destin Jenkins and Justin Leroy (New York: Columbia University Press, 2021), 85–110.

14   On financial history and, more generally, the new history of capitalism, see Sven Beckert, "History of American Capitalism," in *American History Now*, ed. Eric Foner and Lisa McGirr (Philadelphia: Temple University Press, 2011), 314–35; Seth Rockman, "What Makes the History of Capitalism Newsworthy?," *Journal of the Early Republic* 34 (January 2014): 439–66; Jeffrey Sklansky, "The Elusive Sovereign: New Intellectual and Social Histories of Capitalism," *Labor* 11 (Spring 2014): 23–46; and Jeremy Adelman and Jonathan Levy, "The Fall and Rise of Economic History," *Chronicle of Higher Education*, December 1, 2014. Landmark recent financial histories include Mihm, *A Nation of Counterfeiters*; Judith Stein, *Pivotal Decade: How the United States Traded Factories for Finance in the Seventies* (New Haven, CT: Yale University Press, 2010); Louis Hyman, *Debtor Nation: The History of America in Red Ink* (Princeton, NJ: Princeton University Press, 2011); Scott Reynolds Nelson, *A Nation of Deadbeats: An Uncommon History of America's Financial Disasters* (New York: Knopf, 2012); Edward E. Baptist, "Toxic Debt, Liar Loans, Collateralized and Securitized Human Beings, and the Panic of 1837," in *Capitalism Takes Command: The Social Transformation of Nineteenth-Century America*, ed. Michael Zakim and Gary J. Kornblith (Chicago: University of Chicago Press, 2012), 69–92; Jonathan Levy, "Accounting for Profit and the History of Capital," *Critical Historical Studies* 1 (Fall 2014): 171–214; Kim Phillips-Fein, *Fear City: New York's Fiscal Crisis and the Rise of Austerity Politics* (New York:

Metropolitan Books, 2017); Josh Lauer, *Creditworthy: A History of Consumer Surveillance and Financial Identity in America* (New York: Columbia University Press, 2017); and Jenkins, *The Bonds of Inequality*.

15 On the close connection between labor and finance that the new history of capitalism often effaces, see Jeffrey Sklansky, "Labor, Money, and the Financial Turn in the History of Capitalism," *Labor: Studies in Working-Class History of the Americas* 11 (2014): 23–46. On debt, coercion, and labor generally, see Sven Beckert, "Emancipation and Empire: Reconstructing the Worldwide Web of Cotton Production in the Age of the American Civil War," *American Historical Review* 109 (December 2004): 1405–38; David Graeber, *Debt: The First 5,000 Years* (New York: Melville House, 2011); Paula Chakravarty and Denise Ferreira da Silva, eds., "Race, Empire, and the Crisis of the Subprime," special issue, *American Quarterly* 64 (September 2013); Tim di Muzzio and Richard H. Robbins, *Debt as Power* (Manchester: Manchester University Press, 2016); K-Sue Park, "Money, Mortgages, and the Conquest of America," *Law and Social Inquiry* 41 (Fall 2016): 1006–35; and Peter James Hudson, *Bankers and Empire: How Wall Street Colonized the Caribbean* (Chicago: University of Chicago Press, 2017).

16 Karl Polanyi, *The Great Transformation: The Political and Economic Origins of Our Times* (Boston: Beacon, 1944). Especially influential legal histories of debt, dealing largely with the periods before and after this study, are Mann, *Republic of Debtors*; Anne Fleming, *A Century of Fringe Finance* (Cambridge, MA: Harvard University Press, 2018); and Claire Priest, *Credit Nation: Property Laws and Legal Institutions in Early America* (Princeton, NJ: Princeton University Press, 2021). On the construction and contestation of freedom in related areas of law generally, see C. B. Macpherson, *The Political Theory of Possessive Individualism: Hobbes to Locke* (New York: Oxford University Press, 1962); P. S. Atiyah, *The Rise and Fall of Freedom of Contract* (New York: Oxford University Press, 1979); Carole Pateman, *The Sexual Contract* (Cambridge: Cambridge University, 1988); Margaret Jane Radin, *Contested Commodities* (Cambridge, MA: Harvard University Press, 1993); Charles Mills, *The Racial Contract* (Ithaca, NY: Cornell University Press, 1997); Gregory S. Alexander, *Commodity and Propriety: Competing Visions of Property in American Legal Thought, 1776–1970* (Chicago: University of Chicago Press, 1997); Stanley, *From Bondage to Contract*; Robert J. Steinfeld, *Coercion, Contract, and Free Labor in the Nineteenth Century* (Cambridge: Cambridge University Press, 2001); Barbara Young Welke, *Recasting American Liberty: Gender, Race, Law, and the Railroad Revolution, 1865–1920* (Cambridge: Cambridge University Press, 2001); and Jennifer Nedelsky, *Law's Relations: A Relational Theory of Self, Autonomy, and Law* (New York: Oxford University Press, 2011).

17 Irving Fisher, "Senses of 'Capital,'" *Economic Journal* 7 (June 1897): 206. On capitalist epistemologies, see Sklansky, "The Elusive Sovereign," 23–46; Levy, "Accounting for Profit," 171–214; and Eli Cook, *The Pricing of Progress: Economic Indicators and the Capitalization of American Life* (Cambridge, MA: Harvard University Press, 2017). Scholars have not ignored the profound cultural work involved in naturalizing finance, but much of the literature focuses on the fictions of certainty that counterbalanced the inherent uncertainty of the financial marketplace. See Michael O'Malley, "Specie and Species: Race and the Money Question in Nineteenth-Century America," *American Historical Review* 99 (April 1994): 369–95; Ann Fabian, *Card Sharps and Bucket Shops: Gambling in Nineteenth-*

Century America (New York: Routledge, 1999); Mary Poovey, *Genres of the Credit Economy: Mediating Value in Eighteenth- and Nineteenth-Century Britain* (Chicago: University of Chicago Press, 2008); and Peter Knight, *Reading the Market: Genres of Financial Capitalism in Gilded Age America* (Baltimore: Johns Hopkins University Press, 2015). This book's interest, on the other hand, is in how the ownership rights in the person that Fisher and others have observed were understood.

CHAPTER ONE

1   "The Ludlow-Street Jail," *New York Times*, October 30, 1871.
2   "Imprisonment for Debt," *Albany Law Journal*, June 15, 1872, 387; Thomas Hertell, *Remarks on the Law of Imprisonment for Debt* (New York, 1823), 6; *Speech of Col. Richard M. Johnson of Kentucky, on a Proposition to Abolish Imprisonment for Debt* (Boston, 1822), 3; Joseph D. Fay, *Essays of Howard; or, Tales of Prison* (New York, 1811), 15; Thomas W. Palmer quoted in *The History of Woman Suffrage*, ed. Susan B. Anthony and Ida Husted Harper (4 vols., Rochester, 1902), 4:63. On the abolition of imprisonment for debt, see George Philip Bauer, "The Movement against Imprisonment for Debt in the United States" (PhD diss., Harvard University, 1935); Peter J. Coleman, *Debtors and Creditors: Insolvency, Imprisonment for Debt, and Bankruptcy, 1607–1900* (Madison: State Historical Society of Wisconsin, 1974); and Bruce H. Mann, *Republic of Debtors: Bankruptcy in the Age of American Independence* (Cambridge, MA: Harvard University Press, 2009). A midpoint in the abolition of the debtors' prison was the rise of the poor debtor's oath, which, once sworn, shielded the impoverished debtor (who had not attempted to flee the debt) from imprisonment. See Charles E. Grinnell, *A Study of the Poor Debtor Law of Massachusetts* (Boston, 1883).
3   William Blackstone, *Commentaries on the Laws of England* (5 vols., London, 1765–1769), 3:42; Theophilus Parsons, *Law of Contracts* (2 vols., Boston, 1853); 1:9–10; A. D. Smith, review of Marshall M. Strong's speech, *Milwaukee Courier*, in *The Struggle over Ratification, 1846–1847*, ed. Milo M. Quaife (Madison: State Historical Society of Wisconsin, 1918), 575–76. On the historical linkages (and important differences) between debt and slavery, see Orlando Patterson, *Slavery and Social Death: A Comparative Study* (Cambridge, MA: Harvard University Press, 1982), 124–26; David Graeber, *Debt: The First 5,000 Years* (New York: Melville House, 2011), 80–87; and Amanda Bailey, *Of Bondage: Debt, Property, and Personhood in Early Modern England* (Philadelphia: University of Pennsylvania Press, 2013). On the language of debt slavery in the antebellum United States, see Scott A. Sandage, "Deadbeats, Drunkards, and Dreamers: A Cultural History of Failure in America, 1819–1893" (PhD. diss, Rutgers University, 1995), 122–50.
4   McDonald v. Campbell, 57 Tex. 614 (1882) at 18. The touchstone of the view that credit enacts freedom was Jeremy Bentham, *Defence of Usury* (London, 1787). American renditions were found in the Boston Merchants Petition Massachusetts General Court for a Law Repealing the Statutory Maximum on Interest Rates (Boston, 1834); and Richard H. Dana, *Speech [. . .] on the Repeal of Usury Laws* (New York, 1872). See also Franklin W. Ryan, *Usury and Usury Laws* (Boston, 1924). On postbellum political economy, see Eric Foner, *Reconstruction: America's Unfinished Revolution, 1863–1877* (New York: Harper and Rowe, 1988); Richard Franklin Bensel, *Yankee Leviathan: The Origins of Central State Authority in America, 1859–1877* (Cambridge: Cambridge University Press, 1990); Amy Dru Stanley,

From Bondage to Contract: Wage Labor, Marriage, and the Market in the Age of Slave Emancipation (Cambridge: Cambridge University Press, 1998); Stephen Mihm, *A Nation of Counterfeiters: Capitalists, Con Men, and the Making of the United States* (Cambridge, MA: Harvard University Press, 2009); and Jonathan Levy, *Freaks of Fortune: The Emerging World of Capitalism and Risk in America* (Cambridge, MA: Harvard University Press, 2014). On the protective and regulatory state in this period, see William J. Novak, *The People's Welfare: Law and Regulation in Nineteenth-Century America* (Chapel Hill: University of North Carolina Press, 1995); Michele Landis Dauber, *The Sympathetic State: Disaster Relief and the Origins of the American Welfare State* (Chicago: University of Chicago Press, 2013); and Susan J. Pearson, "A New Birth of Regulation: The State of the State After the Civil War," *Journal of the Civil War Era* 5 (2015): 422–39. On contract and risk-taking as measures of freedom, see Morton J. Horwitz, *The Transformation of American Law, 1780–1860* (Cambridge, MA: Harvard University Press, 1977); Thomas Bender, ed., *The Anti-slavery Debate: Capitalism and Abolitionism as Problems in Historical Interpretation* (Berkeley: University of California Press, 1992); Stanley, *From Bondage to Contract*; Roy Krittner, *Calculating Promises: The Emergence of Modern American Contract Doctrine* (Stanford: Stanford University Press, 2007); and Levy, *Freaks of Fortune*.

5   [Frederick Douglass], *Life and Times of Frederick Douglass* (Boston, 1892), 429; James A. Garfield (1865) quoted in Eric Foner, "The Meaning of Freedom in the Age of Emancipation," *Journal of American History* 81 (September 1994): 435–60; "Order by the Commander of the Northern District of the Department of the South, June 24, 1865," in *Land and Labor, 1865*, ed. Steven Hahn, Steven F. Miller, Susan E. O'Donovan, John C. Rodrigue, and Leslie S. Rowland, ser. 3, vol. 1, of *Freedom: A Documentary History of Emancipation, 1861–1867* (Chapel Hill: University of North Carolina Press, 2008), 351. On Reconstruction and the law, see Michael Vorenberg, *Final Freedom: The Civil War, the Abolition of Slavery, and the Thirteenth Amendment* (Cambridge: Cambridge University Press, 2004); Kate Masur, *An Example for All the Land: Emancipation and the Struggle over Equality in Washington, D.C.* (Chapel Hill: University of North Carolina Press, 2011); Laura F. Edwards, *A Legal History of the Civil War and Reconstruction: A Nation of Rights* (Cambridge: Cambridge University Press, 2015); Martha Jones, *Birthright Citizens: A History of Race and Rights in Antebellum America* (Cambridge: Cambridge University Press, 2018); Eric Foner, *The Second Founding: How the Civil War and Reconstruction Remade the Constitution* (New York: W. W. Norton, 2019); and Stephanie McCurry, "Reconstructing Belonging: The Thirteenth Amendment at Work in the World," in *Intimate States: Gender, Sexuality, and Governance in Modern U.S. History*, ed. Margot Canaday, Nancy F. Cott, and Robert O. Self (Chicago: University of Chicago Press, 2021), 19–40.

6   On law and free labor, see Robert J. Steinfeld, *The Invention of Free Labor: The Employment Relation in English and American Law and Culture, 1350–1870* (Chapel Hill: University of North Carolina Press, 1991); Christopher L. Tomlins, *Law, Labor, and Ideology in the Early American Republic* (Cambridge: Cambridge University Press, 1993); and Robert J. Steinfeld, *Coercion, Contract, and Free Labor in the Nineteenth Century* (Cambridge: Cambridge University Press, 2001). On African American experiences of work after emancipation, see W. E. B. Du Bois, *Black Reconstruction in America, 1860–1880* (New York: Free Press, 1998 [1935]); Leon Litwack, *Been in the Storm So Long: The Aftermath of Slavery* (New York: Vintage,

1980); Barbara Jeanne Fields, *Slavery and Freedom on the Middle Ground: Maryland during the Nineteenth Century* (New Haven, CT: Yale University Press, 1985); Julie Saville, *The Work of Reconstruction: From Slave to Wage Labor in South Carolina, 1860–1870* (New York: Cambridge University Press, 1996); Tera W. Hunter, *To 'Joy My Freedom: Southern Black Women's Lives and Labors after the Civil War* (Cambridge, MA: Harvard University Press, 1998); Thavolia Glymph, *Out of the House of Bondage: The Transformation of the Plantation Household* (Cambridge: Cambridge University Press, 2008); and Susan Eva O'Donovan, *Becoming Free in the Cotton South* (Cambridge, MA: Harvard University Press, 2010).

7   Sarah, a Woman of Color, v. Borders, 4 Scam. 341 (Ill. 1843), at 347; Parsons v. Trask, 73 Mass. 473 (1856), at 478; The Case of Mary Clark, a Woman of Color, 1 Blackf. 122 (Ind. 1821), at 126; Steinfeld, *Coercion, Contract, and Free Labor*, 284.

8   William H. Corwin to William H. Seward, September 10, 1865, extract, included in "Slavery or Peonage in Mexico," Ex. Doc. No. 13, 39th Cong., 1st Sess. 2, 3; H. Romero to William H. Seward, October 5, 1865, included in "Slavery or Peonage in Mexico," Ex. Doc. No. 13, 39th Cong., 1st Sess. 9; Benjamin F. Flanders (1865) in Foner, *Reconstruction: America's Unfinished Revolution*, 199; "Peonage at the South," *New York Daily Tribune*, July 10, 1865; "African Peonage," *Liberator*, August 25, 1865; "From New Orleans," *New York Daily Tribune*, December 8, 1865). On Indigenous bondage, see James F. Brooks, *Captives and Cousins: Slavery, Kinship, and Community in the Southwest Borderlands* (Chapel Hill: University of North Carolina Press, 2002); Andrés Reséndez, *The Other Slavery: The Uncovered Story of Indian Enslavement in America* (New York: Mariner, 2016); and William S. Kiser, *Borderlands of Slavery: The Struggle over Captivity and Peonage in the American Southwest* (Philadelphia: University of Pennsylvania Press, 2017). On indentured Chinese labor, see Evelyn Hu-DeHart, "Chinese Coolie Labour in Cuba in the Nineteenth Century: Free Labour or Neoslavery?," *Slavery and Abolition* 14 (April 1993), 38–54; Moon-Ho Jung, *Coolies and Cane: Race, Labor, and Sugar in the Age of Emancipation* (Baltimore: Johns Hopkins University Press, 2008); and Stacey L. Smith, *Freedom's Frontier: California and the Struggle over Unfree Labor, Emancipation, and Reconstruction* (Chapel Hill: University of North Carolina Press, 2013).

9   Charles Sumner, Cong. Globe, 39th Cong., 2d Sess. 240 (1867) (statement of Charles Sumner); Senate Bill 543, Cong. Globe, 39th Cong., 2d Sess. 764 (1867).

10 Cong. Globe, 39th Cong., 2d Sess. 1571–72 (1867) (emphasis added).

11 Proclamation of New Mexico Governor Robert Mitchell quoted in Kiser, *Borderlands of Slavery*, 164. On the campaign against peonage in New Mexico, see Kiser, 164–69. While the Peonage Act did not meet with significant resistance, it is notable that Congress considered, and ultimately rejected, a provision that would have voided the peon's debts entirely. Indebted laborers could not be made to work, but, by the Peonage Act, they would not be relieved of the obligation to repay.

12 US Const. art I, § 8; Barbara Weiss, *The Hell of the English: Bankruptcy and the English Novel* (Lewisburg, PA: Bucknell University Press, 1986), 14. On bankruptcy in the nineteenth century, see Charles Warren, *Bankruptcy in United States History* (Cambridge, MA: Harvard University Press, 1935); Edward J. Balleisen, *Navigating Failure: Bankruptcy and Commercial Society in Antebellum America* (Chapel Hill: University of North Carolina Press, 2001); David A. Skeel Jr., *Debt's Dominion: A History of Bankruptcy Law in America* (Princeton, NJ: Princeton University Press, 2001); John Fabian Witt, "Narrating Bankruptcy/Narrating

Risk," *Northwestern University Law Review* 98 (Fall 2003): 303–34; and Mann, *Republic of Debtors*. On Jenckes and the Bankruptcy Act of 1867 specifically, see Scott A. Sandage, *Born Losers: A History of Failure in America* (Cambridge, MA: Harvard University Press, 2005), 189–225.

13   Debtors quoted in Sandage, *Born Losers*, 199, 202–3. On the national economy of slavery, see Sven Beckert and Seth Rockman, eds., *Slavery's Capitalism: A New History of American Economic Development* (Philadelphia: University of Pennsylvania Press, 2016). The bankruptcy law would also have the benefit of helping northern creditors conclude their business with southern debtors, then seeking to guard their property using stay laws and retroactive exemption laws of doubtful constitutionality. See Kenneth Edson St. Clair, "Debtor Relief in North Carolina during Reconstruction," *North Carolina Historical Review* 18 (July 1941): 215–35; Armstead L. Robinson, "Beyond the Realm of Social Consensus: New Meanings of Reconstruction for American History," *Journal of American History* 68 (September 1981): 276–97; and Dan T. Carter, *When the War Was Over: The Failure of Self-Reconstruction in the South, 1865–1867* (Baton Rouge: Louisiana State University Press, 1985).

14   "An Act to Establish a Uniform System of Bankruptcy throughout the United States," Cong. Rec., 39th Cong., 2nd Sess. 536, 521 (1867).

15   Lysander Spooner, *Poverty: Its Illegal Causes and Legal Cure* (Boston, 1846), 7; "Creditor vs. Debtor," *Hunt's Merchants' Magazine and Commercial Review*, August 1860, 267; J. F. B., "Expediency of a Bankruptcy Law," *American Law Register*, June 1865, 459; John Tyler Morgan quoted in "The Bankrupt Bill," *Christian Advocate*, July 12, 1866, 220; Cong. Globe, 38th Cong., 1st Sess. (1864) 2638 (statement of Thomas A. Jenckes); Cong. Globe, 39th Cong., 1st Sess. 2742 (1866) (statement of Thomas A. Jenckes) (emphasis added); Cong. Globe, 37th Cong., 3d Sess. 224 (1863) (statement of Owen Lovejoy). On free-labor ideology, see Eric Foner, *Free Soil, Free Labor, Free Men: The Ideology of the Republican Party before the Civil War* (New York: Oxford University Press, 1970); Jonathan A. Glickstein, *Concepts of Free Labor in Antebellum America* (New Haven, CT: Yale University Press, 1991); and Alex Gourevitch, *From Slavery to the Cooperative Commonwealth: Labor and Republican Liberty in the Nineteenth Century* (Cambridge: Cambridge University Press, 2015).

16   Cong. Globe, 37th Cong., 3d Sess. 224 (1863) (statement of Owen Lovejoy); Cong. Globe, 39th Cong., 1st Sess. 2742 (1866) (statement of Thomas A. Jenckes); Cong. Globe, 38th Cong., 1st Sess. (1864) 2638 (statement of Thomas A. Jenckes); Sandage, *Born Losers*, 203; J. F. B., "Expediency of a Bankruptcy Law," 459. On the imperative to work, see Rodgers, *The Work Ethic in Industrial America*.

17   On homelife in relation to slavery and freedom, see Amy Dru Stanley, "Home Life and the Morality of the Market," in *The Market Revolution in America: Social, Political, and Religious Expressions, 1800–1880*, ed. Melvyn Stokes and Stephen Conway (Charlottesville: University Press of Virginia, 1996), 74–96; Laura F. Edwards, "'The Marriage Covenant Is at the Foundation of All Our Rights': The Politics of Slave Marriages in North Carolina after Emancipation," *Law and History Review* 14 (Spring 1996): 81–124; and McCurry, "Reconstructing Belonging." Home is offered as a central theme of the postbellum era in Richard White, *The Republic for Which It Stands: The United States during Reconstruction and the Gilded Age, 1865–1896* (New York: Oxford University Press, 2017).

18   Cong. Globe, 39th Cong., 2d Sess. 981 (1867) (statement of Reverdy Johnson);
     Cong. Globe, 38th Cong., 1st Sess. 2637 (1864) (statement of Thomas A. Jenckes).
19   Cong. Globe, 39th Cong., 1st Sess. 1698 (1866) (statement of Thomas A Jenckes);
     "A Bankrupt Law," *New York Independent*, December 1864; petition quoted in
     Sandage, *Born Losers*, 195.
20   *Expense of Proceedings in Bankruptcy in United States Courts*; Senate Executive
     Document 19. 43rd Cong. 1st Sess., 1580. On the role of the Bankruptcy Act in
     preserving the power of large planters, see Elizabeth Lee Thompson, *The Recon-
     struction of Southern Debtors: Bankruptcy after the Civil War* (Athens: University
     of Georgia Press, 2004). On Republican developmental policies in this period, see
     Heather Cox Richardson, *The Greatest Nation of the Earth: Republican Economic
     Policies during the Civil War* (Cambridge, MA: Harvard University Press, 1997).
21   Bankruptcy Act of 2 March 1867, 14 Stat. 517, § 13. The incorporation of property
     exemption law into the Bankruptcy Act thus represented a merging of liberal
     understandings of freedom—with an emphasis on freedom of contract—and
     republican understandings of freedom—with a view that freedom was rooted in
     the control over productive property.
22   The major treatises on exemption laws in this period are John H. Smyth, *The
     Law of Homestead and Exemptions* (San Francisco, 1875); Alexander M. Burill,
     *A Treatise on the Law and Practice of Voluntary Assignments for the Benefit of
     Creditors* (New York, 1877); and Rufus Waples, *A Treatise on Homestead and
     Exemptions* (Chicago, 1893). See also "State Homestead Exemption Laws," *Yale
     Law Journal* 46 (April 1937): 1023–41; Joseph W. McKnight, "Protection of the
     Family Home from Seizure by Creditors: The Sources and Evolution of a Legal
     Principle," *Southwest Historical Quarterly* 86 (1983): 369–99; Paul Goodman, "The
     Emergence of Homestead Exemption Laws in the United States: Accommodation
     and Resistance to the Market Revolution, 1840–1880," *Journal of American History*
     80 (September 1993): 470–98; and James W. Ely Jr., "Homestead Exemption and
     Southern Legal Culture," in *Signposts: New Directions in Southern Legal History*,
     ed. Sally E. Hadden and Patricia Hagler Minter (Athens: University of Georgia
     Press, 2013), 298–314.
23   Significantly, the exemptions could be understood—with good reason—as signify-
     ing the retreat of the state rather than its advance. "My path lies with less Govern-
     ment, less power, less machinery," said an Ohio exemption advocate in 1850. "Let
     credit be free—trusting in the sense of honesty in men, rather than to the law."
     *Convention Reports: Official Report of Debates and Proceedings in the Convention to
     Form a New Government for the State of Ohio* (2 vols., 1850) 2:1103.
24   Wood v. Wheeler, 7 Tex. 22 (1851), Nevada Constitutional Convention (1864), and
     Walker v. Darst, 31 Tex. 682 (1869), cited in Smyth, *Law of Homestead and Exemp-
     tions*, 49–52; Franklin v. Coffee, 18 Tex. 413 (1857); Samuel Kingman quoted in
     Kansas Constitutional Convention (Topeka, 1859), 377.
25   "Exemption of Real Estate," in *The Struggle over Ratification, 1846–1847*, ed. Milo
     M. Quaife (Madison: State Historical Society of Wisconsin, 1918), 473; "The
     Issue," in *The Movement for Statehood, 1845–1846*, ed. Milo M. Quaife (Madison:
     State Historical Society of Wisconsin, 1918), 163–64; Clark v. Shannon, 1 Nev. 568
     (1865), at 571; Harris v. Haynes, 30 Mich. 140 (1874), at 141; Smyth, *Law of Home-
     stead and Exemptions*, 377; Waples, *Treatise on Homestead and Exemptions*, 793,
     795; S. A. Kingman quoted in *Kansas Constitutional Convention* (Topeka, 1859),

337. In Illinois, for example, a homestead exemption act passed in 1851 shielded the lot and home of the householder, valued up to $1,000. An amended act, passed in 1861, expanded the protection to include the debtor's family pictures and schoolbooks, household furniture, one yoke of oxen, one plow and harness, and "the tools and implements of any mechanic . . . not exceeding one hundred dollars, used for the purpose of carrying on his trade or profession, whether he be the head of a family or not" (Illinois 22nd General Assembly, Public Laws, 1st Sess. (1861), 121–22). The amended act of 1871 pressed further, naming apparel, one sewing machine, the tools and instruments of trade, the implements of any professional man, and the materials and stock necessary for carrying on business.

26 Brown v. Hebard, 20 Wis. 326 (1866), at 330; Caraker v. Matthews, 25 Ga. 571 (1858), at 571; Lehigh V. R. Co. v. James Woodring, 116 Penn. 519 (1887), at 519. In most states, it fell within the wage earner's rights to assign a portion of his un-earned wages for credit, with the largest exception being public interest laws that denied that right to government employees. On wage assignments, see Emery v. Lawrence, 62 Mass. 51 (1851); Field v. Mayor, etc., of New-York, 6 N.Y. 179 (1852); and Thayer & Williams v. Kelley, 28 Vt. 19 (1855). On garnishment and attachment, see Rufus Waples, *A Treatise on Attachment and Garnishment* (Chicago, 1895); and Roswell Shinn, *A Treatise on the American Law of Attachment and Garnishment* (Indianapolis, 1896).

27 Grimes v. Bryne, 2 Minn. 89 (1858), at 104; Brief and Argument of Appellant, Amend v. Murphy (1873), Vault No. 18662, Illinois State Archives; Wilkinson v. Alley, 45 N.H. 551 (1864). See also Perkins v. Wisner, 9 Iowa 320 (1859); Springer v. Lewis, 22 Pa. 191 (1853); Jenkins v. McNall, 27 Kan. 532 (1882); and Hickman v. Cursie 72 Ia. 528 (1887). On debt relief and planter power, see supra 13.

28 Harris v. Haynes, 30 Mich. 140 (1874), at 142; Sellers v. Bell, 94 F. 801 (1899), at 812. The record of appellate litigation indicates how often property exemptions were used. Alison Morantz finds around four thousand exemption cases reaching high state courts in the nineteenth century, "with the bulk of appellate litigation occur-ring after the Civil War." This contrasts with "appeals involving fugitive slave laws, state and federal land grants . . . and miscegenation [which] numbered only in the dozens or hundreds." Alison D. Morantz, "There's No Place Like Home: Homestead Exemption and the Constructions of Family in Nineteenth-Century America," *Law and History Review* 24 (Summer 2006): 248, 248n10. Paul Goodman, citing the low rates of exemption registrations in states that required the homesteader to formally claim the exemption, argues that the exemptions were less relevant to economic life. Between these two claims—supported by two types of evidence—may be homesteaders who were disinclined to claim the exemption when it might limit their access to credit but who were eager to use it once their gambles had failed. See Goodman, "Emergence of Homestead Exemption Laws," 497.

29 The Marshall lawsuit is also discussed in Morantz, "There's No Place Like Home," 245–95.

30 Race v. Oldridge, 90 Ill. 250 (1878), at 252–54.

31 Howard v. Marshall, 48 Tex. 471 (1878), at 5–7. On slaveholders' narratives of the plantation family, see Eugene D. Genovese, *Roll, Jordan, Roll: The World the Slaves Made* (New York: Vintage, 1974).

32 Race v. Oldridge, at 254; Howard v. Marshall, at 7.

33 Morantz notes that the Lettie Marshall case "raised the even more frightening

prospect of freed slaves preventing the lawful heirs of their former masters from acquiring family land." Morantz, "There's No Place Like Home," 290.

34 Mark Twain and Charles Dudley Warren, *The Gilded Age: A Tale of Today* (New York: Library of America, 2002 [1872]), 145, 271.

35 "Bankrupt Laws," *North-American Review* 7 (May 1818): 25.

36 John Commons, Ulrich B. Phillips, Eugene A. Gilmore, Helen L. Sumner, and John B. Andrews, eds., *A Documentary History of American Industrial Society* (5 vols., Cleveland: Arthur H. Clark, 1910), 5:28; W. G. Maxwell, "The Rights of Debtors," *Albany Law Journal*, March 20, 1889, 311. On private mechanisms of risk management, see Levy, *Freaks of Fortune*. On the saga of bankruptcy law, see David Skeel, *Debt's Dominion: A History of Bankruptcy Law in America* (Princeton, NJ: Princeton University Press, 2001). On Populism and the currency question, see Lawrence Goodwyn, *Democratic Promise: The Populist Moment in America* (New York: Oxford University Press, 1976); Elizabeth Sanders, *Roots of Reform: Farmers, Workers, and the American State, 1877–1917* (Chicago: University of Chicago Press, 1999); and Charles Postel, *The Populist Vision* (New York: Oxford University Press, 2007).

37 W. E. B. Du Bois, *The Souls of Black Folk* (New York: Oxford University Press, 2007 [1903]), 88.

CHAPTER TWO

Portions of chapter 2 were originally published in Daniel Platt, "The Domestication of Credit," *History of the Present* 9, no. 2: 142–65, copyright 2019 Illinois University Press. All rights reserved. Republished by permission of the present publisher, Duke University Press.

1 Ella Gertrude Clanton Thomas, *The Secret Eye: The Journal of Ella Gertrude Clanton Thomas, 1848–1889*, ed. Virginia Ingraham Burr (Chapel Hill: University of North Carolina Press, 1990), 291, 364, 310. On the experiences of indebted planters, see David Silkenat, *Moments of Despair: Suicide, Divorce, and Debt in Civil War Era North Carolina* (Chapel Hill: University of North Carolina Press, 2011); and Elizabeth Lee Thompson, *The Reconstruction of Southern Debtors: Bankruptcy after the Civil War* (Athens: University of Georgia Press, 2004).

2 Thomas, *Secret Eye*, 364, 326. While Thomas claimed to be at peace with the abolition of slavery, she also resisted the loss of "her negroes" and sought to keep one formerly enslaved child as a servant in her family against the child's mother's wishes. Thomas, 267–68, 370; see also Stephanie McCurry, "Reconstructing Belonging: The Thirteenth Amendment at Work in the World," in *Intimate States: Gender, Sexuality, and Governance in Modern U.S. History*, ed. Margot Canaday, Nancy F. Cott, and Robert O. Self (Chicago: University of Chicago Press, 2021), 28–30.

3 Thomas, *Secret Eye*, 318, 351.

4 Cong. Globe, 39th Cong., 2d Sess. 981 (1867) (statement of Reverdy Johnson). On the gendered experience of failure generally, see Toby Ditz, "Shipwrecked; or, Masculinity Imperiled: Mercantile Representations of Failure and the Gendered Self in Eighteenth-Century Philadelphia," *Journal of American History* 81, no. 1 (June 1994): 51–80; and Scott Sandage, "Gender and the Economics of the Sentimental Market in Nineteenth-Century America," *Social Politics* 6 (Summer 1999): 105–30.

5 This chapter draws on a robust literature on married women's property and contract

rights that, generally speaking, has not been incorporated into the new history of capitalism. This omission is peculiar, given that married women's commercial rights were directly implicated in the legal history of risk, financialization, and dynastic wealth. See Norma Basch, *In the Eyes of the Law: Women, Marriage, and Property in Nineteenth-Century New York* (Ithaca, NY: Cornell University Press, 1982); Richard H. Chused, "Late Nineteenth Century Married Women's Property Law: Reception of the Early Married Women's Property Acts by Courts and Legislatures," *American Journal of Legal History* 29 (January 1985): 3–35; Amy Dru Stanley, "Conjugal Bonds and Wage Labor: Rights of Contract in the Age of Emancipation," *Journal of American History* 75 (September 1988): 471–500; Reva Siegel, "The Modernization of American Status Law: Adjudicating Wives' Rights to Earnings, 1860–1930," *Georgetown Law Journal* 82 (1994): 2127–211; and Ariela R. Dubler, "In the Shadow of Marriage: Single Women and the Legal Construction of the Family and the State," *Yale Law Journal* 112 (May 2003): 11641–715. On feminism in this period generally, see Suzanne M. Marilley, *Woman Suffrage and the Origins of Liberal Feminism in the United States, 1820–1920* (Cambridge, MA: Harvard University Press, 1996); Rebecca Edwards, *Angels in the Machinery: Gender in American Party Politics from the Civil War to the Progressive Era* (New York: Oxford University Press, 1997); Ellen Carol DuBois and Richard Cándida Smith, eds., *Elizabeth Cady Stanton: Feminist as Thinker* (New York: New York University Press, 2007); and Christine Stansell, *The Feminist Promise, 1792 to the Present* (New York: Modern Library, 2010).

6   Harriet Bailey Blaine to Mrs. James G. Blaine, August 14, 1879, in *Letters of Mrs. James G. Blaine*, ed. Harriet S. Blaine Beale (2 vols., 1908), 1:159; Cong. Rec., 55th Cong., 1st Sess. 733 (1890). The new history of capitalism has been criticized for effacing women's presence in the financial economy. See Ellen Hartigan-O'Connor, "Gender's Value in the History of Capitalism," *Journal of the Early Republic* 36 (Winter 2016): 613–35; and Amy Dru Stanley, "Histories of Capitalism and Sex Difference," *Journal of the Early Republic* 36 (Summer 2016): 343–50. Recent correctives to this trend include Shennette Garrett-Scott, *Banking on Freedom: Black Women in U.S. Finance before the New Deal* (New York: Columbia University Press, 2019); Stephanie E. Jones-Rogers, *They Were Her Property: White Women as Slave Owners in the American South* (New Haven, CT: Yale University Press, 2019); and Sara T. Damiano, *To Her Credit: Women, Finance, and the Law in Eighteenth-Century New England Cities* (Baltimore: Johns Hopkins University Press, 2021).

7   Browne family account books in Additional Papers of the Albert Gallatin Browne Family, 1805–1997, series II, Schlesinger Library, Harvard University; Beth G. Crabtree and James W. Patton, eds., *Journal of a Secesh Lady: The Diary of Catherine Ann Devereux Edmondston, 1860–1866*, (Raleigh, 1879), 4; [Alice B. Haven], *Cousin Alice: A Memoir of Alice B. Haven*, ed. Cornelia H. B. Richards (1868), 175; Jeanne Boydston, *Home and Work: Housework, Wages, and the Ideology of Labor in the Early Republic* (New York: Oxford University Press, 1990), 109. Thavolia Glymph suggests that household accounting did not generally fall to white plantation women of the South until after the Civil War. Thavolia Glymph, *Out of the House of Bondage: The Transformation of the Plantation Household* (Cambridge: Cambridge University Press, 2008), 63–97.

8   Luna Kellie, *A Prairie Populist: The Memoirs of Luna Kellie* (Iowa City: University of Iowa Press, 1992 [1925]), 84–85. Scott Sandage notes that women often wrote begging letters on behalf of their husbands during periods of financial distress. See Sandage, "Gender and the Sentimental Market," 105–30.

9   *Six Hundred Dollars a Year: A Wife's Effort at Low Living, under High Prices* (1867), 72; Elise Amalie Tyede Waerenskjold to Emilie Syversten, June 9, 1869, in *The Lady with the Pen: Elize Waerenskjold in Texas*, ed. C. A. Clausen (1961), 74; Kellie, *Prairie Populist*, 101.

10   John Ise, *Sod and Stubble*, unabridged and annotated ed., with additional material by Von Rothenberger (Topeka: University Press of Kansas, 1996 [1936]), 166, 197. The wife's advisory role was also double edged, in that having played some role in the decision to contract the debt—even if that role was simply saying nothing as the husband did as he wished—she was also available to be blamed for the debt if it became oppressive.

11   Thomas, *Secret Eye*, 353, 406.

12   Wendy A. Woloson, *In Hock: Pawning in America from Independence through the Great Depression* (Chicago: University of Chicago Press, 2009), 94; G. Frank Brockway to "Friend Jones" (1875) in Woloson, *In Hock*, 93; William Pickens, *Bursting Bonds* (Boston: Jordan & More, 1929), 26; William H. Holtzclaw, *The Black Man's Burden* (New York: Neale, 1915), 35. Wendy Woloson observes that women were better equipped to borrow at the pawnshop because "More than men, women knew the relative values of various domestic articles (including linens, clothing, and kitchen utensils)." Woloson, *In Hock*, 94.

13   Cong. Rec., 55th Cong., 1st Sess. 733 (1890); Thomas, *Secret Eye*, 326.

14   Hamlin Garland, "A Good Fellow's Wife," *Main-Travelled Roads* (New York: Harper & Brothers, 1956 [1891]), 246.

15   George E. Harris, *A Treatise on the Law of Contracts by Married Women* (Albany, 1887), 638, 6; *Chicago Legal News*, October 31, 1868, quoted in Stanley, "Conjugal Bonds and Wage Labor," 485. On the reform of coverture, see supra 5; and Hendrik Hartog, *Man and Wife in America: A History* (Cambridge, MA: Harvard University Press, 2002). On key differences between laws protecting the wife's property and laws protecting her earnings, see Stanley, "Conjugal Bonds and Wage Labor," 492–93.

16   Frecking v. Rolland, 53 N.Y. 423 (1873), at 425; Cashman v. Henry, 75 N.Y. 103 (1878), at 113, 115. See also Siegel, "Modernization of American Status Law," 2150–54. On the legal construction of responsibility generally, see Susanna L. Blumenthal, *Law and the Modern Mind: Consciousness and Responsibility in American Legal Culture* (Cambridge, MA: Harvard University Press, 2016).

17   De Vries v. Conklin, 22 Mich. 255 (1871), at 259–60. On the doctrine of charging, see David Stewart, "Contracts of Married Women," *Albany Law Journal* 20 (1879): 244–46. On gift and consideration, see Roy Kreitner, *Calculating Promises: The Emergence of Modern American Contract Doctrine* (Palo Alto, CA: Stanford University Press, 2007), 15–42.

18   Bailey v. Hill, 77 Va. 492 (1888), at 496; Marietta Stow, *Probate Confiscation: Unjust Laws which Govern Women* (Boston, 1876), 73; May Wright Sewall, "Business Education for Women," *Woman's Journal*, December 1884, 111.

19   John Whitehead, "The Legal Status of Woman—no. 2," *Woman's Journal*, October 29, 1870, 338; Amy Dru Stanley, *From Bondage to Contract: Wage Labor, Marriage, and the Market in the Age of Slave Emancipation* (Cambridge: Cambridge University Press, 1998), 212; "Fraudulent Conveyances to Wife," *Central Law Journal*, December 13, 1878, 464; Emma R. Coe quoted in *National Citizen*, April 1880; "Legal Rights of Married Women," *Friends' Intelligencer*, October 11, 1884, 558. On fraud, commingling, and the question of which of the wife's labors

constituted "house work" and thus remained the property of the husband, see
Birkbeck v. Ackroyd, 74 N.Y. 356 (1878); Dawes v. Rodier, 125 Mass. 421 (1878);
Cunningham v. Hanney, 12 Ill. App. 437 (1883); Coleman v. Burr, 93 N.Y. 17 (1883);
Siegel, "Modernization of American Status Law," 2168–96; and Stanley, "Conjugal
Bonds and Wage Labor," 495–99.

20 Illinois Rev. Stat. § 68.15 (1874); "An Important Decision Touching the Liabilities
of a Married Woman," *Chicago Daily Tribune*, October 11, 1882, 12; Keller v. Phillips, 7 Trans. App. 124, at 129.

21 Susan B. Anthony and Ida Husted Harper, eds., *The History of Woman Suffrage*
(4 vols., Rochester, 1902), 4:326, 793; Marquardt v. Flaugher, 60 Iowa 148; Watkins v. Mason, 11 Ore 72, at 74; Frost v. Parker, 65 Iowa 178, at 181; "Husband and
Wife," *Michigan Law Review* 19 (April 1921): 658; "Statutory Liability of Wife for
Necessaries for Family," *Central Law Journal* 27 (September 21, 1888): 279.

22 Smedley v. Felt, 41 Iowa 591 (1875), and Lawrence v. Sinnamon, 24 Iowa 82 (1867),
quoted in "Statutory Liability of Wife," 279.

23 William W. Story, *A Treatise on the Law of Contracts*, 4th ed. (Boston, 1856), 148;
Elizabeth Cady Stanton, Susan B. Anthony, and Matilda Joslyn Gage, eds., *History
of Woman Suffrage* (3 vols., Rochester, NY, 1886), 3:324; Stow, *Probate Confiscation*, 73.

24 Smedley v. Felt, 41 Iowa 591 (1875), in "Statutory Liability of Wife," 279; Thomas,
Secret Eye, 319.

25 *Kansas Constitutional Convention* (Topeka, 1859), 700, 337.

26 Chase v. Abbott, 20 Iowa 154 (1866), at 15. On dower, see Marylynn Salmon,
Women and the Law of Property in Early America (Chapel Hill: University of
North Carolina Press, 1986). These two positions mirrored the divide between
liberal and sentimental feminism in the late nineteenth century. See Stansell, *The
Feminist Promise*, 119–46.

27 E. M. Randall, "Homestead Exemption, Married Women's Rights, Etc., in
Florida," *Semi-tropical*, March 1, 1876, 131. On sentimental feminism, see Paula
Baker, "The Domestication of Politics: Women and American Political Soci-
ety, 1780–1920," *American Historical Review* 89 (June 1984): 620–47; Elizabeth
Maddock Dillon, *The Gender of Freedom: Fictions of Liberalism and the Literary
Public Sphere* (Palo Alto, CA: Stanford University Press, 2004); and Stansell, *The
Feminist Promise*, 119–46. On sentiment and the rights claims of other dependents,
see Susan J. Pearson, *The Rights of the Defenseless: Protecting Animals and Children
in Gilded Age America* (Chicago: University of Chicago Press, 2011).

28 Elizabeth Fries Ellet, *The New Cyclopaedia of Domestic Economy* (1872), 17; Catharine Beecher, *A Treatise on Domestic Economy* (1845), 188; *Six Hundred Dollars a
Year*, 11; Peter E. Earling, *Whom to Trust: A Practical Treatise on Mercantile Credits*
(1890), 149; S. D. Power, *Anna Maria's Housekeeping Book* (1884), 64–65.

29 *Convention Reports: Official Report of Debates and Proceedings in the Convention
to Form a New Government for the State of Ohio* (2 vols., 1850) 2:1103; Samuel
W. Small, ed., *A Stenographic Report of the Proceedings of the Constitutional
Convention Held in Atlanta, Georgia* (Atlanta, 1877), 464; *Kansas Constitutional
Convention* (Topeka, 1920 [1859]), 318. *Report of the Debates and Proceedings of
the Convention for the Revision of the Constitution of the State of Indiana* (2 vols.,
1850), 1:757; David A. Noggle, "Exemption and the Rights of Married Women,"
speech, December 7, 1846, in *The Convention of 1846*, ed. Milo M. Quaife
(1919), 662.

30   *Debates and Proceedings of the Constitutional Convention of the State of California* (3 vols., 1881), 2:1127, 1128.

31   Morris v. Ward, 5 Kan. 239 (1869), at 697; Helm v. Helm, 11 Kan. 19 (1873); Hotchkiss v. Brooks, 93 Ill. 386 (1879), at 387.

32   Speidel v. Schlosser, 13 W. Va. 686 (1879), at 697; Jane M. Slocum, "The Law of Coverture," *Woman's Journal*, September 5, 1874, 289; Roach v. Karr, 18 Kan. 529 (1877), at 533.

33   *Debates and Proceedings of California*, 1127; Mutual Loan Co. v. Martell, 222 U.S. 225 (1911), at 226; *Charlotte News*, February 8, 1889; Cong. Rec., 55th Cong., 1st Sess. (1890), 735 (statement of J. C. Spooner).

34   Small, *Stenographic Report of the Constitutional Convention in Atlanta*, 464.

35   T[homas] W[entworth] H[igginson], "The Honesty of Women," *Harper's Bazaar*, September 3, 1887, 610.

36   Thomas, *Secret Eye*, 318, 351; Mary A. Lipscomb, "Woman as a Financier," in *The Congress of Women Held in the Women's Building, World's Columbian Exposition, Chicago, USA, 1893* (1894), 469; Mrs. E. B. B. Reesor, "Women as Bankers," *Bankers' Magazine*, October 1909, 513. On women in banking during this period, see Genevieve Gildersleeve, *Women in Banks: The History of the National Association of Bank Women* (Washington, DC: Public Affairs Press, 1959); Nancy Marie Robertson, "'The Principles of Sound Banking and Financial *Noblesse Oblige*': Women's Departments in U.S. Banks at the Turn of the Twentieth Century," in *Women and Their Money, 1700–1950: Essays on Women and Finance*, ed. Anne Laurence, Josephine Maltby, and Janette Rutterford (London: Routledge, 2008), 243–53; and Garrett-Scott, *Banking on Freedom*. On feminism in the early twentieth century, see Baker, "The Domestication of Politics," 620–47; and Stansell, *The Feminist Promise*, 119–76.

37   Ella A. Trapp, "The Loan Business from a Woman's Point of View," *Industrial Lender News*, July 1923, 5; William Hirsch, letter to the editor, *Industrial Lender News*, April 1924, 6; E. I. Levitt, "Service and Advertising," *Industrial Lender News*, December 1924, 10.

38   *Social and Labor Needs of Farm Women*, US Department of Agriculture, report no. 103 (Washington, DC: Government Printing Office, 1915), 44.

CHAPTER THREE

1   Theodore Rosengarten, *All God's Dangers: The Life of Nate Shaw* (Chicago: University of Chicago Press, 1974), 106–8, 181.

2   W. E. B. Du Bois, *The Souls of Black Folk* (New York: Oxford University Press, 2007 [1903]), 87. George K. Holmes, "The Peons of the South," *Annals of the American Academy of Political and Social Science* 4 (September 1893): 267. On the political economy of the postbellum South, see C. Vann Woodward, *Origins of the New South, 1877–1913* (Baton Rouge: Louisiana State University Press, 1951); Steve Hahn, *The Roots of Southern Populism: Yeoman Farmers and the Transformation of the Georgia Upcountry, 1850–1890* (New York: Oxford University Press, 1983); Jacquelyn Dowd Hall, James L. Leloudis, Robert R. Korstad, Mary Murphy, and Lu Ann Jones, eds., *Like a Family: The Making of a Southern Cotton Mill World* (New York: W. W. Norton, 1987); Harold D. Woodman, "The Political Economy of the New South: Retrospects and Prospects," *Journal of Southern History* 67 (November 2001): 789–810; and Roger L. Ransom and Richard P. Sutch, *One Kind of Freedom: The Economic Consequences of Emancipation*, 2nd ed. (Cambridge: Cambridge University Press, 2001).

3   Holmes, "Peons of the South," 267; Herbert D. Ward, "Peonage in America," *Cosmopolitan*, August 1905, 423; George W. Cable, *The Negro Question* (New York, 1898), 148–49; Du Bois, *Souls of Black Folk*, 81, 103, 88. On the centrality of indebted labor to agriculture globally in this era, see Sven Beckert, *Empire of Cotton: A Global History* (New York: Vintage, 2015), 274–339; and Mishal Khan, "The Indebted among the 'Free': Producing Indian Labor through the Layers of Racial Capitalism," in *Histories of Racial Capitalism*, ed. Destin Jenkins and Justin Leroy (New York: Columbia University Press, 2021), 85–110.

4   Interview with Sylvia Cannon, South Carolina, WPA Narratives. On debt and indebted labor as central to modern African American history, see Saidiya Hartman, *Scenes of Subjection: Terror, Slavery, and Self-Making in Nineteenth-Century America* (New York: Oxford University Press, 1997); Leon F. Litwack, *Trouble in Mind: Black Southerners in the Age of Jim Crow* (New York: Vintage, 1998), 114–78; Aaron Carico, "Freedom as Accumulation," *History of the Present* 6 (Spring 2016): 1–31; and Destin Jenkins and Justin Leroy, eds., *Histories of Racial Capitalism* (New York: Columbia University Press, 2021). On reconciliation, see Nina Silber, *The Romance of Reunion: Northerners and the South, 1865–1900* (Chapel Hill: University of North Carolina Press, 1993); David W. Blight, *Race and Reunion: The Civil War in American Memory* (Cambridge, MA: Harvard University Press, 2001); and Caroline Janney, *Remembering the Civil War: Reunion and the Limits of Reconciliation* (Chapel Hill: University of North Carolina Press, 2013). On unfree labor in this era generally, see Alex Lichtenstein, *Twice the Work of Free Labor: The Political Economy of Convict Labor in the New South* (London: Verso, 1996); Gunther Peck, *Reinventing Free Labor: Padrones and Immigrant Workers in the North American West, 1880–1930* (Cambridge: Cambridge University Press, 2000); Rebecca McLennan, *The Crisis of Imprisonment: Protest, Politics, and the Making of the American Penal State, 1776–1941* (Berkeley: University of California Press, 2008); and Sarah Haley, *No Mercy Here: Gender, Punishment, and the Making of Jim Crow Modernity* (Chapel Hill: University of North Carolina Press, 2016).

5   Du Bois, *Souls of Black Folk*, 102; Eric Foner, *Reconstruction: America's Unfinished Revolution, 1863–1877* (New York: Harper and Rowe, 1988), 365, 379. The first Black governor of Louisiana was P. B. S. Pinchback. The first Black lieutenant governors of Louisiana, Mississippi, and South Carolina were Pinchback, Alexander K. Davis, and Alonzo Ransier, respectively. The Black US Congressmen representing southern states in this era were, from Alabama, Jeremiah Haralson, James T. Rapier, and Benjamin S. Turner; from Florida, Josiah T. Walls; from Georgia, Jefferson Long; from Louisiana, Charles E. Nash; from Mississippi, Blanche K. Bruce, John R. Lynch, and Hiram Revels; from North Carolina, John A. Hyman; from South Carolina, Richard H. Cain, Robert C. DeLarge, Robert B. Elliot, Joseph H. Rainey, Alonzo J. Ransier, and Robert Smalls. See Eric Foner, *Freedom's Lawmakers: A Directory of Black Officeholders during Reconstruction* (Baton Rouge: Louisiana State University Press, 1996).

6   *Proceedings of the Constitutional Convention of South Carolina* (Charleston, 1868), 727, 725, 881–82; J. Henri Burch quoted in *Report and Testimony of the Select Committee of the United States Senate to Investigate the Causes of the Removal of the Negroes from the Southern States to the North States*, S. Rpt. 693 (3 vol., Washington DC, 1880), 2:220; Georgia, Session Laws of 1870, title X, no. 62, 70–74; *Brenham (TX) Weekly Banner*, January 1, 1878. On Sledge, the Black legislator from Texas, see Nell Irvin Painter, *Exodusters: Black Migration to Kansas after Reconstruction*

(New York: W. W. Norton, 1992), 37. Burch also testified about proposing a law that would have prohibited whites from lending to Blacks.

7 Burch quoted in *Report and Testimony*, 2:220; W. J. Whipper, *Proceedings of South Carolina*, 463; Foner, *Reconstruction: America's Unfinished Revolution*, 374.

8 Quoted in Foner, *Reconstruction: America's Unfinished Revolution*, 590. Political exclusion was not instantaneous and took place in the context of Populist political organizing among Black and white farmers—a project in which justice in debt was paramount. See Woodward, *Origins of the New South*; Jane Dailey, *Before Jim Crow: The Politics of Race in Postemancipation Virginia* (Chapel Hill: University of North Carolina Press, 2000); and Michael Perman, *Struggle for Mastery: Disfranchisement in the South, 1888–1908* (Chapel Hill: University of North Carolina Press, 2001).

9 P. H. Edge quoted in Samuel W. Small, ed., *A Stenographic Report of the Proceedings of the Constitutional Convention Held in Atlanta, Georgia* (Atlanta, 1877), 451; Burch quoted in *Report and Testimony*, 2:220 (see also "A Wholesome Reform," *Times-Democrat* [New Orleans], January 12, 1876); Du Bois, *Souls of Black Folk*, 116. A. D. Smith, review of Marshall M. Strong's speech, *Milwaukee Courier*, in *The Struggle over Ratification, 1846–1847*, ed. Milo M. Quaife (Madison: State Historical Society of Wisconsin, 1918), 575–76. The exemption waiver—whether entrusted to both husband and wife or only one spouse—was an important technology in the repeal effort, as lawmakers could introduce waivers confident that furnishing merchants would then require poor borrowers to waive their rights if they were to receive credit. At the same time, trespassing and enclosure laws (which had been suspended under Republican rule) were renewed and enhanced to prevent poor Blacks from subsisting on common lands. See Foner, *Reconstruction: America's Unfinished Revolution*, 589, 593–98. Another measure of the white South's turn against protective debt law was its withdrawn support for the Bankruptcy Act of 1867, which was repealed with southern votes in 1878. This was likely less because of the release that bankruptcy could offer to African Americans and more because of the projection of federal power that bankruptcy represented. See Elizabeth Lee Thompson, *The Reconstruction of Southern Debtors: Bankruptcy after the Civil War* (Athens: University of Georgia Press, 2004), 135–41.

10 Clarence H. Poe, "Rich Kingdom of Cotton," *World's Work* 9 (November 1904), quoted in Carico, "Freedom as Accumulation," 9. See also Harold D. Woodman, "Post–Civil War Southern Agriculture and the Law," *Agricultural History* 53 (January 1979): 332–33; Harold D. Woodman, *New South—New Law: The Legal Foundations of Credit and Labor Relations in the Postbellum Agricultural South* (Baton Rouge: Louisiana State University Press, 1995); Scott P. Marler, "Two Kinds of Freedom: Mercantile Development and Labor Systems in Louisiana Cotton and Sugar Parishes after the Civil War," *Agricultural History* 85 (Spring 2011): 225–51; and Adam Wolkoff, "Every Man His Own Avenger: Landlord Remedies and the Antebellum Roots of the Crop Lien and Chattel Mortgage in the United States," *Law and History Review* 35 (February 2017): 131–54. Crop liens also limited the kinds of crops that could be grown, for merchants and landowners would not generally lend on security other than for tobacco or cotton. This further eroded the opportunities for subsistence farming and made farmers more dependent on market prices and credit. See Hall et al., *Like a Family*, 5.

11 Testimony of Henry Adams, Shreveport, *Report and Testimony*, 3:117; Charles Otken, *The Ills of the South or Related Causes Hostile to the General Prosperity of the Southern People* (New York, 1894), 11; "'Pernicious Measure' Passed in House,"

Morning Sun (Tallahassee, Florida), May 7, 1907. On surety and false-pretense laws, along with other measures intended to limit Black mobility and labor choice, see Pete Daniel, *The Shadow of Slavery: Peonage in the South, 1901–1969* (Urbana: University of Illinois Press, 1972); William Cohen, *At Freedom's Edge: Black Mobility and the Southern White Quest for Racial Control, 1861–1915* (Baton Rouge: Louisiana State University Press, 1991); and Douglas A. Blackmon, *Slavery by Another Name: The Re-enslavement of Black Americans from the Civil War to World War II* (New York: Random House, 2008).

12   Du Bois, *Souls of Black Folk*, 81.

13   William Pickens, *Bursting Bonds* (Boston: Jordan & More, 1929), 28–29; O. S. B. Wall, *Report and Testimony*, 1:29; Testimony of Ike Worthy, *Born in Slavery*, Arkansas Narratives, vol. 2, accessed July 15, 2021, http://memory.loc.gov/ammem/snhtml/snhome.html; Testimony of "Aunt" Hannah Allen, *Born in Slavery*, Missouri Narratives, vol. 10, accessed July 15, 2021, http://memory.loc.gov/ammem/snhtml/snhome.html; Joseph Holley, *You Can't Build a Chimney from the Top: The South through the Life of a Negro Educator* (New York: William-Frederick Press, 1948), 161. See also Leon Litwack, *Been in the Storm So Long: The Aftermath of Slavery* (New York: Vintage, 1980), 387–449.

14   Du Bois, *Souls of Black Folk*, 101; Arkansas freedman quoted in Foner, *Reconstruction: America's Unfinished Revolution*, 408; Mary and Aaron Matthews quoted in *Such as Us: Southern Voices of the Thirties*, ed. Tom E. Terrill and Jerrold Hirsch (Chapel Hill: University of North Carolina Press, 1939), 89; Pickens, *Bursting Bonds*, 29. The language in the Matthews quotation has been altered to remove the written dialect that many white ethnographers used when recording Black speech in this period. For a longer comment on the problem of written dialect, and the appropriateness of standardizing it, see Carole Emberton, *To Walk About in Freedom: The Long Emancipation of Priscilla Joyner* (New York: W. W. Norton, 2022), xxv. On theft and forms of everyday resistance to Jim Crow, see Robin D. G. Kelley, "'We Are Not What We Seem': Rethinking Black Working-Class Opposition in the Jim Crow South," *Journal of American History* 80 (June 1993): 75–112. On accounting and power generally, see Caitlin Rosenthal, *Accounting for Slavery: Masters and Management* (Cambridge, MA: Harvard University Press, 2018); and Michael Zakim, *Accounting for Capitalism: The World the Clerk Made* (Chicago: University of Chicago Press, 2018). Examples of African Americans successfully using account books in litigation—primarily when they were creditors rather than debtors and largely before 1900—are found in Melissa Melewski, *Litigating across the Color Line: Civil Cases between Black and White Southerners from the End of Slavery to Civil Rights* (New York: Oxford University Press, 2018), 98–108.

15   Testimony of Henry Blake, *Born in Slavery: Slave Narratives from the Federal Writers' Project, 1936–1938*, Arkansas Narratives, vol. 2, accessed July 15, 2021, http://memory.loc.gov/ammem/snhtml/snhome.html; letter from the Laboring Men and Women of Alabama, in *Report and Testimony*, 3:147; William H. Holtzclaw, *The Black Man's Burden* (New York: Neale, 1915), 148–49, 138.

16   Jake Dunwoodie quoted in Carico, "Freedom as Accumulation," 1; Holtzclaw, *The Black Man's Burden*, 138. On the discourse of savings and thrift generally, see James Livingston, *Against Thrift: Why Consumer Culture Is Good for the Economy, the Environment, and Your Soul* (New York: Basic Books, 2011); and Nicholas Osborne, "Little Capitalists: The Social Economy of Saving in the United States, 1816–1914" (PhD diss., Columbia University, 2014). On the expression of the self-help ethic in

the rise of Black-owned financial institutions, see Mehrsa Baradaran, *The Color of Money: Black Banks and the Racial Wealth Gap* (Cambridge, MA: Harvard University Press, 2019); and Shenette Garrett-Scott, *Banking on Freedom: Black Women in U.S. Finance before the New Deal* (New York: Columbia University Press, 2019).

17 Edward Leonard, St. Louis, testimony, in *Report and Testimony*, 2:61; Henry Adams, Shreveport, testimony, in *Report and Testimony*, 3:117. See also Painter, *Exodusters*.

18 Pickens, *Bursting Bonds*, 13, 29.

19 Ex parte Riley, 94 Ala. 82 (1891), at 85; State v. Leak, 62 S.C. 405 (1902); "Constitutional Law—Imprisonment for Debt—Peonage," *Michigan Law Review* 6 (April 1908): 504; State v. Williams, 150 N.C. 802 (1909), at 803; "Petition for Writ of Habeas Corpus for Enoch and Elijah Drayton," February 28, 1907, box 21, file 50–354, Department of Justice, National Archives II, Record Group 60 (hereafter DOJ, NA, RG 60). On African American legal resistance to Jim Crow, see Barbara Young Welke, *Recasting American Liberty: Gender, Race, Law, and the Railroad Revolution, 1865–1920* (Cambridge: Cambridge University Press, 2001), 249–375; Kate Masur, *An Example for All the Land: Emancipation and the Struggle over Equality in Washington, D.C.* (Chapel Hill: University of North Carolina Press, 2011); Melewski, *Litigating across the Color Line*; and Myisha Shuntez Eatmon, "Public Wrongs, Private Rights: African Americans, Private Law, and White Violence during Jim Crow" (PhD diss., Northwestern University, 2020).

20 Andrew Salter to William H. Armbrecht, January 20, 1911, box 12, file 50–106, DOJ, NA, RG 60; Alexander Ackerman, assistant US Attorney for the Southern District of Georgia, report, November 9, 1910, box 1, file 50–0, DOJ, NA, RG 60; Corrie Mason to Judge Thomas G. Jones, July 2, 1912, box 13, 50–119, DOJ, NA, RG 60; D. P. Johnson to attorney general, March 30, 1907, box 12, file 50–85, DOJ, NA, RG 60; Warren Reese to Attorney General James C. McReynolds, June 4, 1912, box 13, 50–122, DOJ, NA, RG 60; Lettie James, Viola James, Sam James, and Ed James, affidavit, and B. C. Barganeer to Lettie James, letter dated January 5, 1912, included in William H. Armbrecht to George Wickersham, April 6, 1912, box 13, file 50–116, DOJ, NA, RG 60.

21 Bailey v. Alabama, 219 U.S. 219 (1911), at 227–28.

22 Booker T. Washington, "The Atlanta Exposition Address," in *Up from Slavery* (New York: Doubleday, Page, 1901), 218. The most thorough investigation of Washington's role in the *Bailey* case (which was not made known to the public at the time) is Daniel, *Shadow of Slavery*, 65–81. Discussions of the legal dimensions of the case include Benno C. Schmidt Jr., "Principle and Prejudice: The Supreme Court and Race in the Progressive Era: Part 2: The Peonage Cases," *Columbia Law Review* 82 (May 1982): 646–718; Aziz Huq, "Peonage and Contractual Liberty," *Columbia Law Review* 101 (2001): 351–91; Robert J. Steinfeld, *The Invention of Free Labor: The Employment Relation in English and American Law and Culture, 1350–1870* (Chapel Hill: University of North Carolina Press, 1991), 278–85; and Noah Zatz, "State Power and the Construction of Contractual Freedom: Labor and Coercion in *Bailey v. Alabama*," *LPE Blog*, November 24, 2017, https://lpeproject.org/blog/state-power-and-the-construction-of-contractual-freedom -labor-and-coercion-in-bailey-v-alabama.

23 Brief for the U.S. Attorney General as Amicus Curiae, *Bailey v. Alabama*, 219 U.S. 219, at 21; Brief for Plaintiff (by Fred S. Ball), *Bailey v. Alabama*, 219 U.S. 219, at 22.

24 Cong. Globe, 39th Cong., 2d Sess. 240 (1867) (statement of Charles Sumner); Brief for the U.S. Attorney General, Bailey, at 24; Brief for Plaintiff (Ball), Bailey,

at 20, 45. The question of whether it fell within Congress's authority to enact the Peonage Act—which regulated "ordinary relations of individuals to individual [which were typically] subject to the control of the states and not to that of the general government"—was decided affirmatively in Clyatt v. U.S., 197 U.S. 207 (1905); Clyatt, at 207.

25 Brief for Defendant (by Alexander M. Garber and Thomas W. Martin), Bailey v. Alabama 219 U.S. 219, at 13–14; Supplemental Brief for Defendant (by Alexander M. Garber and Thomas W. Martin), Bailey v. Alabama, 219 U.S. 219, at 13.

26 Brief for Defendant (by Garber and Martin), Bailey, at 23, 25; Soon Hing v. Crowley, 113 U.S. 703 (1885), at 710–11.

27 Tillman quoted in Woodward, *Origins of the New South*, 73; Civil Rights Cases, 109 U.S. 3 (1883); Plessy v. Ferguson, 163 U.S. 537 (1896); Williams v. Mississippi, 170 U.S. 213 (1898). See also Benno C. Schmidt, Jr., "Principle and Prejudice: The Supreme Court and Race in the Progressive Era: Part 1: The Heyday of Jim Crow," *Columbia Law Review* 82 (April 1982): 444–24; Schmidt Jr., "Principle and Prejudice: Part 2: The Peonage Cases"; Benno C. Schmidt Jr., "Principle and Prejudice: The Supreme Court and Race in the Progressive Era: Part 3: Black Disenfranchisement from the KKK to the Grandfather Clause," *Columbia Law Review* 82 (June 1982): 835–905; and Michael J. Klarman, *From Jim Crow to Civil Rights: The Supreme Court and the Struggle for Racial Equality* (New York: Oxford University Press, 2004).

28 "Jim Crow credit regime" refers here to a regime of labor coercion through debt. This is different from the regime of exclusionary credit policy, enacted in the New Deal era, that Mehrsa Baradaran describes using the same term. See Mehrsa Baradaran, "Jim Crow Credit," *UC Irvine Law Review* 9 (May 2019): 887–952.

29 *Bailey*, at 245, 246.

30 Lochner v. New York, 198 U.S. 45 (1905), at 76. On the social turn in modern thought, see Dorothy Ross, *The Emergence of American Social Science* (Cambridge: Cambridge University Press, 1990); James T. Kloppenberg, *Uncertain Victory: Social Democracy and Progressivism in European and American Thought, 1870–1920* (New York: Oxford University Press, 1986); James Livingston, *Pragmatism and the Political Economy of Cultural Revolution, 1850–1940* (Chapel Hill: University of North Carolina Press, 1994); Wilfred McClay, *The Masterless: Self and Society in Modern America* (Chapel Hill: University of North Carolina Press, 1994); Louis Menand, *The Metaphysical Club: A Story of Ideas in America* (New York: Farrar, Straus and Giroux, 2001); and Jeffrey Sklansky, *The Soul's Economy: Market Society and Selfhood in American Thought, 1820–1920* (Chapel Hill: University of North Carolina Press, 2002). On Holmes and the revolt against laissez-faire, see Morton J. Horowitz, *The Transformation of American Law, 1870–1960: The Crisis of Legal Orthodoxy* (Cambridge, MA: Harvard University Press, 1992).

31 Bailey, at 245; Holmes to Frederick Pollock, August 30, 1929, in Mark de Wolfe Howe, ed., *Homes–Pollock Letters: The Correspondence of Mr. Justice Holmes and Sir Frederick Pollock, 1847–1932* (2 vols., Cambridge, MA: Harvard University Press, 1941), 2:252.

32 Bailey, at 231, 238, 242, 219; Hodges v. United States, 203 U.S. 1 (1906).

33 "The Peonage System Given a Knock-Out Blow by the Taft Administration," *Washington Bee*, February 24, 1912, 1; "The Courts," *Crisis*, February 1, 1911, 6; Washington quoted in Daniel, *Shadow of Slavery*, 77; "A Blow at Peonage," *Outlook*, January 14, 1911, 47–48; "The Last Traces of Peonage," *Independent*, January 26, 1911, 214. On the southern response to the case, see Daniel, *Shadow*

of Slavery, 78–79. On criticism of Holmes's dissent, see Schmidt Jr., "Principle and Prejudice: Part 2," 868–69.

34 Edwin Mins, "A Liberal Southerner's View of the Negro Problem," *Congregationalist and Christian World*, August 29, 1903, 288.

35 Mins, "Liberal Southerner's View," 288; Brief for the U.S. Attorney General, 21. On white economic interests in *Hodges*, see Pamela S. Karlan, "Contracting the Thirteenth Amendment: *Hodges v. United States*," *Boston University Law Review* 85 (June 2005): 786–87. Aziz Huq argues that the majority also assumed the Black worker's incapacity, in ways similar to Holmes in his concurrence in *Reynolds*, discussed below. This is possible, but it is not how the majority presented its judgment, nor would even a paternalistic regard for Black rights have fit with the Court's record in this era. See Huq, "Peonage and Contractual Liberty," 382–87. A critical interpretation closer to the one offered in this chapter is found in Randall Kennedy, "Race Relations Law and the Tradition of Celebration: The Case of Professor Schmidt," *Columbia Law Review* 86 (December 1986): 1622–61. Kennedy asserts that "avoiding sectional recrimination and silence on the race issue were twin aspects of the tacit deal that was struck in American political culture after the destruction of Reconstruction in the late 1870's" and that Hughes's "rhetoric" in the *Bailey* opinion "paid homage" to this truce. Kennedy, "Race Relations Law," 1648.

36 U.S. v. Reynolds, 235 U.S. 133 (1914), at 150; David Starr Jordan, "The Blood of the Nation," *Popular Science Monthly*, May 1901, 95. The *Reynolds* concurrence coincided with Holmes's more forthright embrace of eugenics. If human progress could be "helped by conscious, coordinated human effort," he wrote in 1915, it would not come through "tinkering with the institution of property, but only by taking life in hand and trying to build a race." Oliver Wendell Holmes Jr., "Ideals and Doubts," *Illinois Law Review* 10 (1915): 3.

37 Dean C. Worcester, *Slavery and Peonage in the Philippine Islands* (Manila: Bureau of Printing, 1913), 4. On the endurance of false-pretense laws in the South, see W. Cohen, *At Freedom's Edge*, 293. On the peonage controversy in the Philippines, see Michael Salman, *The Embarrassment of Slavery: Controversies over Bondage and Nationalism in the American Colonial Philippines* (Berkeley: University of California Press, 2001), 199–222.

38 Carter G. Woodson, *A Century of Negro Migration* (Washington: Association for the Study of Negro Life and History, 1918), 154; transcript of Mose Hamilton by H. C. Tinney quoted in Sydney Nathans, "'Gotta Mind to Move, a Mind to Settle Down': Afro-Americans and the Plantation Frontier," in *A Master's Due: Essays in Honor of David Herbert Donald*, ed. William J. Cooper Jr., Michael F. Holt, and John McCardell (Baton Rouge: Louisiana State University Press, 1985), 215n18. The language in this closing quotation has been standardized; see supra 14. On peonage and the Great Migration, see W. Cohen, *At Freedom's Edge*, 294–98. On the endurance of peonage into the 1930s and 1940s, see Daniel, *Shadow of Slavery*, 170–92; and Risa L. Goluboff, *The Lost Promise of Civil Rights* (Cambridge, MA: Harvard University Press, 2010).

CHAPTER FOUR

Portions of chapter 4 were originally published in Daniel Platt, "The Natures of Capital: Jewish Difference and the Decline of American Usury Law, 1910–1925,"

Journal of American History 104, no. 4 (March 2018): 863–78, and appear here by permission of Oxford University Press.

1   "Bankrupt Wage-Earners and Wives," *Harper's Bazaar*, December 22, 1900, 2210, 2211.

2   Abraham Lincoln, "Address before the Wisconsin State Agricultural Society, Milwaukee, Wisconsin," in *The Collected Works of Abraham Lincoln*, ed. Roy P. Basler (9 vols., New Brunswick: Rutgers University Press, 1953), 3:478. On the ideology of savings, see Nicholas Osborne, "Little Capitalists: The Social Economy of Saving in the United States, 1816–1914" (PhD diss., Columbia University, 2014). On wage assignments, see *Emery v. Lawrence*, 62 Mass. 51 (1851); *Field v. Mayor, etc., of New-York*, 6 N.Y. 179 (1852); and *Thayer & Williams v. Kelley*, 28 Vt. 19 (1855). On wage garnishment, see Rufus Waples, *A Treatise on Attachment and Garnishment* (Chicago, 1895); and Roswell Shinn, *A Treatise on the American Law of Attachment and Garnishment* (Indianapolis, 1896). On the dilemmas of wage labor generally, see Daniel T. Rodgers, *The Work Ethic in Industrial America, 1850–1920* (Chicago: University of Chicago Press, 1978); Sean Wilentz, *Chants Democratic: New York City and the Rise of the American Working Class, 1788–1850* (New York: Oxford University Press, 1984); Leon Fink, *Workingman's Democracy: The Knights of Labor and American Politics* (Champaign: University of Illinois Press, 1985); David Montgomery, *The Fall of the House of Labor: The Workplace, the State, and American Labor Activism, 1865–1925* (New York: Cambridge University Press, 1987); Lawrence B. Glickman, *A Living Wage: American Workers and the Making of Consumer Society* (Ithaca, NY: Cornell University Press, 1997); and Rosanne Currarino, *The Labor Question in America: Economic Democracy in the Gilded Age* (Champagne: University of Illinois Press, 2011).

3   "Thirty Thousand Pairs of Blankets Pawned," *Workingman's Advocate*, June 18, 1870, 2; "Bankrupt Wage-Earners and Wives," 2211. For an illuminating discussion of the pawnshop and the material history of class, see Peter Stallybrass, "Marx's Coat," in *Border Fetishisms*, ed. Patricia Spyer (New York: Routledge, 1998), 183–207.

4   On progressivism generally, see Daniel T. Rodgers, "In Search of Progressivism," *Reviews in American History* 10 (December 1982): 113–32; Daniel T. Rodgers, *Atlantic Crossings: Social Politics in a Progressive Era* (Cambridge, MA: Harvard University Press, 1998); Alan Dawley, *Changing the World: American Progressives in War and Revolution* (Princeton, NJ: Princeton University Press, 2003); Michael McGerr, *A Fierce Discontent: The Rise and Fall of the Progressive Movement in America* (New York: Oxford University Press, 2003); Shelton Stromquist, *Reinventing "The People": The Progressive Movement, the Class Problem, and the Origins of Modern Liberalism* (Champaign: University of Illinois Press, 2006); and Maureen A. Flanagan, *America Reformed: Progressives and Progressivisms 1890s–1920s* (New York: Oxford University Press, 2007). The Russell Sage Foundation's anti-usury campaign does not appear in the leading accounts of the progressive movement, likely because it fits uncomfortably with the notion that progressivism entailed a rejection of markets in favor of the state. For a new interpretation of progressivism that foregrounds the era's promarket themes, see Eli Cook, "The Neoclassical Club: Irving Fisher and the Progressive Origins of Neoliberalism," *Journal of the Gilded Age and Progressive Era* 15 (July 2016): 246–62.

5   The anti-usury campaign has been analyzed by other scholars principally as an

episode in the rise of consumer credit. This chapter builds on those accounts but is more interested in what it meant to approach working-class indebtedness as a financial problem (rather than as a social dilemma of welfare or the wage). See Lendol Calder, *Financing the American Dream: A Cultural History of Consumer Credit* (Princeton, NJ: Princeton University Press, 1999); Louis Hyman, *Debtor Nation: The History of America in Red Ink* (Princeton, NJ: Princeton University Press, 2011); and Anne Fleming, *A Century of Fringe Finance* (Cambridge, MA: Harvard University Press, 2018).

6   Irwin Ellis, "In the Grip of the Loan Shark," *Chicago Daily Tribune*, January 14, 1912; "Loan Shark's Victims Cry for Retribution," *San Francisco Chronicle*, February 20, 1912; J. B. Hippler, "Organization to Fight Loan Shark," *Detroit Free Press*, October 3, 1909.

7   Community Service Society quoted in Fleming, *Century of Fringe Finance*, 18. See also Susan Porter Benson, *Household Accounts: Working-Class Family Economies in the Interwar United States* (Ithaca, NY: Cornell University Press, 2007).

8   Fleming, *Century of Fringe Finance*, 22. See also Benson, *Household Accounts*; and Wendy A. Woloson, *In Hock: Pawning in America from Independence through the Great Depression* (Chicago: University of Chicago Press, 2009).

9   Lee K. Frankel, "The Cost of Living in New York," *Charities and the Commons* 19 (November 1907): 1049–54; Robert Coit Chapin, *The Standard of Living Among Workingmen's Families in New York City* (New York, 1909), 235–44; Margaret F. Byington, *Homestead: The Households of a Mill Town* (New York, 1910), 206–13; W. R. Patterson, "Pawnbroking in Europe and the United States," *U.S. Department of Labor Bulletin* 4 (March 1899): 288; Peter R. Shergold, "The Loan Shark: The Small Loan Business in Early Twentieth-Century Pittsburgh," *Pennsylvania History* 3 (July 1978): 203, 209, 210.

10   Irwin Ellis, "The Vicious Wolf under a Sheep's Skin—the Loan Shark," *Chicago Daily Tribune*, March 17, 1912; Lyman Beecher Stowe, "Credit versus Charity: The Morris Plan," *Outlook*, March 17, 1915, 645; "A Loan Shark's Victim," *New York Times*, April 4, 1905.

11   Lewis Edwin Theiss, "Loan Slaves and Their Emancipation," *Independent*, November 5, 1908; R. W. Sharp, *The Chattel Mortgage Loan Business: The Disease and the Remedy* (Newark, 1910), 12; Irwin Ellis, "The Hungry Child Is a Product of the Loan Shark System," *Chicago Daily Tribune*, March 31, 1912; Ellis, "In the Grip of the Loan Shark"; Irwin Ellis, "If Not Your Salary, the Loan Shark May Get Your Home," *Chicago Daily Tribune*, March 3, 1912; James H. Collins, "Where—and How—to Borrow Money," *McClure's Magazine*, August 1917, 39.

12   Ellis, "If Not Your Salary."

13   Calder, *Financing the American Dream*, 124–28. On the foundation generally, see David C. Hammack and Stanton Wheeler, eds., *Social Science in the Making: Essays on the Russell Sage Foundation* (New York: Russell Sage Foundation, 1995).

14   "Usury and Usury Laws," *Bankers' Magazine and Statistical Register* 9 (July 1874): 49; Henry Charles Carey, *Of the Rate of Interest; and of Its Influence on the Relations of Capital and Labor* (Philadelphia, 1873), 3; Gordon L. Clark, *Shylock: As Banker, Bondholder, Corruptionist, Conspirator* (Washington, 1894), 20, 6; Sharp, *The Chattel Mortgage Loan Business*, 6; "Extract from Report of Fulton County, Georgia, Grand Jury, Fall Term, 1903," box 16, RSF-LOC; "Report of the Operations of the Citizens' Permanent Relief Committee of Philadelphia," quoted in Louis N. Robinson and Rolf Nugent, *Regulation of the Small Loan Business*

(New York, 1935), 48. On US usury laws, see Ransom H. Tyler, *A Treatise on the Law of Usury, Pawns or Pledges, and Maritime Loans* (Albany: W. Gould & Sons, 1873); Sidney Perley, *Principles of the Law of Interest* (Boston: G. B. Reed, 1893); and Lawrence M. Friedman, "Usury Laws of Wisconsin: A Study in Legal and Social History," *Wisconsin Law Review* 515 (July 1963): 515–65. On the nineteenth-century concept of Jewish business, see David A. Gerber, "Cutting Out Shylock: Elite Anti-Semitism and the Quest for Moral Order in the Mid-nineteenth-century American Market Place," *Journal of American History* 69 (December 1982): 615–37.

15 Calder, *Financing the American Dream*, 128–32; "Remedial Loan Societies," *Outlook*, February 24, 1915, 416.

16 Arthur Ham, memorandum on Morris Plan, April 14, 1915, box 26, RSF-RAC; Arthur Ham to John M. Glenn, December 10, 1914, box 26, RSF-RAC.

17 Calder, *Financing the American Dream*, 121; Robinson and Nugent, *Regulation of the Small Loan Business*, 84.

18 Arthur Ham, "The Remedial Loan Movement," *Survey*, August 27, 1910, in box 111, RSF-LOC; confidential memorandum, January 30, 1911, box 33, folder 262, RSF-RAC; Arthur Ham to John M. Glenn, November 5, 1912, box 6, folder 199, RSF-RAC; "Conference Notes: Credit Unions and Morris Plan," May 2, 1914, box 139, RSF-LOC.

19 Roy F. Bergengren, *CUNA Emerges* (Madison: Credit Union National Association, 1938), 2, 20; "May Deal Death Blow to Loan Shark," *New York Times*, October 25, 1914; John M. Glenn to Julius Rosenwald, March 1, 1915, box 26, folder 198, RSF-RAC; John M. Glenn to Judge Julian W. Mack, March 24, 1914, box 26, folder 198, RSF-RAC. See also J. Carroll Moody and Gilbert C. Fite, *The Credit Union Movement: Origins and Development, 1850 to 1950* (Dubuque: Kendall/Hunt, 1984).

20 Sharp, *The Chattel Mortgage Loan Business*, 18.

21 Ellis, "If Not Your Salary"; Arthur Ham to Hugh Cavanaugh, March 10, 1916, box 111, RSF-LOC; Arthur Ham to Charles Whitman, December 30, 1912, box 26, RSF-RAC. On the persistence of loansharking, see Earle Edward Eubank, "Loan Sharks and Loan Shark Legislation in Illinois," *Journal of the American Institute of Criminal Law and Criminology* 8 (May 1917): 69–81.

22 Samuel Crowther (1922) quoted in Lawrence B. Glickman, *A Living Wage: American Workers and the Making of Consumer Society* (Ithaca, NY: Cornell University Press, 1997), 133; George Perkins (1902) quoted in Rosanne Currarino, *The Labor Question in America: Economic Democracy in the Gilded Age* (Champaign: University of Illinois Press, 2011), 53. Adkins v. Children's Hospital, 261 US 525 (1923). On labor politics in this era generally, see also Montgomery, *Fall of the House of Labor*; Julie Greene, *Pure and Simple Politics: The American Federation of Labor and Political Activism, 1881–1917* (Cambridge: Cambridge University Press, 1998); and Joseph A. McCartin, *Labor's Great War: The Struggle for Industrial Democracy and the Origins of Modern American Labor Relations, 1912–1921* (Chapel Hill: University of North Carolina Press, 1998). On the meaning of labor's needs, see Dana Simmons, "The Living Wage, 'That Reproductive Ferment,'" *History of the Present* 7 (2017): 96–121.

23 On the early US welfare state, see Theda Skocpol, *Protecting Soldiers and Mothers: The Political Origins of Social Policy in the United States* (Cambridge, MA: Harvard University Press, 1992); Linda Gordon, *Pitied but Not Entitled: Single Mothers and the History of Welfare, 1890–1935* (New York: Free Press, 1994); Rodgers, *Atlantic*

Crossings; Beatrix Hoffman, *The Wages of Sickness: The Politics of Health Insurance in Progressive America* (Chapel Hill: University of North Carolina Press, 2001); Jennifer Klein, *For All These Rights: Business, Labor, and the Shaping of the Public-Private Welfare State* (Princeton, NJ: Princeton University Press, 2006); and Nate Holdren, *Injury Impoverished: Workplace Accidents, Capitalism, and Law in the Progressive Era* (New York: Cambridge University Press, 2020.)

24   Arthur Ham to John M. Glenn, September 13, 1915, box 26, folder 199, RSF-RAC; "Extract from a Paper by Mr. Stroup in Discussion of Problems of Newly Organized Remedial Loan Societies," c. 1915, box 26, folder 199, RSF-RAC.

25   "The Loan Shark Bill," *New Orleans States*, June 11, 1924. On later narratives of market beneficence, see Daniel T. Rodgers, *Age of Fracture* (Cambridge, MA: Harvard University Press, 2011); and Angus Burgin, *The Great Persuasion: Reinventing Free Markets since the Depression* (Cambridge, MA: Harvard University Press, 2012).

26   Julia Ott, *When Wall Street Met Main Street: The Quest for an Investor's Democracy* (Cambridge, MA: Harvard University Press, 2011), 58, 59; "As to Shylock," *Bankers' Magazine*, October 1926, 451. On popular finance, see William Leach, *Land of Desire: Merchants, Power, and the Rise of a New American Culture* (New York: Vintage, 1993), 298–322; Calder, *Financing the American Dream*, 211–61; David Hochfelder, "'Where the Common People Could Speculate': The Ticker, Bucket Shops, and the Origins of Popular Participation in Financial Markets, 1880–1920," *Journal of American History* 93 (September 2006): 335–58; and Peter Knight, *Reading the Market: Genres of Financial Capitalism in Gilded Age America* (Baltimore: Johns Hopkins University Press, 2016).

27   Arthur Ham to Frank Marshall White, October 12, 1916, box 36, RSF-LOC; Arthur Ham, "Remedial Loans as Factors in Family Rehabilitation," *Proceedings of the National Federal of Remedial Loan Associations* (Baltimore: Lucas Brothers, 1912), 9.

28   William Stanley Jevons, *The Theory of Political Economy* (London, 1871), 72. On the stringency of state supervision under the USLL, see Samuel Grafton, "Need, Gold, and Blood," *North American Review* 227 (March 1929): 334–42; and Leon Henderson, "An Authority Speaks," *North American Review* 227 (May 1929): 132–33.

29   Arthur Ham to Frank Marshall White, October 12, 1916, box 36, RSF-LOC; "A Law Needed to Protect Borrowers of Small Sums," 1917, box 23, RSF-LOC; John M. Glenn to Roy Bergengren, April 29, 1922, box 26, folder 200, RSF-LOC.

30   Sharp, *The Chattel Mortgage Loan Business*, 12; Leon Henderson, "Memo: The Salary Buying Loan Shark," c. 1927, box 26, RSF-RAC; Elizabeth Stern, "Loan Shark Is Now Vanishing," *New York Times*, March 7, 1926; Ella A. Trapp, "The Loan Business from a Woman's Point of View," *Industrial Lender News*, July 1923, 5; F. H. Love Grove, "Educating the General Public to the Small Loan Business Through Advertising of Character," *Industrial Lender News*, May 1924, 2; Blaine McGrath, "Ethics that Build Public Faith in the Industrial Lenders' Business," *Industrial Lender News*, July 1924, 12; Rev. Arthur J. Folsom, Manager's Convention in Fort Wayne, IN, quoted in *Industrial Lender News* 7 (March 1923): 3.

31   Wilford I. King, *The Small Loan Situation in New Jersey* (Trenton, 1929), 94; Henry Fitzwilliam Woods, "Usurious Credit Charges Bleed American Workers," *Industrial Banker*, January 1928, 16; Clarence Hodson, *The Banks and Small Loans* (1922), box 36, Russell Sage Foundation Records (Library of Congress); Robinson and Nugent, *Regulation of the Small Loan Business*, 145, 73.

32   James M. Cox, *Industrial Lender News*, February 1920, 2; W. G. Wood, *Loan*

Gazette, September 1916, 2, 3; C. H. Stratton, *Loan Gazette*, November 1923, 3; C. H. Stratton, *Loan Gazette*, December 1923, 3; "Financing a War on the Loan Shark Evil," *Bankers' Magazine*, March 1923, 493.

33 Arthur Ham, "The Trend and Progress of the Movement to Improve Small Loan Conditions," address before the Convention of the American Industrial Lenders' Association, September 23, 1921, box 2, RSF-LOC; Louis N. Robinson, "Changes in the Small Loan Business," September 10, 1923, box 26, folder 201, RSF-RAC; James C. Sheppard, "California Adopts the Small Loan Law," ca. 1931, memo, California Litigation and Decisions, *Beneficial Loan Society v. Haight* 1932 folder, box 71, RSF-LOC. For more on this theme, see Daniel Platt, "The Natures of Capital: Jewish Difference and the Decline of American Usury Law, 1910-1925," *Journal of American History* 104 (March 2018): 863-78.

34 Robinson, "Changes in the Small Loan Business"; Arthur Ham to Frank Marshall, Oct 12, 1916, box 36, RSF-LOC; "Your Right to Borrow Money," Chattel Loan Society of New York, c. 1924, box 33, RSF-RAC; Ham, "Remedial Loans as Factors," 9.

35 *Sixth Annual Report of the Bureau of Statistics of Labor* (Boston, 1875), 447, 449; Arthur Ham to John M. Glenn, September 25, 1911, box 26, RSF-RAC; Stern, "Loan Shark Is Now Vanishing."

36 "Loan Sharks," *Atlanta Jeffersonian Searchlight*, April 16, 1927; "Data on Mr. Heilborn's Trip to West Virginia," January 30, 1919, box 26, folder 198, RSF-RAC; John S. Radway to Leon Henderson, November 5, 1929, box 26, RSF-RAC; "Sage Foundation Assailed by Neil," *Des Moines Register-Leader*, October 18, 1914.

37 "Why Former Usury Laws Were Failures," *Tampa Tribune*, April 23, 1922; Robinson and Nugent, *Regulation of the Small Loan Business*, 134-36. On labor's support for the USLL, see R. B. Ackerman, "Organized Labor Views Uniform Small Loan Law," n.d., box 4, RSF-LOC; and Gilbert E. Hyatt, "The Uniform Small-Loan Law," *American Federationist*, October 1932, 1146-51.

38 John M. Glenn to Leon Henderson, July 9, 1925, box 24, folder 187, RSF-RAC; Arthur Ham to Roy Bergengren, March 2, 1922, box 23, RSF-LOC; Leon Henderson to John M. Glenn, April 28, 1928, box 24, folder 187, RSF-RAC.

39 John M. Glenn to Arthur Ham, July 31, 1925, box 26, folder 200, RSF-RAC; George Upson to Joyn Ryan, February 26, 1930, in "Memorandum on Interest Rate on Small Loans in New Jersey, March 1930," box 32, RSF-LOC.

40 Arthur Ham to John M. Glenn, February 23, 1927, box 24, folder 187, RSF-RAC. On the foundation's retreat from legislative activity, see John M. Glenn, Lilian Brandt, and F. Emerson Andrews, *Russell Sage Foundation, 1907-1946* (2 vols., New York: Russell Sage Foundation, 1947), 2:531-21.

41 *Industrial Lender News* quoted in Grafton, "Need, Gold, and Blood," 337.

42 "Bankrupt Wage-Earners and Wives"; Ham, "Remedial Loans as Factors," 9.

CHAPTER FIVE

1 "Marshal Victor in Barbed Wire Eviction Battle," *New York Herald-Tribune*, July 28, 1936.

2 "3 More Houses Sold at Auction in Sunnyside," *New York Herald-Tribune*, December 20, 1935.

3 Letters to Franklin and Eleanor Roosevelt in *Down & Out in the Great Depression: Letters from the Forgotten Man*, ed. Robert S. McElvaine (Chapel Hill: University of North Carolina Press, 1983), 72, 110, 64. On Sunnyside, see Jeffrey Andrew

Kroessler, "Building Queens: The Urbanization of New York's Largest Borough" (PhD diss., City University of New York, 1991), 359–411. On the genre of begging letters, see Scott Sandage, "Gender and the Economics of the Sentimental Market in Nineteenth-Century America," *Social Politics* 6 (Summer 1999): 105–30."

4   Edwards v. Kearzey, 95 U.S. 595 (1877); Home Building & Loan Association v. Blaisdell, 290 U.S. 398 (1933); Huey Long, "Share the Wealth," in Robert S. McElvaine, *The Depression and New Deal: A History in Documents* (New York: Oxford University Press, 2000), 99; Charles Coughlin quoted in Christopher W. Shaw, *Money, Power, and the People: The American Struggle to Make Banking Democratic* (Chicago: University of Chicago Press, 2019), 204. On state moratoria, see Douglass Poteat, "State Legislature Relief for the Mortgage Debtor During the Depression," *Law and Contemporary Problems* 5 (1938): 517–44; and John A. Fliter and Derek S. Hoff, *Fighting Foreclosure: The Blaisdell Case, the Contract Clause, and the Great Depression* (Lawrence: University Press of Kansas, 2012). On federal farm-property moratoria, see John Hanna, "New Frazier–Lemke Act," *Missouri Law Review* 1 (1936): 1–20. On federal banking politics in the 1930s, see Shaw, *Money, Power, and the People*; and Sarah Quinn, Mark Igra, and Selen Guler, "'A Modern Financial Tool Kit': Lessons from Adolf A. Berle for a More Democratic Financial System," in *Democratizing Finance: Restructuring Credit to Transform Society*, ed. Fred Block and Robert Hockett (London: Verso, 2022), 189–222. On Long and Coughlin, see Alan Brinkley, *Voices of Protest: Huey Long, Father Coughlin, and the Great Depression* (New York: Vintage, 1983). Older debtor protections, such as property exemptions and garnishment laws, also remained relevant. See Mary Eschelbach Hansen and Bradley A. Hansen, "Crisis and Bankruptcy: The Mediating Role of State Law, 1820–1932," *Journal of Economic History* 72 (June 2012): 448–68.

5   Marriner Eccles, *Beckoning Frontiers: Public and Personnel Recollections* (New York: Knopf, 1951), 144.

6   Jonathan Levy, *Ages of American Capitalism: A History of the United States* (New York: Random House, 2021), 392; *Moody's Analysis of Investments* (New York: Moody Investor Service, 1923), xiii. That the National Housing Act both promoted a political economy of personal debt and encouraged discriminatory lending practices is known. This chapter argues that those developments were causally linked through the discourse of predictive economics, which taught that rational market entanglements were benign and which defined rationality through the avoidance of high-risk businesses, places, and people. On the market as an object of knowledge, see Philip Mirowski, *More Heat Than Light: Economics as Social Physics; Physics as Nature's Economics* (Cambridge: Cambridge University Press, 1989); and Margaret Schabas, *The Natural Origins of Economics* (Chicago: University of Chicago Press, 2006). On the culture of prediction, see Gerd Gigerenzer, Zeno Swijtink, Theodore Porter, Lorraine Daston, John Beatty, and Lorenz Krüger, *The Empire of Chance: How Probability Changed Science and Everyday Life* (Cambridge: Cambridge University Press, 1989); Walter A. Friedman, *Fortune Tellers: The Story of America's First Economic Forecasters* (Princeton, NJ: Princeton University Press, 2014); and Jamie Pietruska, *Looking Forward: Prediction and Uncertainty in Modern America* (Chicago: University of Chicago Press, 2017). On discrimination in the National Housing Act, see Kenneth T. Jackson, "Race, Ethnicity, and Real Estate Appraisal: The Home Owners Loan Corporation and the Federal Housing Administration," *Journal of Urban History* 6 (1980): 419–52;

David Freund, *Colored Property: State Policy and White Racial Politics in Suburban America* (Chicago: University of Chicago Press, 2007); and Jennifer Light, "Nationality and Neighborhood Risk at the Origins of FHA Underwriting," *Journal of Urban History* 36 (2010): 1–38.

7　Letters in McElvaine, *Down & Out in the Great Depression*, 159, 106, 158; Edward Archbold, *Report of the Debates and Proceedings of the Convention for the Revision of the Constitution of the State of Ohio*, (2 vols. Columbus: S. Medary, 1851), 2:470. On older narratives of failure, see Scott A. Sandage, *Born Losers: A History of Failure in America* (Cambridge, MA: Harvard University Press, 2005); and Jonathan Levy, "The Freaks of Fortune: Moral Responsibility for Booms and Busts in Nineteenth-Century America," *Journal of the Gilded Age and Progressive Era* 10 (October 2011): 435–46.

8　George M. Coleman, "1904—the Babson Statistical Organization—1929," Babson Statistical Organization Box 1, Roger W. Babson Collection, Horn Library, Babson College (hereafter RWBC). See also Roger W. Babson, *Actions and Reactions: An Autobiography of Roger W. Babson* (New York: Harper & Bros., 1935), 74–96, 133–58.

9　Sandage, *Born Losers*, 46. See also Josh Lauer, *Creditworthy: A History of Consumer Surveillance and Financial Identity in America* (New York: Columbia University Press, 2017).

10　"United States Bulletin Services," January 1, 1921, box "Business Series RWB," RWBC; Roger W. Babson, "Scientific Forecasting of Business Conditions," c. 1919, box "Business Series RWB," RWBC; Roger W. Babson, "Do You Want More Money for Your Business?," *Saturday Evening Post*, September 6, 1913. On the larger culture of outlines and digests for busy professionals, see Joan Shelley Rubin, *The Making of Middlebrow Culture* (Chapel Hill: University of North Carolina Press, 1992).

11　Babson, "Do You Want More Money?"; Roger W. Babson, "Barometric Indices of the Condition of Trade," *Annals of the American Academy of Political and Social Science* 35 (May 1910): 111, 112, 118; Roger W. Babson, "Ascertaining and Forecasting Business," *Publications of the American Statistical Association* 13 (March 1912): 41. See also Susan Buck-Morss, "Envisioning Capital: Political Economy on Display," *Critical Inquiry* 21 (Winter 1995): 434–67; Mary S. Morgan, "Models, Stories, and the Economic World," *Journal of Economic Methodology* 8 (2001), 361–84; and Mary Poovey, *Genres of the Credit Economy: Mediating Value in Eighteenth- and Nineteenth-Century Britain* (Chicago: University of Chicago Press, 2008); W. A. Friedman, *Fortune Tellers*, 1–11; and Pietruska, *Looking Forward*.

12　"Trade Cycles Have Made New Experts," *New York Times*, November 27, 1927. See also W. A. Friedman, *Fortune Tellers*, 31–40, 51–85, 118–65. Forecasting did not map cleanly, for example, onto the divide between neoclassical economics and institutional economics, which is often linked to the divide between laissez-faire and regulationism in US political economy. As a field, forecasting at once described the economy as a natural entity and suggested that knowledge of its natural features could be used to govern it more effectively. See W. A. Friedman, 189–93.

13　Babson, "Ascertaining and Forecasting Business," 42; Melvin Copeland (1915) quoted in W. A. Friedman, *Fortune Tellers*, 2. On the predictive context of financial forecasting, see Pietruska, *Looking Forward*; and Dan Bouk, "The History and Political Economy of Personal Data over the Last Two Centuries in Three Acts," *Osiris* 32 (2017): 95–101.

14   Louis N. Robinson and Rolf Nugent, *Regulation of the Small Loan Business* (New York, 1935), 244. Walter Friedman links Babson and other forecasters to the emergence of the concept of "the economy," understood as "a complex but unified system that operated according to its own internal logic and hence could be predicted by means of sustained, systematic study." W. A. Friedman, *Fortune Tellers*, 13. On "the economy" concept generally, see Timothy Mitchell, "Fixing the Economy," *Cultural Studies* 12 (1998): 82–101. In a different province of professional economics, it was also in this period that Frank Knight distinguished uncertainty and risk, with the former being simply the unknown and the latter being events that one could probabilistically evaluate. See Frank Knight, *Risk, Uncertainty, and Profit* (Boston: Houghton Mifflin, 1921).

15   Paul Clay, "How to Do Your Own Business Forecasting," *Forbes*, May 1, 1924.

16   W. A. Friedman, *Fortune Tellers*, 90. On Moody's early life, see John Moody, *The Long Road Home* (New York: Macmillan, 1937); and John Moody, *Fast by the Road* (New York: Macmillan, 1942).

17   *Moody's Manual of Industrial and Miscellaneous Securities* (New York: O. C. Lewis, 1900).

18   "Rating Investments," *Outlook*, March 14, 1923; *Moody's Weekly Bond Letter* (1931) quoted in Gilbert Harris, *Bond Ratings as an Investment Guide* (New York: Ronald Press, 1938), 135; Gilbert Harris, "Bond Ratings before the Jury," *Barron's*, February 25, 1935. See also *Poor's Three Thirds Service*, pamphlet, 1924, box "Correspondence," folder "Standards and Poor's," RWBC.

19   "Rating Investments," *Outlook*, March 15, 1923; Gilbert Harris, "Do Bond Ratings Forecast the Market?," *Barron's*, December 31, 1934.

20   *Moody's Municipal & Government Manual* (New York: Moody Investor Service, 1920), 7, 4.

21   *Moody's Municipal & Government Manual* (New York: Moody Investor Service, 1923), xii; *Moody's Municipal & Government Manual* (New York: Moody Investor Service, 1926), xvi.

22   John Moody, *Profitable Investing: Fundamentals of the Science of Investing* (New York: B. C. Forbes, 1925), 130–31; *Moody's Municipal & Government Manual* (New York: Moody Investor Service, 1928), xv, xvi.

23   *Moody's* (1928), xx, xiv, 845; *Moody's Municipal & Government Manual* (New York: Moody Investor Service, 1925), 584, 653.

24   *Moody's* (1928), xiv, xvii; *Moody's Municipal & Government Manual* (New York: Moody Investor Service, 1935), vii; *Moody's* (1928), xvii; *Moody's* (1925), 498; A. Emil Davies, *Investments Abroad* (Chicago: A. W. Shaw, 1927), 190. On the discourse of civilization, see Gail Bederman, *Manliness and Civilization: A Cultural History of Gender and Race in the United States, 1880–1917* (Chicago: University of Chicago Press, 1995); and Ntina Tzouvala, *Capitalism as Civilization: A New History of International Law* (Cambridge: Cambridge University Press, 2020). On race and the marketing of domestic bonds, see Destin Jenkins, "Ghosts of the Past: Debt, the New South, and the Propaganda of History," in *Histories of Racial Capitalism*, ed. Destin Jenkins and Justin Leroy (New York: Columbia University Press, 2021), 185–214.

25   *Speech of Col. Richard M. Johnson of Kentucky, on a Proposition to Abolish Imprisonment for Debt* (Boston, 1822), 6. On risk and personhood in this period, see Dan Bouk, *How Our Days Became Numbered: Risk and the Rise of the Statistical*

Individual (Chicago: University of Chicago Press, 2015). On an analogous transformation in criminological thought, see Michel Foucault, "About the Concept of
the 'Dangerous Individual' in 19th-Century Legal Psychiatry," trans. Alain Baudot
and Jane Couchman, *International Journal of Law and Psychiatry* 1 (1978): 1–18.

26 "Comptroller of Currency Liberalizes Rules on Depreciated Government, State
and Municipal Bonds," *Commercial and Financial Chronicle*, September 12, 1931;
Banking Act of 1933, 48 Stat. 162 (1933).

27 *Moody's Analysis of Investments* (1923), xiii; James Ford (1931) and Robert Lamont
(1932) quoted in Freund, *Colored Property*, 144; Catherine Bauer, *Modern Housing*
(Boston: Houghton Mifflin, 1931), xvii.

28 Freund, *Colored Property*, 109. Eccles, *Beckoning Frontiers*, 144; Judge Glock,
"Keynesian Mortgage Policy in the 1937 Recession" (paper in author's possession,
2017) 2. Important elements of this theoretical diagnosis were supplied by the
economist John Maynard Keynes, whose analysis of the Great Depression both
revived important elements of the older neoclassical economics (with its vision
of economic change as a natural process) and supported the newer institutional
economist's view that "the market was not an optimum self-equilibrating process
and that the intervention of government was necessary to achieve democratic
social goals." Dorothy Ross, *The Origins of American Social Science* (Cambridge:
Cambridge University Press, 1991), 419.

29 See Gail Radford, *Modern Housing for America: Policy Struggles in the New Deal
Era* (Chicago: University of Chicago Press, 1996); Glock, "Keynesian Mortgage
Policy"; Freund, *Colored Property*; Jason Scott Smith, *Building New Deal Liberal-
ism: The Political Economy of Public Works, 1933–1956* (Cambridge: University of
Cambridge Press, 2009); and Monica Prasad, *The Land of Too Much: American
Abundance and the Paradox of Poverty* (Cambridge, MA: Harvard University
Press, 2012).

30 Frederick Babcock, *The Appraisal of Real Estate* (New York: Macmillan, 1927),
74, 65. The person who mattered in predictive discourse was not the autonomous
individual of old but rather the statistical individual, who was fit into models of
aptitude and trajectory using aggregate, typological data. See Bouk, "History and
Political Economy of Personal Data."

31 Babcock, *Appraisal of Real Estate*, 70–71; FHA, *Underwriting Manual* (1936 edition), vol. 2, sec. 2, p. 224. On race and ethnicity in rational lending discourse, see
Light, "Nationality and Neighborhood Risk."

32 Homer Hoyt, *One Hundred Years of Land Values in Chicago: The Relationship of the
Growth of Chicago to the Rise in Its Land Values, 1830–1933* (Chicago: University of
Chicago Press, 1933), 311, 314; Ernest M. Fisher, "Can We 'Immunize' Mortgages?,"
Insured Mortgage Portfolio 1 (July 1936): 17.

33 Cong. Rec., 73rd Cong., 2nd Sess. 78 (1934); Judge Glock, *The Dead Pledge: The
Origins of the Mortgage Market and Federal Bailouts, 1913–1939* (New York: Columbia University Press, 2021), 366.

34 "Memorandum on Mortgage Financing (April 17, 1934)," in *Documentary History
of the National Housing Act: Releases and Memoranda*, box 1, Office of the Com-
missioner, Federal Housing Administration, National Archives II, record group 31
(hereafter FHA, NA, RG 31). Exemption laws were not targeted by federal policymakers, likely because the laws had no power to protect the home from creditors
who had financed the purchase of said home.

35   Phillips Goldsborough, Henry Steagall, and Marie L. Obenauer quoted in *National Housing Act: Hearings before the Committee on Banking and Currency, House of Representatives, Seventy-Third Congress, Second Session, on H.R. 9620* (Washington, DC: Government Printing Office, 1934), 94–95, 28, 322. The nongovernmental House witnesses to which Obenauer referred were Albert L. Deane, president of General Motors; Henry I. Harriman, president of the US Chamber of Commerce; Charles A. Miller, president of the Savings Banks & Trust Co.; Hugh Potter, president of the National Association of Real Estate Boards; Morton Bodfish, executive vice president of the United States Building and Loan League; and Don A. Loftus, president of Homer Permanesque. Appearing before the Senate, the Roosevelt administration representatives were joined by witnesses from finance, the construction industry, and the building trades.

36   Henry Luce quoted in *National Housing Act: Hearings on H.R. 9620*, 73; "Marshal Victor in Barbed Wire Eviction Battle"; McDonald v. Campbell, 57 Tex. 614 (1882), at 18.

37   Quotes from *National Housing Act: Hearings on H.R. 9620*: Francis Perkins, 74; Morton Bodfish, 261; Frank Watson, 158; Orrin Lester quoted in *National Housing Act: Hearings on the Committee on Banking and Currency, United States Senate, Seventy-Third Congress, Second Session, on S. 3603*, 314.

38   Hopkins quoted in Freund, *Colored Property*, 149, 152.

39   Julian H. Zimmerman, *The FHA Story in Summary, 1934–1959* (Washington, DC: Federal Housing Administration, 1959), 8; "*Home* [. . .]" (c. 1934), Printed Materials Box 136, FDR Presidential Library and Museum; *How Owners of Homes & Business Property Can Secure the Benefit of the National Housing Act* (c. 1934), Printed Materials Box 136, FDR Presidential Library and Museum.

40   *Selling Better Housing* (1935), 15, 10, Printed Materials Box 136, FDR Presidential Library and Museum; Zimmerman, *FHA Story in Summary*, 9. The gendering of loan marketing carried into real estate brokering. Reported one realtor in 1941, "The man customer likes to deal with a woman in real estate. . . . He's amazed and delighted to find someone who can *handle* business like a man, and *still* make him feel like a superior being." See Jeffrey M. Hornstein, "'Rosie the Realtor' and the Re-gendering of Real Estate Brokerage, 1930–1960," *Enterprise & Society* 3 (June 2002): 318–51, quotation on 318.

41   Zimmerman, *FHA Story in Summary*, 10.

42   "What Can Families Pay for Housing?," *Insured Mortgage Portfolio* 1 (August 1936): 7; Fisher, "Can We 'Immunize' Mortgages?," 17.

43   *Illustrate Case: Mortgagee's Application for Insurance* (1936), in Printed Materials Box 136, FDR Presidential Library and Museum; "The Risk Rating of Mortgages," *Architectural Forum*, September 1935, 213.

44   On risk and the marriage rate, see "Housing Market Analysis: Washington, D.C., 1937," pp. 84–93, box 17, FHA, NA, RG 31.

45   "Instructions to Enumerators on Land Use and Dwelling Survey," c. 1939, box 18, FHA, NA, RG 31; "Housing Market Analysis: San Mateo, California," 1939, p. 1, box 14, FHA, NA, RG 31; "N. Missouri Security Map and Area Descriptions #2," p. 4, box 2, Records Relating to the City Survey File, 1935–40, FHA, NA, RG 31; "Report on the Negro Rental Market," 1938, p. 2, box 17, FHA, NA, RG 31; "Housing Market Analysis: Camden, New Jersey," 1940, p. 48, box 3, FHA, NA, RG 31; "Housing Market Analysis: Trenton, New Jersey," 1940, p. 32, box 16, FHA, NA,

RG 31; "Housing Market Analysis: Baltimore, Maryland," 1939, p. 52, box 2, FHA, NA, RG 31 (emphasis added).

46 Deuteronomy 23:20; E. M. Gibson, "Going into Business," *Ballou's Magazine*, quoted in Edward J. Balleisen, *Navigating Failure: Bankruptcy and Commercial Society in Antebellum America* (Chapel Hill: University of North Carolina Press, 2001), 203.

47 Walter L. Greene, address before the National Urban League, Cleveland, Ohio, September 2, 1952, box 4, FHA, NA, RG 31; "Memorandum (to the NAACP) Prepared by the FHA," c. 1944, box 4, FHA, NA, RG 31.

CONCLUSION

1 Louis Hyman, *Debtor Nation: The History of America in Red Ink* (Princeton, NJ: Princeton University Press, 2011), 130. Statistics on consumer borrowing drawn from Kenneth Snowden, "Table Dc929–949: Mortgage Debt, by Type of Property, Holder, and Financing: 1939–1999," in *Historical Statistics of the United States*, ed. Susan B. Carter and Richard Sutch (Cambridge: Cambridge University Press); and "Consumer Credit," in *Supplement to Banking and Monetary Statistics* (Washington: Government Printing Office, 1965), 33–37. The increase in home debt (604 percent) far outpaced the increase in the US population (35 percent) between 1940 and 1960. See also Andrea Ryan, Gunnar Trumbull, and Peter Tufano, "A Brief Postwar History of U.S. Consumer Finance," *Business History Review* 85 (Autumn 2011): 461–98. On mass consumption generally, see Lizabeth Cohen, *A Consumer's Republic: The Politics of Mass Consumption in Postwar America* (New York: Vintage, 2003); and Meg Jacobs, *Pocketbook Politics: Economic Citizenship in Twentieth-Century America* (Princeton, NJ: Princeton University Press, 2005); and Hyman, *Debtor Nation*.

2 US House Subcommittee on Domestic Finance and Committee on Banking and Currency, *A Study of Federal Credit Programs* (Washington: Government Printing Office, 1964); Murray L. Weidenbaum, "An Economic Analysis of the Federal Government's Credit Programs" (Working Paper #18, Center for the Study of American Business, Washington University, St. Louis, 1977), 1. On federal credit programs, see Sarah L. Quinn, *American Bonds: How Credit Markets Shaped a Nation* (Princeton, NJ: Princeton University Press, 2019); and Elizabeth Tandy Shermer, *Indentured Students: How Government-Guaranteed Loans Left Generations Drowning in College Debt* (Cambridge, MA: Harvard University Press, 2021). Private finance also claimed the territory ceded by the retreat of wages and welfare spending after the 1970s. See Hyman, *Debtor Nation*, 220–80; and Greta Krippner, *Capitalizing on Crisis: The Political Origins of the Rise of Finance* (Cambridge, MA: Harvard University Press, 2012). On public debt and postwar liberalism, see Destin Jenkins, *The Bonds of Inequality: Debt and the Making of the Modern American City* (Chicago: University of Chicago Press, 2021); and Michael R. Glass and Sean H. Vanatta, "Frail Bonds of Liberalism: Pensions, Schools, and the Unraveling of Fiscal Mutualism in Postwar New York," *Capitalism* 2 (Summer 2021): 427–72.

3 S. Rep. No. 93–278, 93rd Cong., 1st Sess. 19 (1973). On debtors' rights after the 1930s, see Anne Fleming, *City of Debtors: A Century of Fringe Finance* (Cambridge, MA: Harvard University Press, 2018). On the ECOA, see "The Impact of Michigan's

Common-Law Disabilities of Coverture on Married Women's Access to Credit," *Michigan Law Review* 74 (November 1975): 76–105; Susan Smith Blakely, "Credit Opportunity for Women: The ECOA and Its Effects," *Wisconsin Law Review* (1981): 655–96; and Winnie F. Taylor, "The ECOA and Disparate Impact Theory: A Historical Perspective," *Journal of Law and Policy* 26 (2018), 575–635. On antidiscrimination law generally, see Nancy MacLean, *Freedom Is Not Enough: The Opening of the American Workplace* (Cambridge, MA: Harvard University Press, 2006); Felicia Kornbluh, *The Battle for Welfare Rights: Politics and Poverty in Modern America* (Philadelphia: University of Pennsylvania Press, 2007); Serena Mayeri, *Reasoning from Race: Feminism, Law, and the Civil Rights Revolution* (Cambridge, MA: Harvard University Press, 2014); Katherine Turk, *Equality on Trial: Gender and Rights in the Modern American Workplace* (Philadelphia: University of Pennsylvania Press, 2017); Deborah Dinner, "Beyond 'Best Practices': Employment-Discrimination Law in the Neoliberal Era," *Indiana Law Journal* 92 (Summer 2017): 1059–118; and Caley Horan, *Insurance Era: Risk, Governance, and the Privatization of Security in Postwar America* (Chicago: University of Chicago Press, 2021).

4   On African American access to finance before and after the Fair Housing Act, see Beryl Satter, *Family Properties: How the Struggle over Race and Real Estate Transformed Chicago and Urban America* (New York: Metropolitan Books, 2010); Keeanga-Yamahtta Taylor, *Race for Profit: How Banks and the Real Estate Industry Undermined Black Homeownership* (Chapel Hill: University of North Carolina Press, 2019); Mehrsa Baradaran, "Jim Crow Credit," *UC Irvine Law Review* 9 (May 2019): 887–952; and Rebecca K. Marchiel, *After Redlining: The Urban Reinvestment Movement in the Era of Financial Deregulation* (Chicago: University of Chicago Press, 2020). On antidiscrimination law as legitimizing indebtedness, see Louis R. Hyman, "Ending Discrimination, Legitimating Debt: The Political Economy of Race, Gender, and Credit Access in the 1960s and 1970s," *Enterprise & Society* 12 (2011): 200–232. On the "acoustic separation" of credit and debt in this period—wherein Congress made it easier for marginalized groups to get credit while doing little to ease the condition of indebtedness—see Abbye Atkinson, "Borrowing Equality," *Columbia Law Review* 120 (October 2020): 1403–69.

5   A. D. Smith, review of Marshall M. Strong's speech, 575–76; "The Exemptions," *Wisconsin Democrat* (August 22, 1846) in *The Movement for Statehood, 1845–1846*, ed. Milo M. Quaife (Madison: State Historical Society of Wisconsin, 1918), 163–64; Francis Fontaine quoted in Samuel W. Small, ed., *A Stenographic Report of the Proceedings of the Constitutional Convention Held in Atlanta, Georgia* (Atlanta, 1877), 450.

6   "Bankrupt Laws," *North-American Review* 7 (May 1818): 25.

7   See Maurizio Lazzarato, *The Making of the Indebted Man: An Essay on the Neoliberal Condition* (Cambridge: MIT Press, 2012); M. H. Miller, "Been Down So Long It Looks Like Debt to Me," *Baffler* 40 (July 2018): 82–90; Ryan D. Doerfler, "Executive Orders and Smart Lawyers Won't Save Us," *Jacobin*, December 1, 2019, https://jacobin.com/2019/12/executive-orders-supreme-court-law-college-debt; Luke Herrine, "Executive Action as Power Building: A Response to Professor Doerfler," *LPE Project Blog*, December 10, 2019, https://lpeproject.org/blog/executive-action-as-power-building-a-response-to-professor-doerfler; and Astra Taylor, "Make Americans' Crushing Debt Disappear," *New York Times*, July 2, 2021. For a parallel attempt to hail a new revolutionary constituency, see Guy Standing, *The Precariat: The New Dangerous Class* (London: Bloomsbury, 2011).

Index

Page numbers in italics refer to figures.